Revised First Edition

BASIC AND PRACTICAL MICROBIOLOGY

Lab Manual

By Mette Prætorius Ibba and Katherine Elasky
The Ohio State University

cognella® academic publishing

Bassim Hamadeh, CEO and Publisher
Jess Estrella, Senior Graphic Designer
Sean Adams, Project Editor
Luiz Ferreira, Licensing Specialist
Natalie Piccotti, Director of Marketing
Kassie Graves, Vice President of Editorial
Jamie Giganti, Director of Academic Publishing

Copyright © 2019 by Cognella, Inc. All rights reserved. No part of this publication may be reprinted, reproduced, transmitted, or utilized in any form or by any electronic, mechanical, or other means, now known or hereafter invented, including photocopying, microfilming, and recording, or in any information retrieval system without the written permission of Cognella, Inc.

Trademark Notice: Product or corporate names may be trademarks or registered trademarks, and are used only for identification and explanation without intent to infringe.

Cover image copyright © iStockphoto LP/olikim.

Printed in the United States of America

ISBN: 978-1-5165-4446-2 (pbk) / 978-1-5165-4447-9 (br) / 978-1-5165-4445-5 (ap) / 978-1-5165-4448-6 (pf)

cognella
academic publishing
www.cognella.com   800-200-3908

Contents

ACKNOWLEDGEMENTS   VII

MODULE ONE

Lab Safety, Microscopes, Microbial Diversity and Ubiquity

    Lab Safety 1

        Exercise 1-1 Laboratory safety rules and procedures...................... 4

    Microscopes, Microbial Diversity And Ubiquity.......................... 11

        Exercise 1-2 Where do the parts belong on the microscope? 19

        Exercise 1-3 Using the microscope 22

        Exercise 1-4 Getting familiar with microbes and their sizes 27

        Exercise 1-5 Microbial motility and pond water microbes
        (hay infusion) 33

        Exercise 1-6 Fungi and molds 38

MODULE TWO

Cultivation and Staining Bacterial Cells for Microscopy

    Cultivation of Bacteria 41

        Exercise 2-1 Streaking Microorganisms to Obtain
        Single Isolated Colonies... 46

        Exercise 2-2 Streaking Bacterial Organisms to Examine
        Nutritional Needs 50

Exercise 2-3 Streaking Microorganisms to Examine Temperature Requirements 53

Exercise 2-4 Isolating and Characterizing Bacteria from a Mixed Culture 58

Exercise 2-5 Dilution and Enumeration Using Spread Plate Technique 67

Staining Bacterial Cells for Microscopy 76

Exercise 2-6 Simple Stain: Crystal Violet 81

Exercise 2-7 Differential Stain: Gram Stain 85

Exercise 2-8 Acid-fast Stain 91

Exercise 2-9 Capsule Stain 96

Exercise 2-10 Observation of Endospores—Crystal Violet Stain 101

Exercise 2-11 The Endospore Stain 106

Exercise 2-12 The Flagella Stain 109

MODULE THREE
The Microbes Around Us

Environmental microbiology 111

Exercise 3-1 Sampling the Environment 118

Exercise 3-2 Biofilm Formation Using Pond Water Sample 122

Exercise 3-3 Isolation of Biofilm-Forming Bacteria from Soil 126

Food Microbiology 131

Exercise 3-4 Examination of microbes in milk and juice 133

Exercise 3-5 Examination of microbes in meat and cheese 139

Exercise 3-6 The Symbiotic Relationship of Bacteria in Yogurt Production 147

MODULE FOUR
Bacterial Metabolism

Metabolic diversity of bacteria 151

Carbohydrate Usage 155

Exercise 4-1 Carbohydrate utilization 163

Protein Utilization 170

Interpretation of Amino Acid and Gelatin Breakdown 171

Exercise 4-2 Protein Utilization 174

Catalase and Oxidase Activities.. 179

Exercise 4-3 Catalase and Oxidase Activities 181

Aerobic and Anaerobic Growth.. 184

Exercise 4-4 Aerobic and Anaerobic Growth............................. 186

Anaerobic Respiration and Nitrate Reduction 189

Exercise 4-5 Anaerobic Respiration and Nitrate Reduction 191

Selective, Differential, and Selective-Differential Media 195

Exercise 4-6 Selective, Differential, and Selective-Differential Media 200

MODULE FIVE

Identification of Unknown Bacteria

Identification of Infectious agents in the Clinical Setting 205

Exercise 5-1 Identification of Unknown Bacteria in the Clinic ..209

Identification of Unknown Bacteria in the Laboratory 214

Exercise 5-2 Identification of Unknown Bacteria in the Laboratory 215

MODULE SIX

Control of Bacterial Growth

Physical Factors Controlling Bacterial Growth 231

Exercise 6-1 Growth Curve 238

Exercise 6-2 Effect of pH on Bacterial Growth...........................245

Exercise 6-3 Effects of Osmotic Pressure on Bacterial Growth...248

Exercise 6-4 Effect of High Temperature on Viability of Bacteria 251

Exercise 6-5 Effect of UV Radiation on Bacterial Viability............... 254

Chemical Factors Controlling Bacterial Growth 257

Exercise 6-6 The Effectiveness of Handwashing 263

Exercise 6-7 Effects of Mouthwashes and Rinses on Bacterial Growth 267

Exercise 6-8 Effects of Antiseptics and Disinfectants on Bacterial Growth 271

Exercise 6-9 Antibiotics 274

Exercise 6-10 The Action of Natural Antibiotics 285

MODULE SEVEN
Symbiosis, Immunology, and Epidemiology

Symbiosis 289

Exercise 7-1 Mutualism 292

Exercise 7-2 Parasitism 296

Immunology—Nonspecific Host Defense 302

Exercise 7-3 Phagocytosis and Virulence Factors 304

Immunology—Specific Host Defense 309

Exercise 7-4 Antigen-antibody Interactions 311

Epidemiology 317

Exercise 7-5 Epidemiology and ELISA 322

Epidemiology Practice Problem #1 329

Epidemiology Practice Problem #2 330

INDEX   331

Acknowledgements

We would like to thank Mieka Portier, Sean Adams, and all the great people at Cognella, our predecessors who previously taught our microbiology lab courses, our Lecturers, and all of our hardworking staff and TAs in the Department of Microbiology at The Ohio State University. Thank you to Dr. Valerie M. Marshall, Lund University, Sweden, for providing her exercise "Production of Yogurt", which we have adapted. Thank you to our previous TA, George Allen, for his photo contribution.

ATTENDANCE SHEET

Please collect your lab instructor's signature after each lab period.

Your lab instructor will sign off only if the following have been achieved:
- You have been present the entire lab period
- You have worked through and finalized all exercises
- You have properly cleaned your microscope
- You have answered the questions in the lab manual

Lab period	Date	Signature
1		
2		
3		
4		
5		
6		
7		
8		
9		
10		
11		
12		

Lab period	Date	Signature
13		
14		
15		
16		
17		
18		
19		
20		
21		
22		
23		
24		

Lab Safety, Microscopes, Microbial Diversity and Ubiquity

LAB SAFETY

When working in a microbiology lab—whether it is a teaching laboratory, a basic research laboratory, or a research laboratory in a clinical setting—it is extremely important to strictly practice lab safety by following all provided safety rules and guidelines. Microorganisms such as bacteria grow and divide quickly, and if they are introduced to an environment that provides suitable growth conditions and the necessary nutrients, they can easily settle down and make such an environment their new home. As you will learn in this course, we human beings are excellent hosts for many different microbial species.

MODULE 1

> ### Box 1 Clinical and Teaching Microbiology Labs Responsible for *Salmonella* Outbreak
>
> Between August 2010 and June 2011, more than one hundred individuals in the United States were diagnosed with a *Salmonella* infection that was caused by the strain *Salmonella* Typhimurium. This particular *Salmonella* strain, which is commonly used in microbiology teaching labs, is a Biosafety Level 2 (BSL2) organism. Among the infected individuals who participated in the early examinations and investigations regarding the *Salmonella* outbreak were students of microbiology courses and children of healthy parents who attended microbiology courses. These initial results strongly suggested the possibility that the individuals' attendance in microbiology courses was responsible for the outbreak. This was further verified by results from additional investigations and genetic verification of the origin of the strain that caused the infection in the individuals. Throughout the entire time of the outbreak, infections were reported in thirty-eight states, with patients ranging in age from one to ninety-one years old. One death was reported.
>
> **FIGURE 1.1** *Salmonella typhimurium*
>
> The symptoms of *Salmonella* infection are diarrhea, fever, and abdominal cramps that start 12–72 hours after the exposure that led to the infection. Healthy people will normally recover in 4–7 days without treatment. If *Salmonella* is given the opportunity to spread from the intestines to the bloodstream and other parts of the body, it can be life threatening, and immediate antibiotic treatments are crucial.
>
> It is important to note that in this course we will work mostly with BSL1 organisms, and there will be limited exposure to BLS2 organisms in this lab. We will never work with an organism such as S*almonella* Typhimurium. Nevertheless, we can potentially contribute to the spread of other bacterial organisms, which may be a potential risk for elderly people, infants, young children, or individuals with impaired immune systems. Therefore, we cannot emphasize strongly enough the importance of strictly following the lab safety rules and regulations.
>
> ***References***
>
> Hayden, Erika C. "Salmonella Hits U.S. Teaching Labs." *Nature* 473, 132 (May 2011). doi:10.1038/473132a.
>
> "Human *Salmonella* Typhimurium Infections Associated with Exposure to Clinical and Teaching Microbiology Laboratories (Final Update)." Centers for Disease Control and Prevention, January 17, 2012, http://www.cdc.gov/salmonella/2011/lab-exposure-1-17-2012.html.
>
> You can get more information about current and past *Salmonella* outbreaks on the website of the Center for Disease Control and Prevention at: http://www.cdc.gov/.

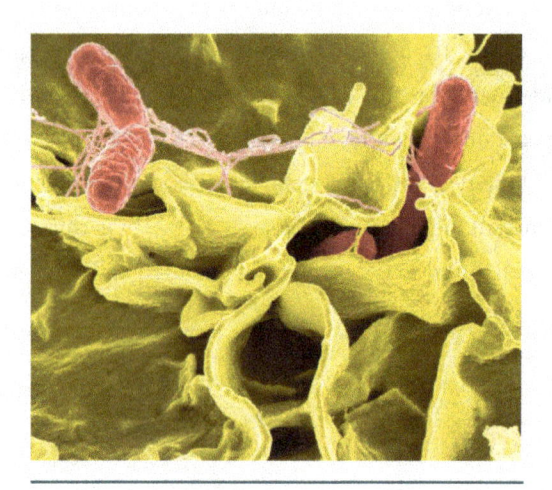

In the lab, we will be working with bacterial organisms belonging to the level of low-risk microbes (Biosafety Level 1, **BSL1**). We will limit the use of potential pathogenic organisms (Biosafety Level 2 bacterial strains, **BSL2**). In contrast to pathogenic strains, the strains we will mostly be working with are unlikely to cause disease in healthy individuals. However, under certain circumstances, many bacterial strains can potentially cause disease (for instance, if bacterial cells in larger quantities come into contact with an immune-compromised individual: a person whose immune defense is weakened and thus is not capable of efficiently eliminating the microbes; such elimination is needed to overcome the bacterial infection). To minimize risk, protect the health of all students and educators in the teaching lab, and avoid spreading bacteria to communities outside of the lab, we are strictly following the rules and guidelines stated in the following exercise. The rules and guidelines that are followed in this course were developed by the American Society for Microbiology (ASM) Task Committee on Laboratory Biosafety. You can read more about the rules and regulations here: https://www.uab.cat/doc/teaching_lab_ASM.

Box 2 Proper Hygiene Decreases Spread of Infectious Diseases

One of the most devastating incidents involving the spread of microbes—a spread mainly caused by the lack of handwashing—was the tragedy of puerperal fever (also called childbed fever). From the 1600s to the late 1800s, an enormous number of women suffered from puerperal fever just after giving birth and while still in the hospital. The number of postpartum mothers who lost their lives just after giving birth was immense. During much of this time, the **germ theory** did not exist, so finding the cause and preventing the disease were complicated and delayed. Ignaz Semmelweis (1818–1865) and Oliver Wendell Holmes (1809–1894), two medical doctors, were among the first to suggest that the spread of the disease among postpartum women was mostly caused by the fact that doctors did not clean their hands in between their different activities in the hospital. Dr. Semmelweis and Dr. Holmes had gained sufficient evidence to prove that, in fact, doctors transferred bacteria to the women giving birth from their previous work tasks in the hospitals, which often involved work such as examinations of cadavers. The bacteria on the hands and clothes of the doctors were directly transferred to the woman giving birth, leading to bacterial infections in the birth canals of the postpartum women. One of the doctors' strongest pieces of evidence was the fact that women giving birth who were only seen by midwives (who did not examine cadavers) did have a considerably lower risk of getting infected. Unfortunately, the two doctors' theory and evidence of proof were not easily acknowledged among their colleagues, and many years passed before proper action was taken to minimize the spread of the bacteria. It was not until the early to mid-1900s (when the germ theory was fully accepted and antibiotics were invented and widely used) that postpartum women suffering puerperal fever could be effectively cured.

Many of the puerperal fever infections were caused by the bacterium *Streptococcus pyogenes, but other bacteria such as chlamydia, clostridium tetani, Clostridium Welchii, Escherichia coli, gonococci, and staphylococci* are also known for causing the disease. Due to the spread of bacteria to the blood, many women died from septicemia or peritonitis (inflammation of the abdominal lining).

Reference
Lane, Hilary J., Nava Blum, and Elizabeth Fee. "Preventing the Transmission of Puerperal Fever." *American Journal of Public Health* 100, no. 6 (June 2010).

Exercise 1-1

Laboratory safety rules and procedures

Learning objectives

To understand and know how to follow microbiology safety rules.

Before you start working in a microbiology lab, it is very important that you familiarize yourself with all the rules and regulations that apply to working in such an environment.

Therefore, please read through the following rules carefully. For your safety, as well as the safety of everyone in the lab, you are expected to strictly follow each one of these rules.

- Wash your hands with soap and water when entering and leaving the lab.

- When indicated, always wear a long-sleeved lab coat to protect your clothes. Wear gloves during the entire lab if you have fresh cuts or abrasions or if you are immunocompromised. Use safety goggles or safety glasses while working with live microorganisms.

- Always wear closed-toed shoes that cover the entire foot.

- Tie back long hair (shoulder length or longer). If you wear a hat, the brim should face backwards; this is because we will be working with Bunsen burners.

- Do not wear dangling jewelry.

- Never bring food or drinks (including water and water bottles) into the lab. Do not chew gum or bite your nails in the lab.

- Never apply cosmetics or lotion, or insert or adjust contact lenses, in the lab.

- Know the location of (and how to operate) fire extinguisher(s), fire blanket(s), eyewash station(s), safety shower(s), and first aid kit(s) in the lab.

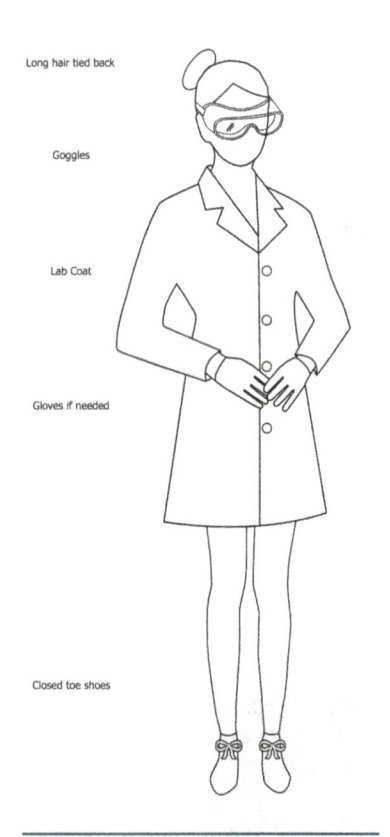

FIGURE 1.2 Lab Safety attire

Exercise 1-1

- Strictly follow the fire-safety regulations (detailed in the fire-safety presentation given by your lab instructor) and read through all fire-safety information posted in lab.

- Notify your lab instructor if you are immunocompromised (or living with or caring for an immunocompromised person), pregnant or may become pregnant, or have any known allergies to components we will be working with in the lab.

For the safety of all students working in the lab, as well as the TAs and instructors, it is very important to strictly follow the procedures described below.

FIGURE 1.3 No food or drinks

- Wipe off the lab bench at the start and end of each lab period with the provided disinfectant and paper towels.

- Label all tubes and plates as indicated in the lab manual so organisms and growth medium can easily be identified.

- Be aware of your own Bunsen burner when it is lit, along with other Bunsen burners in your vicinity. The flames are not always easy to see. Shut off the Bunsen burner when not in use.

- Always inform your TA or lab instructor immediately of any accidents in the lab, including (but not limited to) fire, culture spills, or personal injury of any kind.

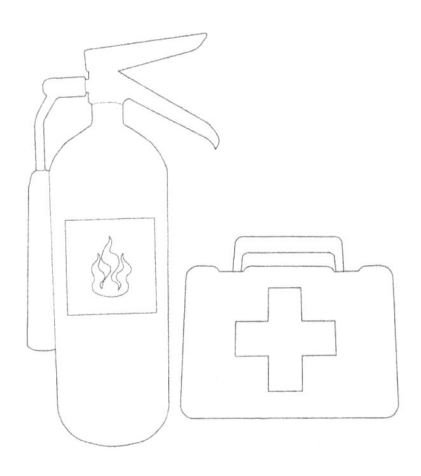

FIGURE 1.4 Fire extinguisher and first aid kit

- If culture is spilled, first notify your TA or lab instructor. Then flood the area with disinfectant and use paper towels to wipe the area dry. Throw away the paper towels and broken glass in the biohazard bins, and wash your hands immediately, using soap and water.

- Be careful not to spill any culture on tablets or laptops that are used in the lab. Contaminated equipment cannot leave the lab until it is disinfected. It is recommended that you protect your tablet while working with cultures by enclosing it in a Ziploc bag or covering it entirely with Saran Wrap.

Exercise 1-1

- Wear gloves when stated in the lab manual (or during the entire lab period if you have fresh cuts on your hands). Discard the gloves in the biohazard bins when the work has been completed and before leaving the lab.

- Return all shared materials to their designated locations when you are done using them.

- To avoid the spread of the microorganisms and to contain them in a safe place prior to their destruction (autoclaving), it is important to know exactly how to dispose of the microbes when you are done working with them:

  - All live cultures on agar plates should always be disposed of in the biohazard bins. These bins are typically red and marked with a biohazard label.

FIGURE 1.5 Sharps and biohazard bin

  - All microbes in culture tubes should be placed in racks designated for cultures to be autoclaved. Remove all tape or writing on the tubes.

  - All material that has been in direct contact with microbial culture should be disposed of in the biohazard bins. This include gloves, microscope slides, pipet tips, serological pipettes, droppers (not the wrappers), swabs (not the wrappers), microcentrifuge tubes, and any other disposable plastic materials.

- Normal trash bins are also present in the lab. Please use these for all material that has not been in direct contact with the microbes, such as:

  - Paper towels used for wiping the benches before and after lab work

  - Gauze

  - Wrappers from swabs, droppers, and serological pipettes

FIGURE 1.6 Trash bin

Exercise 1-1

Results and questions (R & Q)

Explain why drinking and eating are prohibited in the lab.

_____
_____
_____

Where do we discard used gloves?

_____
_____
_____

Explain why we have to remove the gloves when leaving the lab (e.g., when going to the restrooms or to the elevators).

_____
_____
_____

Explain why students with a fresh cut should wear gloves for the entire lab period.

_____
_____
_____

Why is it important to tie back long hair?

_____
_____
_____

Describe three potential risks that could occur if lab safety rules are not followed.

_____
_____
_____

Where do you dispose of used tubes with labels removed?

_____
_____
_____

8

Exercise 1-1

What goes where?

Draw a line from the item to the correct disposal location.

Gloves

Pipette Tips

Slides

Uncontaminated Paper Towels

Contaminated Paper Towels

Microcentrifuge tubes

Wrappers

Droppers

Gauze

Swabs

Exercise 1-1

Laboratory Safety Sign-off Sheet

I have read and understood the rules and guidelines presented to me.

Signature:_____   Date: _____

Print name: _____

Lab day: _____

Lab time: _____

Room number: _____

TA names: _____

Semester: _____

Year: _____

MICROSCOPES, MICROBIAL DIVERSITY AND UBIQUITY

We can easily visualize microbial organisms with the naked eye when they grow up to form colonies on agar plates (solid media) or when they are grown in nutrient-containing broth (liquid media), transforming the media from clear to cloudy. However, we do need a microscope to see the individual microbial cells.

The most common of all microscopes is the compound brightfield microscope (compound microscopes use more than one lens), and this is the type of microscope that we will use most often in the lab. The history of the invention and development of microscopes goes back for centuries. In the 1590s, two Dutch lens grinders, Hans and Zacharias Janssen (1585–1638), developed the very first documented compound microscope. It was simple, consisting of a tube and two lenses, and it magnified images approximately three times. However, long before that, in the twelfth through the fourteenth centuries, the Romans developed the lens-grinding procedure; to improve people's eyesight, they also produced spectacles—a kind of one-lens microscope.

In the early 1600s, Galileo Galilei (1564–1642) further developed the compound microscope by adding convex and concave lenses. However, the first publication describing "objects" visualized with a microscope came from the English scientist Robert Hooke (1635–1703), who published his observations in his book, *Micrographia*, in 1665. Robert Hooke was also the first to name the basic unit of life a "cell." About ten years later, Dutch cloth merchant and scientist Anton van Leeuwenhoek (1632–1723) was the first to actually observe and describe unicellular organisms, including

> *Learn More*
>
> You can follow this link to get a peek at Hooke's *Micrographia*: https://ceb.nlm.nih.gov/proj/ttp/flash/hooke/hooke.html

bacterial cells, through a microscope. He had great expertise in lens grinding and created many very powerful lenses and microscopes. While using his very best lens, he observed a sample of pond water and discovered the world of the tiny microorganisms in their pond-water habitat. Leeuwenhoek reported his observations to the Royal Society in London in the late 1670s, and his reports included many detailed illustrations of (among other things) bacteria and algae. Throughout many years of his career, he continued to report his microscopic observations. He was the first person to improve the compound microscope by applying his powerful lenses, which could magnify objects 200–300 times. You can read more about the history of microscopes, Leeuwenhoek, and other pioneers of microscopy by following this link: http://www.history-of-the-microscope.org/.

Similar to early microscopes, some of the newer, more sophisticated microscopes use visible light (light microscopes) to visualize the specimens, but other, even more powerful, microscopes use electron beams, and electromagnets instead of glass lenses (electron microscopes). The development of these different types of microscopes, along with various related microscopic techniques, have contributed greatly to opening our eyes further and further to the stunning world of microorganisms and, in fact, of all living cells. The microscope not only has been, but still is and will be in the future, an essential instrument for a variety of research-area disciplines (from basic research to applied medical research) and for providing clinicians the necessary insight for the diagnosis of a variety of diseases. It is no wonder that quite a few Nobel Prizes have been awarded to scientists who have worked on microscope inventions and the improvements of these instruments.

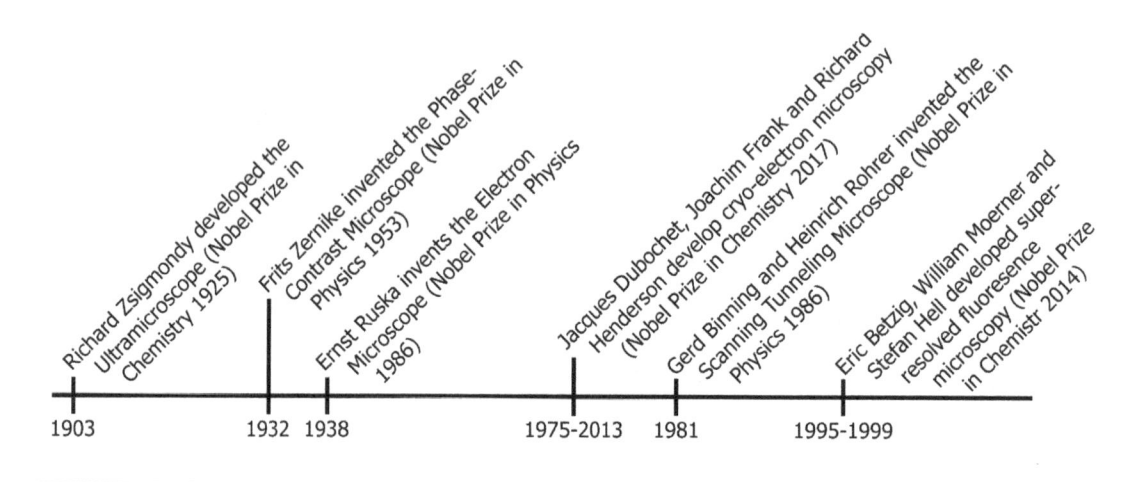

Timeline of microscope developments:
- 1903: Richard Zsigmondy developed the Ultramicroscope (Nobel Prize in Chemistry 1925)
- 1932: Frits Zernike invented the Phase-Contrast Microscope (Nobel Prize in Physics 1953)
- 1938: Ernst Ruska invents the Electron Microscope (Nobel Prize in Physics 1986)
- 1975-2013: Jacques Dubochet, Joachim Frank and Richard Henderson develop cryo-electron microscopy (Nobel Prize in Chemistry 2017)
- 1981: Gerd Binning and Heinrich Rohrer invented the Scanning Tunneling Microscope (Nobel Prize in Physics 1986)
- 1995-1999: Eric Betzig, William Moerner and Stefan Hell developed super-resolved fluoresence microscopy (Nobel Prize in Chemistr 2014)

FIGURE 1.7 Timeline

Today's scientists can choose from a number of different types of microscopes to use for their examinations. Depending on their field of study, they might choose the **compound brightfield microscope** to examine morphology (shape) of live microbial cells, or "fixed specimens." When cells are fixed to a slide by heat, their shapes get distorted, and thus the microbes are no longer present in their native state. It is therefore not possible to examine the native shapes of these fixed microbial cells; however, other interesting characteristics of the microbial cells can be examined by staining the fixed cells (see Module 2 for more on staining). The brightfield microscope is the simplest and most common microscope, and it is found in many research labs. When using the brightfield microscope, specimens look dark against the bright (white) background created by the light. Since the contrast provided by the compound brightfield microscope is low and many bacterial cells are transparent, it is often necessary to stain the cells before performing microscopy of them.

When using a **darkfield microscope** or **phase contrast microscope**, there is no need to stain the specimens. These two microscopes provide better contrast, making it possible to observe more details within the living cells. In contrast to the brightfield microscope, species viewed in the darkfield microscope appear bright against a dark background. A microbiologist choosing to work with a darkfield microscope or a phase contrast microscope would typically examine cell morphology, as well as motility, of living microbial cells in their native state. Also, bacteria, which are difficult to stain, will typically be examined using one of these two microscopes instead of the brightfield microscope.

Of all the three microscopes, the phase contrast microscope has the ability to provide the most detailed image of the species being examined. Thus, in addition to examining morphology and motility, scientists using the phase contrast microscope can also observe certain intracellular structures and inclusions, which are not possible to clearly see using the brightfield or the darkfield microscopes.

When viewing a specimen using a brightfield microscope, the light rays from the light source are transmitted through the specimen. Since the light is restricted upon passing through the specimen to the objective, it makes the cells appear darker or shaded against the bright background. In contrast, the darkfield microscope contains a special condenser, which ensures that only light that is reflected off the specimen will enter the objective. This gives rise to a bright image of the cells against the dark background (greater contrast) and therefore a more detailed image of the cells.

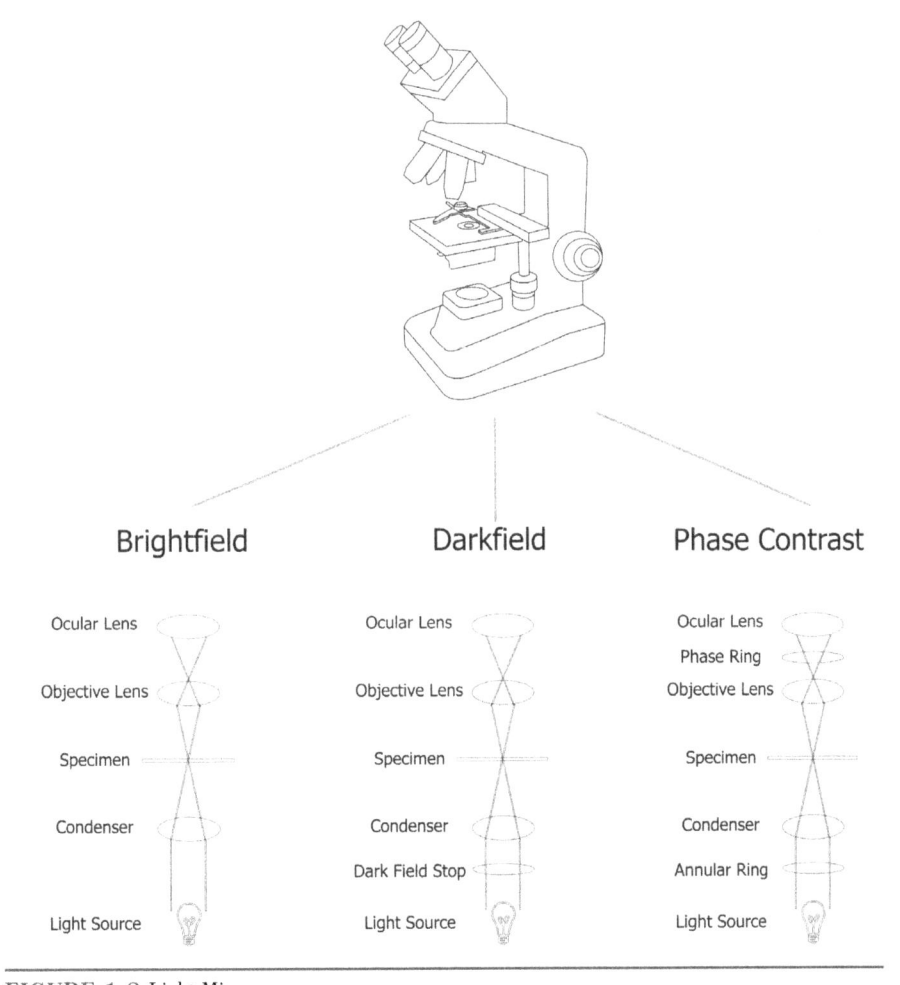

FIGURE 1.8 Light Microscopes

The phase contrast microscope differs from brightfield and darkfield microscopes in that it includes two special optical components: an **annular diaphragm** and a **phase-shifting element**. One of its features (provided by the annular diaphragm) ensures that the light transmitted from the light source is directed into a cone shape onto the specimen. Due to the different densities of the specimen, the light refracts differently. The other feature (provided by the phase-shifting element) is capable of shifting the waves of the refracted light, causing the waves to either add to or subtract from each other. Waves that add to each other are in phase and reinforce each other. This results in an increase in light intensity. Conversely, light waves that are out of phase cancel each other, result in no intensity, and appear dark. The resulting view is a specimen that appears as different levels of dark against a brighter background. The enhanced contrast gives rise to a more improved, detailed image of the cells.

Other microscopes worth mentioning (although they aren't used in this course) are the florescence microscope, the transmission electron microscope, and the scanning electron microscope. Whereas the light microscope magnifies specimens up to 1200–1300 times and the resolution is about 200 nm (i.e., we can see particles as close as 200 nm apart as individual particles), an electron microscope (such as the transmission electron microscope) can magnify images approximately 1,000,000 times, and the resolution is about 0.2 nm. The other type of microscope, the scanning microscope, can amplify images 100,000 times, with a resolution of approximately 3 nm.

The **fluorescence microscope** is also a light microscope; however, it differs from the other light microscopes in that it contains a high-energy mercury vapor lamp. This lamp produces shorter wavelengths of light (in the ultraviolet range), which is necessary for inducing fluorescence. Scientists use the microscope to examine specimens that can fluoresce, which means light of a special wavelength is absorbed by the specimens (atoms or molecules) and reemitted as light of a higher wavelength (lower energy level). Some specimens and objects naturally fluoresce (e.g., minerals, rocks, and chlorophyles); however, in most cases, chemical dyes have to be applied in order for the specimens to fluoresce. This can be obtained by allowing the cells being examined to bind to, or take up, chemicals that fluoresce. Such chemicals, called fluorochromes or fluorophores (or chromophores), can also be conjugated to (bound to) antibodies that are used to recognize specific cell surface components (such as proteins and a variety of intracellular components). The technique is called immunofluorescence microscopy, and it is

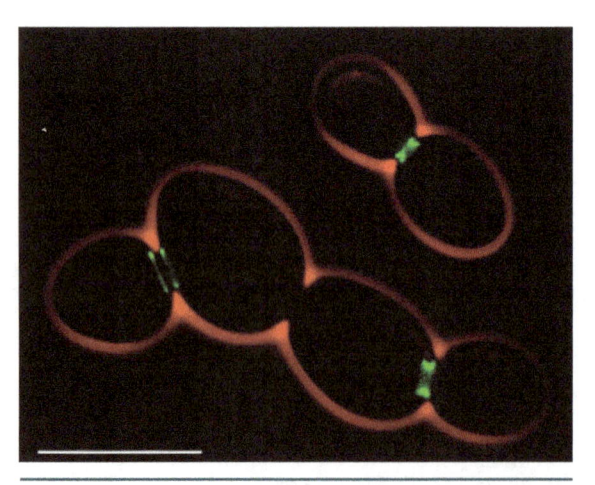

Fluorescent micrograph of *Saccharomyces cerevisiae* with GFP-tagged septins. Scale bar: 10μm

Source: Spitfire ch, https://commons.wikimedia.org/wiki/File:S_cerevisiae_septins.jpg. Copyright in the Public Domain.

a widely used and indispensable technique employed to study various areas of the medical and biological sciences. The microscope contains a darkfield condenser to improve contrast and several filters to adjust wavelengths of the emitted and reemitted light.

Electron microscopes are not light microscopes; instead of light, they employ electron beams, and they use electromagnets instead of lenses to create the magnified image of the specimen. A fluorescence screen is often applied to collect the image. The microscopes produce black-and-white images and, compared to the light microscopes, smaller objects can be viewed in much greater detail. The two different types of electron microscopes, the transmission and scanning electron microscopes, are capable of creating very different images: the transmission electron microscope (TEM) creates an internal view of the specimen (e.g., an internal view of the structures of a bacterial cell), whereas the scanning electron microscope (SEM) creates a external three-dimensional view (e.g., a surface view of a bacterial cell). The difference in the image produced relates to the way that the electrons are either transmitted through the specimen (TEM) or refracted (SEM). In order to view specimens with the electron microscope, they have to undergo lengthy processing, some of which includes fixation, production of very thin sections of the specimen, and staining to increase contrast between the different structures of the viewed specimens. The images appear as dark against a bright background. The development of the transmission electron microscope began in 1931, and in 1935, the scanning electron microscope was developed.

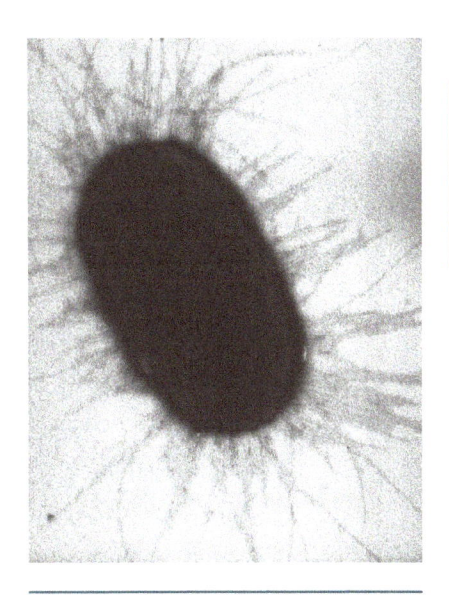

Transmission electron micrograph of *Escherichia coli*

The most recent Nobel Prize within the microscopy field was awarded in 2017 to three scientists whose work helped develope the cryo-electron microscope. With their contributions, it is now possible to generate images of atomic resolution structures of biomolecules in solution. The technique involves freezing biomolecules in a way that that they virtually retain their natural shapes. This methods has been said "to move Biochemistry into a new era".

Another application of the transmission electron microscope is immunoelectron microscopy (IEM), which uses gold-labeled antibodies to visualize specific components of the cells. This technique is commonly used to precisely determine the localization of certain molecules being studied, and it can trace specific molecular processes within the cell. The images created are similar to those of TEM, but they add the dark, electron-dense spots at locations that have been bound by the gold-labeled antibodies.

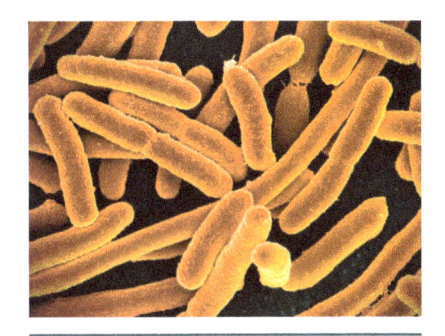

Colorized scanning electron micrograph of *Escherichia coli*

Source: Manu Forero, "Bacterial Fimbriae Designed to Stay with the Flow," PLOS Biology, vol. 4, no. 9, Public Library of Science (PLoS), 2006. Copyright © Public Library of Science (PLoS) (CC by 2.5).
Source: National Institute of Allergy and Infectious Diseases (CC by 2.0) at https://commons.wikimedia.org/wiki/File:E._coli_Bacteria_(16598492368).jpg.

The compound brightfield microscope

Before we start to examine microbes using the compound brightfield microscope, there are some important terms and technical necessities that we need to go through before we are ready to work with the microscope.

Objective and ocular lenses and total magnification: we already learned that light microscopes contain two or more lenses. The compound microscope that we will work with in this course contains an **objective lens** (which is situated close to the specimen) and an **ocular lens** for each of the two eye pieces (which are situated closest to your eyes). The specimen is first magnified by the objective lens according to its magnification capability (4x, 10x, 40, or 100x magnification) and is then further magnified 10 times by the ocular lens (10x).

When calculating the **total magnification** of a given image, it is necessary to multiply the magnifications produced by the objective lens and the ocular lens. So, if you use the objective lens that magnifies 40 times and you know that the ocular lens magnifies 10 times, the total magnification of the specimen is 400 times:

40 times magnification	X	10 times magnification	=	400 times magnification
(Objective lens)	X	(Ocular lens)	=	(Total magnification)

In creating a perfect image of the specimen, the **resolving power** (RP) or **resolution** is equally important, too. The resolving power is the ability of the microscope to distinguish two objects (or points) positioned closely together as being two separate objects (points) instead of one big object. The resolving power is determined by the wavelength of the light used and the **numerical aperture** (NA) of the objective lens, where the numeric aperture is a measure of the quality of the lens with regards to how well the lens can resolve fine details. The numeric value is written on the objective lens; this value reflects how much light can be brought into the lens: the higher the light-gathering ability is (i.e., the bigger the light cone brought into the lens), the higher the numerical aperture is and the better the resolution of the specimen will be.

Resolving power is calculated as:

Resolving Power (RP) = wavelength of light used / 2(Numerical Aperture of the Objective)
                               (500nm)   2(1.25)

The size of the objective lens decreases with increasing magnification. This means that with higher magnification the amount of light that can be brought into the lens gets smaller. This makes the field appear darker. In addition, the amount of light that is able to gather in the objective lens also depends on the refractive properties of the light, so more light will bend away as a result of the light rays moving faster through air than through the glass slide containing the specimen. The iris diaphragm or light rheostat can alter the availability of light when using the 4X, 10X, and 40X objective lenses, but when working with the highest magnifying lens (the 100X lens), **immersion oil** must be applied to the slide in order to increase the amount of light going into the objective lens and obtain a clear image, which otherwise would appear blurry. The reason is that the light rays travel at similar speed through the glass slide and the oil, and this prevents the light from bending away from the specimen, thereby providing sufficient light to view the specimen.

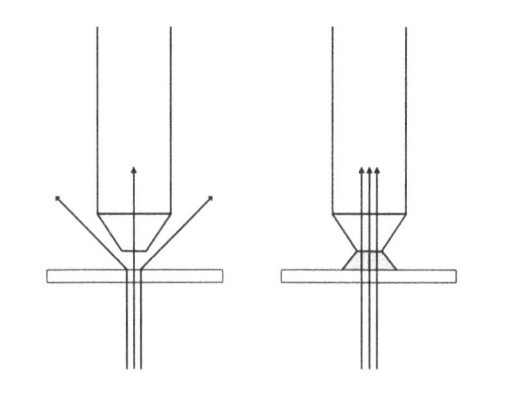

FIGURE 1.9 Light Rays with oil objective

Note: When using the 100X lens, immersion oil must always be applied. This lens is sealed against oil. However, the 4X, 10X, and 40X lenses are not sealed against the immersion oil. They can get damaged, and immersion oil should therefore never be used when working with these lenses. Please immediately clean off any immersion oil that may have unintentionally touched these lenses.

When you start working with the microscope, you will quickly realize that you can easily change from one objective (e.g., 10X) to another (e.g., 40X) and still have the specimen in focus or almost in focus. This feature, called **parfocality**, ensures that the specimens remain in focus while switching from one objective to another. It may be necessary to perform minor adjustments with the **fine focus knob**, though.

Although the contrast or definition is less when viewing the live microbes in the brightfield microscope (compared to dark field or phase contrast microscopes), it is still possible to examine **morphology** and **motility** of the microbes.

In the exercises to follow, we will be looking at prokaryote and eukaryote microbes such as the bacterial organism *Escherichia coli* and the yeast *Saccharomyces cerevisiae* (brewer's or baker's yeast), as well as samples of **hay infusions**, where we also can view protozoa—a unique selection of unicellular eukaryote organisms that normally live in pond water or creek water. We will also be comparing two very different fungi to each other.

When performing the exercises, you will be comparing and familiarizing yourself with the sizes of the different microbes that you are viewing, examining motility (the ability of certain microbes to self-propel though their environment using their **flagella**) and determining the microbes' cell and colony morphology (shape).

As you proceed with the exercises, you should be able to easily distinguish between prokaryote and eukaryote cells and to distinguish true motile organisms from **Brownian motion** and **current flow**. The movement of motile flagellated bacteria often appears directed in straight lines or as rotating tumbles. This should not be confused with Brownian motion, where the bacteria appear to just be vibrating in the same place instead of moving around in their environment. The occurrence of Brownian motion in the cell suspension is a result of random collisions of particle and/or cells. Another phenomenon that should not be confused with true motility of the microbial cell is current flow, which is the simultaneous movement, in one direction, of all particles, cells, etc., that are being viewed on the slide. Current flow is more commonly observed when the slides are starting to dry out.

Microscopes are valuable and very fragile equipment, so it is important to correctly handle and take good care of them. The microscope that you will be working with now is ready to use: the person who worked with it earlier has already cleaned it properly and positioned all of its parts correctly. After you are done working with the microscope, you need to do the same: make sure to clean it and position the parts correctly so the microscope is ready for the next person to use (see "Cleaning the microscope" below).

When carrying a microscope, use one hand to hold the arm of the microscope and place the other hand under the base of the microscope.

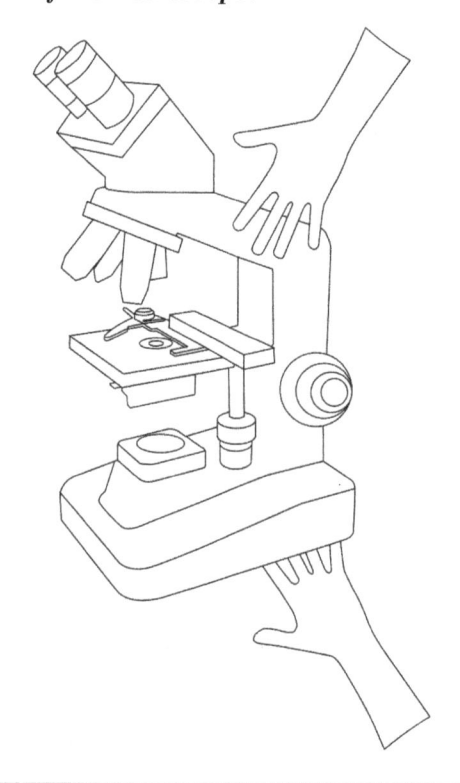

FIGURE 1.10 How to Carry the Scope

Exercise 1-2

Where do the parts belong on the microscope?

Learning objective

To gain competence in working with light microscopes.

Procedure

To familiarize yourself with the brightfield microscope, use the descriptions of each of the parts of the microscope presented below to complete this exercise. A slide will be presented by your TA or lab instructor to check that you have gotten the answers right.

The parts of the compound brightfield microscope

- **Arm:** The arm extends from the base of the microscope and connects the base to the lens systems and stage.

- **Stage:** The stage is the horizontal surface on which the slides containing the specimens are placed for viewing. The mechanical part of the stage includes a clip that holds the slide in place when moving the slide from side to side using the two control knobs located at the base of the mechanical stage.

- **Condenser:** The condenser lens focuses light from the light source onto the specimen. The condenser is positioned just below the stage.

- **Light source:** The light source includes the bulb (typically a halogen lamp) located near the base of the microscope below the condenser. The light rays are transmitted through the slide containing the specimen. The rheostat on the on/off switch is used to adjust the amount of light reaching the specimen.

- **Iris Diaphragm:** The iris diaphragm adjusts the amount of light reaching the specimen, which is done by moving the control lever left and right. The iris diaphragm is positioned between the condenser and the light source.

- **Objectives:** The objectives are the set of lenses which are located closest to the specimen that is being viewed and are attached to the nosepiece. The four objectives that typically are present on the brightfield microscope are the **4X objective** (scanning lens), the **10X objective** (low power lens or

Exercise 1-2

low dry lens), the **40X objective** (the high power lens or high dry lens), and the **100X objective** (the oil-immersion lens).

- **Nosepiece:** The nosepiece is the revolving element that holds the objectives.
- **Coarse- and Fine focus Adjustment Knobs:** These are the two knobs that are used to move the stage in order to bring the specimen into focus. They are commonly located on either side of the stage. The coarse focus adjustment knob moves the stage much larger distances compared to the fine-focus adjustment, which moves the stage very small distances.
- **Oculars or Eyepieces:** The oculars, or eyepieces, are the lenses situated at the very top of the microscope and closest to your eyes. These lenses provide the final 10X magnification of the specimen being viewed. you can slide the oculars back and forth to adjust the distance between the lenses so you can see through both oculars at once; hence, it is a binocular microscope.

Exercise 1-2

R & Q

Draw lines to connect the terms to the microscope.

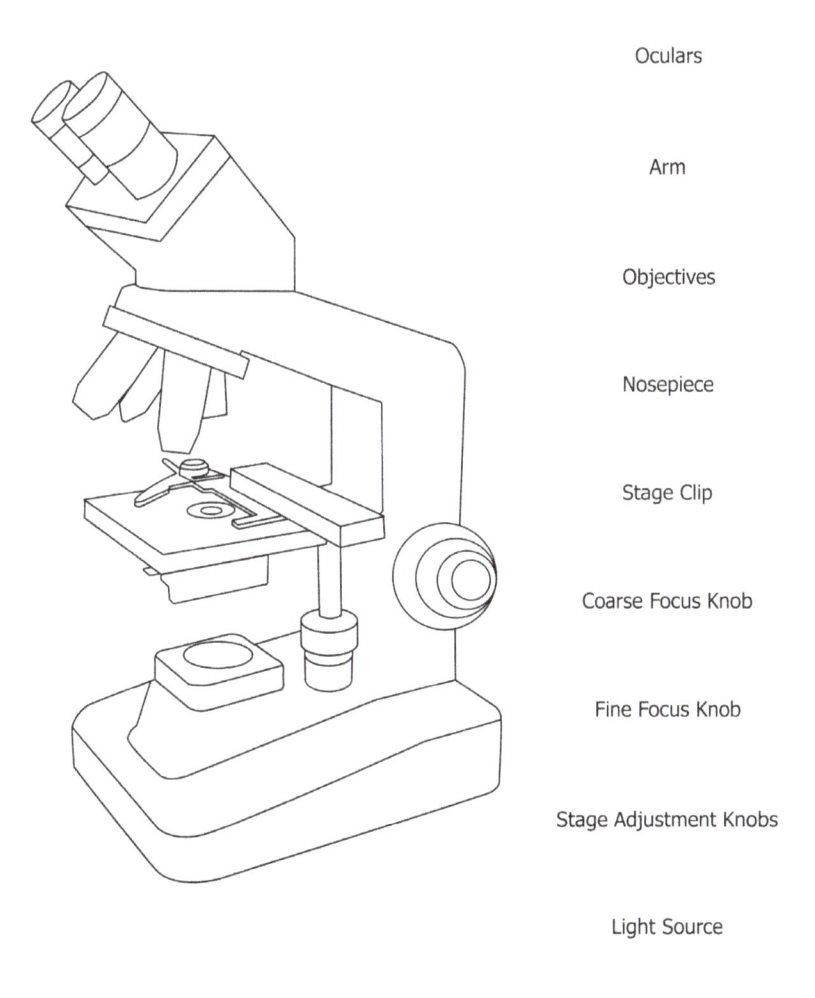

Oculars

Arm

Objectives

Nosepiece

Stage Clip

Coarse Focus Knob

Fine Focus Knob

Stage Adjustment Knobs

Light Source

Exercise 1-3

Using the microscope

Learning Objective

To become familiar with microbes and their sizes.

To practice using the brightfield microscope, you will first examine prepared slides of selected microbes. While looking at these slides, notice the difference in their sizes and other cellular characteristics.

- *E. coli* (bacterium, **prokaryote**, size 0.5–2 µm)
- *S. cerevisiae* (yeast, **eukaryote**, size 5–10 µm)
- *Paramecium* (**protozoa**, eukaryote, size 50–300 µm)

Materials

- Prepared slide of *E. coli*
- Prepared slide of *S. cerevisiae*
- Prepared slide of *Paramecium*
- Compound brightfield microscope

Work in pairs.

Procedure

1. Collect the three prepared slides. You may need to share the prepared slides with other groups in the classroom, so please follow your lab instructor's directions.
2. Carefully position the first slide on the stage by gently pulling back the metal clip and placing the slide horizontally into the metal corner.
3. Use the two control knobs located at the base of the mechanical stage to adjust the slide so the specimen is centered. The upper knob moves the slide forward and backward, and the lower knob moves it left and right.
4. Focus the specimen under the low-power 10X objective by first rotating the nosepiece until you hear objective click into place. Then use the coarse- and fine focus knobs to focus.

5. Once the specimen is in focus under the 10X objective and you switch to the high-power 40X objective with your parfocal microscope, adjustments should only be made with the **fine-adjustment focus knob**.

   Note: The working distance, or the amount of space between the slide and the lens when the specimen is in focus, decreases as the magnification of the lenses increases. Therefore, when the specimen is in focus using the 40X high-power lens or 100X oil-immersion lens, the respective objectives will be positioned relatively close to the slide (in fact, a 100X objective can be as close to the slide as 0.14 mm).

6. Use the iris diaphragm to let more light through or adjust the light intensity using the rheostat so that you can bring the specimen properly into focus. Then use only the fine-focus adjustment knob to focus and make a clear image of the cells on the slide.

   Note: Because the size of the objective lens decreases with increasing magnification, the field will now appear darker, as less light can enter the 40X lens.

7. If appropriate, observe the specimen using the 100X immersion-oil lens. Rotate the nosepiece so that it is positioned halfway between the 40X and 100X objectives. You now have enough room to add oil to the slide.

   Note: It is necessary to use immersion oil when observing the specimen with the 100X lens. However, immersion oil must never be used with any of the other lenses, since they are not sealed and will be damaged by the oil.
   When the oil has been added to the slide, the 40X objective lens cannot be used to observe this same slide before the slide has been properly cleaned.

8. Place a small drop of immersion oil on the slide, just above the light produced by the light source and the condenser lens. Slowly rotate the nosepiece until the 100X objective clicks into place. Because your microscope is parfocal, the specimen is already in focus (or almost in focus). Adjust the light and only use the fine-focus adjustment knob to make a clearer image, if needed.
9. Record your observations in the *R & Q* section.

Exercise 1-3

10. Remove the slide after you have rotated the nosepiece so it is positioned halfway between the two objectives.
11. Repeat steps 2–10 for the specimens on the two remaining slides.
12. When you have finished viewing all three prepared slides, rotate the nosepiece to the 4X objective, pull back the metal clip, and carefully remove the slide. Clean the prepared slides with gauze before returning them to the shared setup area.

R & Q

Calculate the total magnification when viewing specimens using the 10X, 40X, and 100X objectives:

- 10X low dry objective:

- 40X high dry objective:

- 100X oil-immersion objective:

Exercise 1-3

Draw and describe your observation of the prepared slides.

E. coli
100X objective

S. cerevisiae
40X objective

Paramecium
40X objective

Exercise 1-3

Do any of the slides contain stained cells? Which ones? What would the reason be for staining the cells to be viewed?

_____
_____
_____

Explain how the resolving power can be improved.

_____
_____
_____

The smaller the numerical aperture value is, the better the resolving power of the lens used. True or False?

_____
_____
_____

Which objective lens has the numerical aperture value of 1.25?

_____
_____
_____

Why is immersion oil necessary to apply when working with the 100X lens and not with the 40X lens?

_____
_____
_____

Explain parfocality.

_____
_____
_____

Exercise 1-4

Getting familiar with microbes and their sizes

Learning Objective

To increase knowledge about microbes and their sizes.

Now you are ready to make your own slides containing the microbial organisms. You will observe bacterial and yeast cells, and you will prepare the slides from liquid cultures. When you have viewed the organisms using the brightfield microscope, you will transfer your slides to the phase contrast microscope, where you will view the cells using darkfield and phase contrast settings. After recording your observations, you will make a wet mount using "mysterious cells" from broth cultures A and B. Cultures A and B will also be streaked on plates containing rich agar medium so you can see what colonies of culture A and B look like. Hint: one culture contains *E. coli* cells and the other *S. cerevisiae* cells. Which is which?

Materials

- TSB culture of *E. coli*
- TSB + 1% glucose culture of *S. cerevisiae*
- Agar plate A and broth culture A inoculated with *E. coli* or *S. cerevisiae*
- Agar plate B and broth culture B inoculated with *E. coli* or *S. cerevisiae*
- Brightfield microscope, phase contrast microscope
- Slides
- Coverslips
- Inoculating loop
- Droppers

Work in groups of four.

Exercise 1-4

Procedure

Each group of four will prepare and observe a wet mount of *E. coli* and one of *S. cerevisiae* that has been allowed to grow and divide in nutrient-containing broth media. When you are transferring the cells from the culture to the slide, you will use **aseptic technique**, a technique that prevents contamination of the cultures we are working with. We will use aseptic technique throughout this course, so now is a good time for you to familiarize yourself with the techniques.

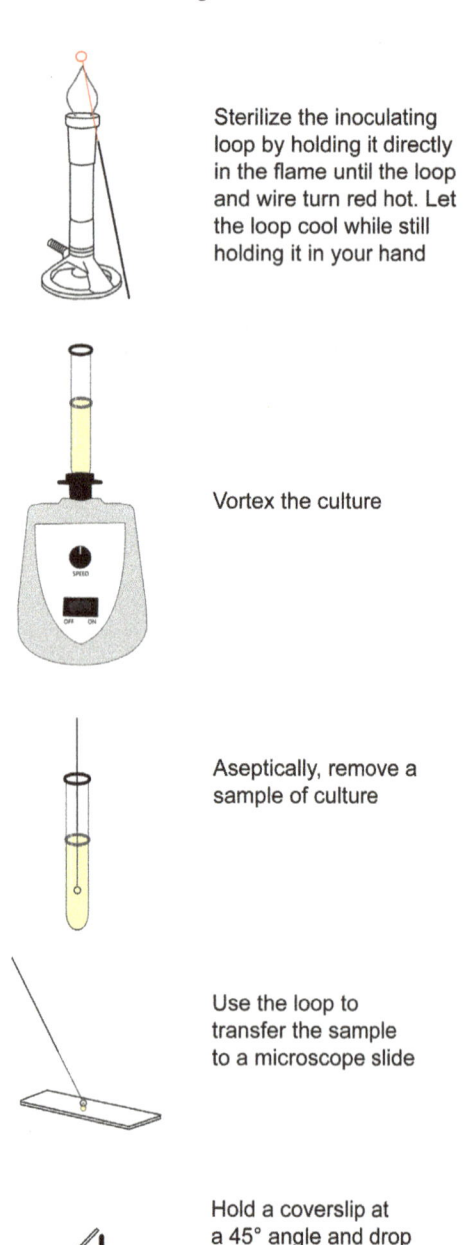

1. Using a wax pencil, label the slides with the respective names of the organisms you are about to view.
2. Ignite your source of open flame.
3. Vortex the broth culture containing *S. cerevisiae*
4. Sterilize the inoculating loop by holding it directly in the flame until the loop and wire turn red-hot. Let the loop cool while still holding it in your hand.
5. Take the culture tube from the rack with your free hand and hold it at a 45° angle. Remove the cap of the culture tube with the two or three fingers that are free on your hand that is holding the loop. Be sure to keep the cap pointed down at all times. Sterilize the lip of the culture tube by passing it through the flame.
6. Dip the loop into the culture and place a loop full of culture on the correctly labeled slide using an inoculation loop (loop).
7. Reflame the lip of the culture tube and replace the cap. Place the culture tube in the rack.
8. Sterilize the loop again by holding it directly in the flame until the entire loop and wire turn red-hot. Put the loop aside.
9. Hold a coverslip at a 45° angle against the microscope slide. Slowly move the edge of the coverslip towards the drop of cells. When the cell suspension spreads across the edge of the coverslip, gently drop the coverslip onto the microscope slide so that it covers the drop.

Sterilize the inoculating loop by holding it directly in the flame until the loop and wire turn red hot. Let the loop cool while still holding it in your hand

Vortex the culture

Aseptically, remove a sample of culture

Use the loop to transfer the sample to a microscope slide

Hold a coverslip at a 45° angle and drop it on the sample

FIGURE 1.11 Aseptic Wetmount Procedure

10. Now place the first wet-mount slide on the stage of the brightfield microscope, focus, and view the cells. Make sure that you have successfully prepared your wet mount (i.e., cells are present). The slide is then ready to be viewed with the phase contrast microscope.
11. Place the slide on the stage of the phase contrast microscope and use the directions provided to view the cells in brightfield mode. Once the cells are in focus using the 10X objective, move the 40X objective into place. Focus using the fine-focus knob only.
12. Use the directions provided to view the cells using the darkfield mode and, finally, the phase contrast mode.
13. Progress to the 100x objective. Rotate the nosepiece so that it is positioned halfway between the 40X and 100X objectives. You now have enough room to add oil to the slide.
14. View the *S. cerevisiae* slide using the 100x objective.
15. Record your observations and answer the questions in the *R & Q* section. Include descriptions of any structures you observe inside the *S. cerevisiae* cells.
16. Repeat steps 1-15 to make, view and record your observations of the *E. coli* wet mount.

Each group of four will prepare and observe wet mounts of cells from cultures A and B and identify the cultures as either bacteria (*E. coli*) or yeast (*S. cerevisiae*). Cells from cultures A and B have been inoculated in rich broth medium as well as streaked on plates containing rich medium. The cells were allowed to grow and divide in the broth medium to form a turbid broth and on the plates to form visible colonies. You will share the broth cultures and plates with the entire class, so these materials will stay in the common bench area.

17. Label a microscope slide "A."
18. Using a dropper, transfer a small drop of broth culture A located on the common area bench to the microscope slide.
19. Add the coverslip.
20. View the cells in the brightfield microscope using the appropriate objectives.
21. Discard slides in the red biohazard container when you are done viewing them.
22. Repeat steps 17–21 for cells in culture B.
23. Record the correct names of the species in the *R & Q* section.

Exercise 1-4

R & Q

Wet mount of *E. coli* and *S. cerevisiae*:

◯ Description: _____
   _____
   Specimen: _____
   Total Magnification: _____

◯ Description: _____
   _____
   Specimen: _____
   Total Magnification: _____

Describe the major differences you see when observing the same specimens in brightfield, darkfield, and phase contrast modes. Include clarity and the background surrounding the cells.

_____
_____
_____

S. cerevisiae is a eukaryotic organism, so the yeast cells have nuclei and other cellular organelles. Describe your observation regarding the appearance of these structures at 1000X total magnification. Did you see any buds (dividing cells)?

_____
_____
_____

Exercise 1-4

Were these structures easily seen using the brightfield, darkfield and phase contrast settings on the phase contrast microscopes?

_____
_____
_____

S. cerevisiae is nonmotile. Do the cells appear to be moving at all on this slide? What could cause nonmotile organisms to appear motile in a wet mount?

_____
_____
_____

Why do we vortex the cultures before transferring cells to the slide?

_____
_____
_____

What does it mean to transfer a sample from a culture tube aseptically? Write down the steps as you remember them. Then check if your answer is correct.

_____
_____
_____

Cultures A and B:

    Below, write the genus and species names of both organisms.

    Capitalize the first letter of the genus name and underline it.

    Do NOT capitalize the first letter of the species name and underline it separately from the genus name.

    Species in culture A:
    _____

    Species in culture B:
    _____

Exercise 1-4

Describe the colonies of Cultures A and B that appeared on the plates.
___

Are there any major differences in the appearance of the colonies?
___

We always underline or write names of the species in *italics* True or False?
___

Our daily lives somewhat depend on the *S. cerevisiae*. Do a bit of research and give two examples of why that could be.
___
___
___

Do some more research and describe a few habitats of *E. coli*.
___
___
___

Exercise 1-5

Microbial motility and pond water microbes (hay infusion)

Learning Objective

To become familiar with microbial motility and microbes around us.

Darkfield microscopy and phase contrast microscopes are very useful for determining bacterial motility. As we already know, cells such as yeast cells are not motile; however, if motile microorganisms are viewed just after a wet mount is prepared of the cells, you can detect their motility.

You will first prepare and view a slide of cells (from the provided culture tube) of the motile bacterium *E. coli* and look at its motility. Thereafter, you will prepare and view a sample from the hay infusion to view the world of diverse microbes that can be found in pond and creek water. The hay infusion is a suspension that has been set up to mimic a natural, pond-like habitat.

Materials

- TSB culture of *E. coli*
- Hay infusion
- Slides
- Coverslips
- Inoculating loop
- Dropper
- Brightfield microscope
- Phase contrast microscope

Work in pairs.

Procedure

1. Each pair in the group labels a slide "*E. coli*" with a wax pencil or, if possible, uses the slide from Exercise 1-4.
2. Vortex the broth culture containing cells of *E. coli*.
3. Flame the inoculating loop until loop and wire turn red-hot.

4. Take the culture tube from the rack with your free hand and hold it at a 45° angle. Remove the cap of the culture tube with the two or three fingers that are free on your hand that is holding the loop. Be sure to keep the cap pointed down at all times. Sterilize the lip of the culture tube by passing it through the flame.
5. Using a sterile inoculating loop, place a drop of the culture onto a clean microscope slide.
6. Sterilize the loop again by holding it directly in the flame until the entire loop and wire turn red-hot. Put the loop aside.
7. Add the coverslip.
8. View the cells with the phase contrast microscope, using brightfield and darkfield mode first and then using phase contrast mode. Finish viewing the specimen at a total of 1000X total magnification. Are the cells motile? Record your observation regarding the motility in the *R & Q* section.

Note: After about five minutes, the amount of oxygen in a wet mount may become depleted, and certain oxygen-dependent organisms will be unable to show motility.

9. Make a wet mount using a sample from the hay infusion.
10. Use a dropper to place a small drop of the hay infusion onto a clean microscope slide. It is not necessary to use aseptic technique when working with the hay infusion.
11. Add the coverslip.

Note: Make sure that you do not add too much liquid from the hay infusion; otherwise the coverslip will float and cells will move with the current, making it difficult to get the cells in focus.

12. Focus using the 10X objective first, and then the 40X objective.
13. Discard slides in the red biohazard container when you are done viewing them.

Exercise 1-5

R & Q

Explain the differences you observed when looking at *E. coli* in the brightfield, darkfield, and phase contrast modes. Focus on the clarity of the image, motility, and cellular details.

_____
_____
_____

Describe the appearance of *E. coli* motility.

_____
_____
_____

E. coli uses its flagella to move. The flagella are located over the entire surface of the cell. Did you see flagella at the magnification you were using?

_____
_____
_____

Why is it recommended to watch motility just minutes after preparing the wet mount?

_____
_____
_____

Which microscope and objective would you recommend that your lab partner use when viewing *E. coli* motility?

_____
_____
_____

Exercise 1-5

In the hay infusion, you most likely saw some of the eukaryotic microbes present at the 100X total magnification. To get a better idea of the diversity of organisms in this sample, you viewed the specimen at 400X total magnification, too. Organisms with different sizes and morphologies were most likely present.

Select two different but motile organisms; draw and describe them below.

Description: _____

_____

Specimen: _____

Total Magnification: _____

Description: _____

_____

Specimen: _____

Total Magnification: _____

Exercise 1-5

Are they protozoa, fungi, or bacteria?
_____

When viewing the sample, how do you identify which are eukaryotic and which are prokaryotic?
_____
_____
_____

Did you see any motile microbes? Explain what you saw regarding motility of the microbes.
_____
_____
_____

Remember that current flow and Brownian motion are not motility. Were you able to easily distinguish between motility, Brownian motion, and current flow?
_____

Why is it not necessary to use aseptic technique when preparing the slide with a sample of hay infusion?
_____
_____
_____

Exercise 1-6

Fungi and molds

Learning Objective

To get acquainted with fungi.

Although the yeast *Saccharomyces cerevisiae* is a fungus, it is not a mold like the fungus *Aspergillus niger*. You will easily be able to distinguish these two fungal genera from each other by looking at the plates (macroscopic) and by examining the wet mounts (microscopic) of the two organisms. These two organisms are excellent examples of the two basic morphologies seen in fungi.

Materials

- Agar plate of *Aspergillus niger*
- Prepared slide of *Aspergillus niger*
- Broth culture of *S. cerevisiae* (from Exercise 1-4)
- Agar plate of *S. cerevisiae* (from Exercise 1-4)

Work in pairs.

Procedure

1. View the agar plate of the hyphal fungus, *A. niger*, under the dissecting microscope. Include the area of the fungus, where the white hyphal mat produces the characteristic black spore-forming structures.
2. View the agar plate of *S. cerevisiae* that you identified in Exercise 1-4 and compare the morphologies of the two fungi. Record your observations in the *R & Q* Section.
3. Examine the prepared slide of *A. niger* using the brightfield microscope. You will be able to locate the spore-bearing structures on this organism. These are usually found at the ends of the hyphae. The spores appear relatively small, and their shapes are round to oval.
4. Compare your microscopic observations of *A. niger* with the observation of *S. cerevisiae* you obtained in Exercise 1-4. You may decide to make a new wet mount of *S. cerevisiae* for the comparison. Record your observations in the *R & Q* section.
5. When you have completed your observations, dispose of any slides that you have prepared (including the coverslips) in the red biohazard container.

Exercise 1-6   39

R & Q

Draw and describe the appearance of the fungus (*Aspergillus niger*) when viewed under the dissecting scope.

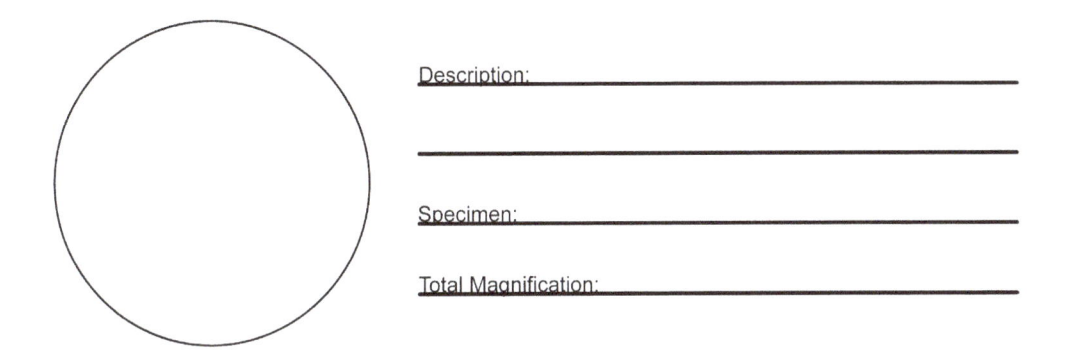

Description: _____

Specimen: _____

Total Magnification: _____

Draw and describe the prepared slide of the spore-forming structure of *Aspergillus niger* and your slide with *S. cerevisiae* when viewed using the brightfield microscope.

Description: _____

Specimen: _____

Total Magnification: _____

Description: _____

Specimen: _____

Total Magnification: _____

Exercise 1-6

Describe dissimilarities between the two fungi (*A. niger* and *S. cerevisiae*) on plates and slides. Did you find any similarities?

_____
_____
_____

Do some research and describe the natural habitats of *A. niger* and *S. cerevisiae*.

_____
_____
_____

Cleaning the microscope

Always clean your microscope thoroughly with lens-cleaning solution and gauze when you are finished using it.

This process includes the following steps:
1. Wipe down oculars
2. Wipe objective lenses from lowest to 100x
3. Dispose of gauze
4. Wipe sides of objectives
5. Wipe down stage
6. Wipe down knobs

It is important to **clean the oil objective last.** This is to avoid spreading oil onto the other objectives, which will damage them.

Discard your used gauze in the **regular trash**.

Show your cleaned microscope to your lab instructor for inspection before you return it to the cabinet.

If you store the microscope in a cabinet, make sure to place it with the arm of the microscope directed outward and the ocular lenses directed toward the back of the cabinet.

Cultivation and Staining Bacterial Cells for Microscopy

CULTIVATION OF BACTERIA

Bacteria and other microbes usually do not live as pure populations of single species in their respective natural habitats but rather together, in clusters consisting of many different species. However, the microbial strains that scientists use for their studies in the laboratories are mostly kept as **pure cultures** of one single species. This means that the individual cultures consist of only one type of microbial cells. Thus, one of the most essential and commonly used techniques in a microbiology lab is the three-phase streak, a procedure that, when performed successfully, will lead to separation (isolation) of individual cells of the microbial organisms on an agar medium. These isolated cells each grow and divide to form single separated colonies on the agar plate. We cannot see the single isolated cells immediately after streaking on the medium; we have to wait until enough cells have been produced from each single cell and a corresponding colony has formed.

The production of singe colonies on agar medium is often done by creating a **three-phase streak** plate using a technique we will learn to master in the upcoming exercises in this module. The entire procedure is done aseptically to minimize the risk of introducing contaminating microbial organisms (**contaminants**) to the cultures being streaked.

Contaminating microbes, whether originally present in our immediate working environment or on us, often benefit hugely from sharing the nutrients on the media that are intended only for the microorganisms of our study. Obviously, having contaminants present in the cultures we are working with will not only interfere with our examinations and observations but will also affect the final results we obtain. Therefore, we keep our cultures pure by employing aseptic technique as we continue to work with them (e.g., when we transfer cells from media to media, or media to slide in case of microscopic examinations). By working aseptically, we greatly reduce the risk of introducing other microbial organisms into our cultures, leaving our examinations and results unaffected and trustworthy.

Box 1 The Beginnings of Bacteriology

Let's go back to the 1860s and 1870s and the famous findings of the French chemist, microbiologist, and main founder of bacteriology, **Louis Pasteur (1822–1895)**. These findings, which explained why the production of wine and beer from time to time was entirely unsuccessful and resulted in an undesirable taste, is a good example of how contaminating microbes can spoil the outcome of a given task. Pasteur saved the wine and beer production of many breweries and wine makers, as he demonstrated that the reason for the unsuccessful production (the bad taste) was due to contamination from bacteria, molds, and undesirable wild yeast species during the different stages of production.

During this time, Pasteur worked with a number of different wine makers and breweries. Among those was the Carlsberg Brewery in Denmark. There, Pasteur worked in close contact with the Danish mycologist and fermentation physiologist **Emil Hansen (1842–1909)** to save the large-scale production of the Danish beers.

Louis Pasteur

By that time, Hansen had isolated yeast for the first time and managed to grow the organism as a pure culture. He saw that more yeast species existed but found that only a few of those species could be successfully used for brewing beer. Hansen shared his yeast, *Saccharomyces carlsbergensis*, with other brewers worldwide who had encountered similar problems with their beer production. *Saccharomyces carlsbergensis* (also named *Saccharomyces pastorianus*) is still used in brewing lager beer today.

Pasteur and **Robert Koch (1843–1910)**—a German physician, main founder of bacteriology, and Nobel prize laureate—were the first to isolate pure cultures of bacteria.

Koch continued work on perfecting bacterial identification techniques and cultivation methods, which also led to the development of solid agar plates. With the help of his postdoctoral assistant, **Walter Hesse (1846–1911)**, who was inspired by his wife Fannie's agar containing jellies and puddings, the solid agar culture media were soon developed. In addition, the petri dish was invented by Koch's assistant, **Julius Richard Petri (1852–1921)**.

During these years, many scientists were inspired to continue Koch's great work, and even today scientists worldwide are employing the research techniques he developed and perfected.

Reference
Blevins, Steve M. and Michael S. Bronze. "Robert Koch and the 'Golden Age' of Bacteriology." *International Journal of Infectious Diseases* 14, no. 9 (September 2010): e744–e751.

Source: https://commons.wikimedia.org/wiki/File:Louis_Pasteur,_Archives_Photographiques.jpg. Copyright in the Public Domain.

In the lab, we will be working with microorganisms that are typically stored as **glycerol stocks** of pure cultures in a −80°C freezer. In order to grow cells from a glycerol culture, a small amount of cells is removed from the stock and transferred to either autoclaved (sterilized) solid growth medium (agar plates containing nutrients) or autoclaved liquid medium (broth medium containing nutrients). Here they are allowed to grow and divide until they have increased sufficiently in cell numbers and produced adequate biomass for us to work with.

Box 2 Autoclaving

At the time Pasteur was engaged in saving the products of wine makers and breweries, he was also executing his pioneer work in connection to the findings and beliefs of the Italian priest, physiologist, and biologist **Lazzaro Spallanzani (1729–1799)**. Spallanzani proposed that microbial cells originated from parent cells and could not appear spontaneously, as was assumed by some scientists at that time. Spallanzani had already shown that, in contrast to unboiled broth, broth that had been boiled did not give rise to the growth of microbes; he had even documented a microscopic observation during which he saw, with his own eyes, a single microbe become two. Despite Spallanzini's experiments and observations, the theory of "spontaneous generation of microbes" was not disproven before the work of Pasteur and the Irish physicist **John Tyndall (1820–1893)**.

Tyndall is also recognized for providing evidence for the importance of sterilizing growth medium to prevent the presence of contaminating microbes. Today, we use the **autoclave** to sterilize the medium prior to use. The autoclave uses heat under pressure and kills all microbes in the vegetative stage, as well as resistant endospores (or spores). Tyndall was able to show a similar sterilization technique simply by repeating cycles of heating and resting; his results showed that such cycles would kill off all vegetative microbes as well as their resistant endospores, which, during the resting period, would germinate and be killed in the following boiling cycle.

FIGURE 2.1 Autoclave

Nutritional needs and temperature requirements

In this module, you will also briefly be introduced to the fact that different kinds of bacteria have specific optimal growth temperatures. The optimal temperatures can differ to such an extent that some microbes prefer to live in cold places, some at body temperature, and others in hot springs. In addition, bacteria also have different nutritional needs. These requirements, as well as their biochemical characteristics, are important traits to have in mind when classifying or grouping individual bacterial microorganisms.

The lab prep staff will provide microbial organisms grown on agar plates or in liquid media for you to work with in this exercise. You will examine those organisms using the brightfield and phase contrast microscopes, and you will learn more about how to **aseptically** (i.e., preventing contamination) handle these cultures as you transfer them from plate to plate, from plate to liquid, from liquid to liquid, or from liquid to plate. You will also learn the very important microbiological technique—the three-phase streak that was briefly mentioned above—to produce **single isolated colonies**. This is an essential technique we will use now, as well as later, to create pure cultures from mixed cultures containing two or more microorganisms.

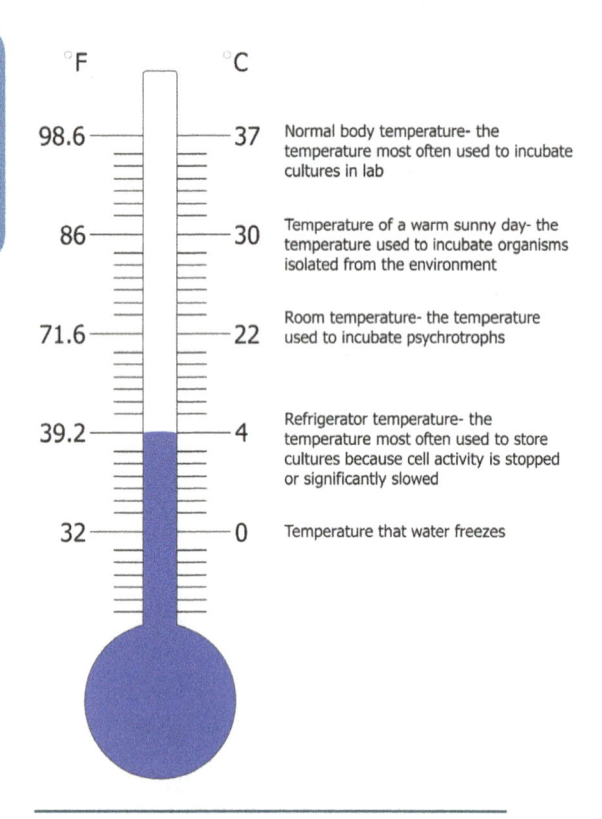

°F	°C	
98.6	37	Normal body temperature- the temperature most often used to incubate cultures in lab
86	30	Temperature of a warm sunny day- the temperature used to incubate organisms isolated from the environment
71.6	22	Room temperature- the temperature used to incubate psychrotrophs
39.2	4	Refrigerator temperature- the temperature most often used to store cultures because cell activity is stopped or significantly slowed
32	0	Temperature that water freezes

FIGURE 2.2 Temperatures in C and F

Enumeration of microbes

Microbiologists in research labs or in various industrial and medical settings often have to determine the concentration of microbes in a given sample (i.e., the number of cells in a given sample). For example, many scientific investigations require a microbial culture to have reached a particular concentration or a certain growth phase before a specific set of experiments can be carried out. In fact, some studies focus directly on the influence that varying the cell size of a microbial population has on the specific phenomenon being investigated.

Analysis of water and food quality also involves enumeration of microbes, and the use of microbes in manufacturing industrial products often includes the maintenance of cultures at a specific cell number or growth phase.

In this exercise, you will learn how to calculate the number of cells in a given liquid culture by appropriately diluting the culture and performing spread plates of the individual dilutions. You will then use the number of colonies appearing on the plate to calculate the number of cells in the original culture.

We learned above the importance of making the work area as sterile as possible by employing aseptic technique and procedures to prevent contaminating the cultures that we are working with. In the first half of Module 2, we will go further into detail with these techniques as we learn how to streak cultures on agar medium and inoculate a bacterial liquid culture. As you proceed through these inoculations successfully, you will know how to 1) obtain pure culture plates containing isolated colonies, 2) initiate the examination of cultures for nutritional needs and temperature requirements, 3) calculate the number of cells in a given culture, and 4) separate organisms from a mixed culture and continue by examining their colony and cell morphologies.

Exercise 2-1

Streaking Microorganisms to Obtain Single Isolated Colonies

Learning Objectives

To master the three-phase streak technique.
To understand the importance of obtaining single isolated colonies.

In order to obtain isolated colonies on a agar plate, we need to streak a given culture of cells in such a way that we end up, in the final streaks, distributing only a few cells along a particular area of the plate. It is sort of a dilution process of the culture that occurs as streaking of the cells across the plate proceeds. This streak procedure, called the three-phase streak technique, increases the chance of obtaining separated individual cells on the agar plates. These separated individual cells will then grow and divide to form a visible colony of cells on the agar plate. We say that each colony originates from one isolated cell, although it is possible for two attached cells to grow up as one colony.

Day 1

Materials

- TSB culture of *E. coli*
- TSA plate
- Inoculation loop

Each student will perform this exercise.

- TSA plate

Entire class will perform this exercise.

Procedure

1. With your marker, label the bottom (the agar part) of a TSA plate with:
   - Name of student
   - Name of organism (remember to underline i.e. <u>E. coli</u>)
   - Medium (TSA)

Exercise 2-1

- Date
- Incubation temperature (37°C)

2. With a marker, divide the plate in three sectors, as shown in Figure 2.3 "Three-phase streak," with the first sector being smaller than the remaining two.

Follow the succeeding steps in order, using aseptic technique as you perform the three-phase streak.

3. Light the Bunsen burner.
4. Sterilize the loop by holding it in the flame until the entire loop and wire turn red-hot. Let the loop cool down while holding it in your hand.
5. Remove a small sample of the TSB culture by dipping the loop into the culture.
6. On the top section of the plate, form the primary streak, starting by lightly dragging the loop across the surface of the medium, as shown in Figure 2.3, "Three-phase streak." Use a zigzag pattern to streak across the area of the primary section. *Do not* overlap any of the streaks.
7. Flame the loop by holding it in the flame until the entire loop and wire turn red-hot. Let the loop cool down while holding it in your hand.

Note: It is important to sterilize the loop between each phase of the streak.

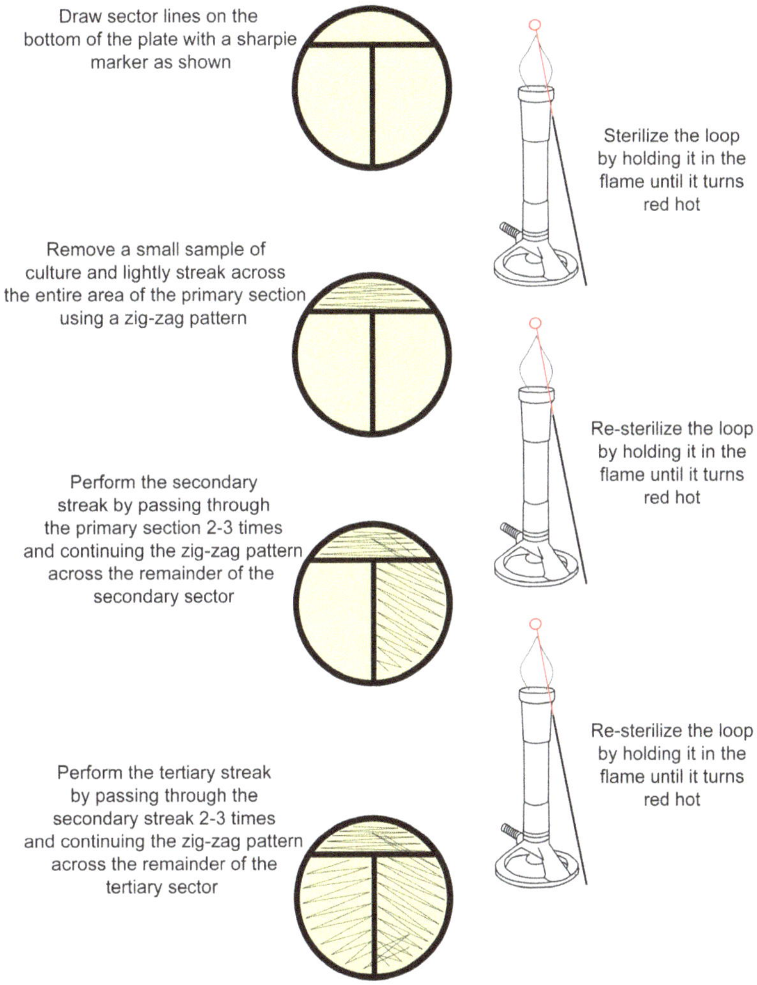

FIGURE 2.3 3-Phase Streak Technique

8. To perform the second streak, start on the right section of the plate, close to the edge. With the resterilized loop, pass through the cells of the primary section 2–3 times and continue spreading the cells, again using the zigzag pattern, across the entire secondary section.
9. Reflame the loop as in step 7.
10. Perform the third streak by starting on the left section of the plate. Pass through the second section 2–3 times while continuing to streak, using the zigzag pattern, across the entire tertiary section.
11. Reflame the loop and set it aside.
12. Incubate the plate at 37°C overnight. Note: When placing your plate to be incubated, invert the plate so that the agar is on top. This will prevent condensation from forming on the surface of the agar.

To examine the likelihood of acquiring contaminants on a TSA plate if aseptic technique was not employed, your instructor will place a TSA plate in the lab with the lid off for the entire period. The plate will be placed away from Bunsen burners. At the end of the lab period, the lid will be placed on the plate and it will be incubated at 30°C for 1–3 days. This exercise can be performed with one TSA plate per lab section.

Day 2

Materials

- TSA plate streaked in previous lab period

Each student will perform this exercise.
- TSA plate left with open lid in previous lab period.

Entire class will perform this exercise.

Procedure

1. Examine the three-phase streak plate and confirm the presence of single isolated colonies in the appropriate sectors of the plate.
2. Ask your lab instructor or TAs to evaluate your plate and answer the questions in the *R & Q* section.
3. Examine the TSA plate that was left without the lid during Day 1. Describe your observations in the *R & Q* section.

Exercise 2-1

R & Q

Day 1

Provide an explanation for why we incubated the plate without a lid (from Day 1) at 30°C for 1–3 days and the three-phase streak plate at 37°C only until the following day.

_____
_____
_____

Why is it necessary to autoclave the bacterial growth media before inoculating the media with the bacterial strains of our studies?

_____
_____
_____

Explain why it is important to always sterilize the loop between streaking each section.

_____
_____
_____

Day 2

Does your three-phase streak have any isolated colonies? Describe the appearance of the three sectors.

_____
_____
_____

If you ended up with only a few or no isolated colonies, suggest what needs to be improved regarding your streak technique. Discuss your answer with the TA or lab instructor.

_____
_____
_____

Observe the plate that your instructor left with the lid off for the entire lab period. Describe what you see on the plate

_____
_____
_____

Exercise 2-2

Streaking Bacterial Organisms to Examine Nutritional Needs

Learning Objectives

To become familiar with the differences in nutritional needs among bacteria.
To begin to gather knowledge about the variety of bacterial growth media.

Bacteria are a diverse group of organisms. They differ largely, not only with respect to their morphological characteristics but also with respect to their nutritional and temperature requirements for growth and biochemical activities. Many of these bacterial traits can also be used to classify the bacterial organisms. In this exercise, we will get an idea of the diversity of bacteria regarding nutritional requirements. We will also reflect on whether an organism is fastidious or non-fastidious, i.e. does the organism require addition of specific and often complex nutrients in the medium to grow.

Organism	MM1	MM1 without glucose	MM1 without sulfur	TSA	BHI
Escherichia coli					
Streptococcus salivarius					
Staphylococcus epidermidis					

Day 1

Materials

- TSB culture of *S. epidermidis*
- TSB culture of *S. salivarius*
- TSB culture of *E. coli*
- MM1 Agar Plate
- MM1 Agar Plate without Glucose

Exercise 2-2

- MM1 Agar Plate without Sulfur
- TSA plate
- BHI plate
- Inoculation loop
- Bunsen burner

Work in groups of four.

Procedure

1. Distribute the five plates among your group of four. Divide each plate into three equally sized sections. Label each section according to the names of each of the three bacteria. Complete labeling your plate with all other required information.
2. Use the loop to streak each of the three organisms in the corresponding section on the plate. Use aseptic technique and streak the organisms using a zigzag pattern. Figure 2.4, "Streaking zigzag pattern"
3. Invert the inoculated plates and incubate at 37°C for 24–48 hours.

   Note: Always sterilize the loop between working with different organisms.

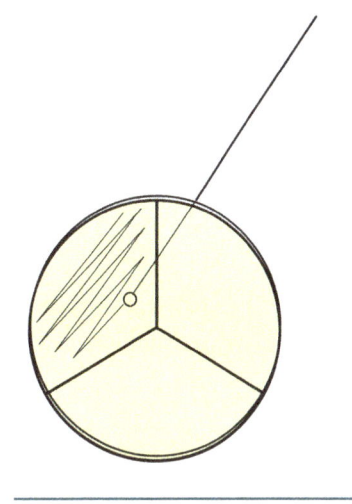

FIGURE 2.4 Streaking zigzag pattern

Day 2

Materials

- Plates streaked in previous lab period

Work in groups of four.

Procedure

1. Record your observations of the TSA plates in the table in the *R & Q* section.

Exercise 2-2

R & Q

Why is it important to always sterilize the loop between streaking the different organisms?

___

A fastidious bacterial organism requires a complex range of nutrients for growth. Can any of the bacterial species tested for growth here be considered fastidious? Explain your answer.

___

Which organism seems to be less demanding in its nutritional requirements?

___

Does the less-nutrition-demanding bacterial organism grow faster or slower than the fastidious organism? Why do you think that is?

___

Exercise 2-3

Streaking Microorganisms to Examine Temperature Requirements

Learning Objective

To become familiar with the differences in temperature requirements of bacteria.

Similar to the previous exercise ("Streaking Bacterial Organisms to Examine Nutritional Needs"), here we will investigate a few bacterial strains for their temperature requirements.

Day 1

Materials

- TSB culture of *Janthinobacterium* sp.
- TSB culture of *S. epidermidis*
- TSB culture of *G. stearothermophilus*
- TSA plates (4)
- Inoculation loop
- Sterile swabs (optional)

Work in groups of four.

Procedure

1. Distribute the four TSA plates among your group of four. Divide each plate into three equally sized sections. Label each section according to the names of each of the three bacteria.
   - *Janthinobacterium* sp.
   - *Staphylococcus epidermidis*
   - *Geobacillus stearothermophilus*

Exercise 2-3

2. Complete labeling your plate with all other required information, including the temperature at which each respective plate will be incubated: 4°C, 22°C, 37°C, or 55°C.
3. Streak the bacterial organisms using zig-zag pattern in the corresponding sectors of the plates. Use aseptic technique.

   Note: Always sterilize the loop between working with different organisms.

   Note: In order for *G. stearothermophilus* to show growth, it is necessary to add several loopfuls of cells to the respective sectors. Alternatively, a swab can be used to plate the cells. Do not flame the swabs!

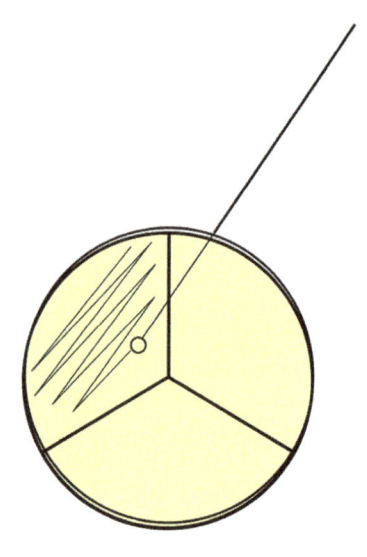

4. Invert the plates when the inocula have dried and incubate the plates at the indicated temperatures for 24–48 hours.

Day 2

Materials

- Plates inoculated in previous lab period

Work in groups of four.

Procedure

1. Record your observations in the table in the *R & Q* section and answer the questions.

Exercise 2-3   55

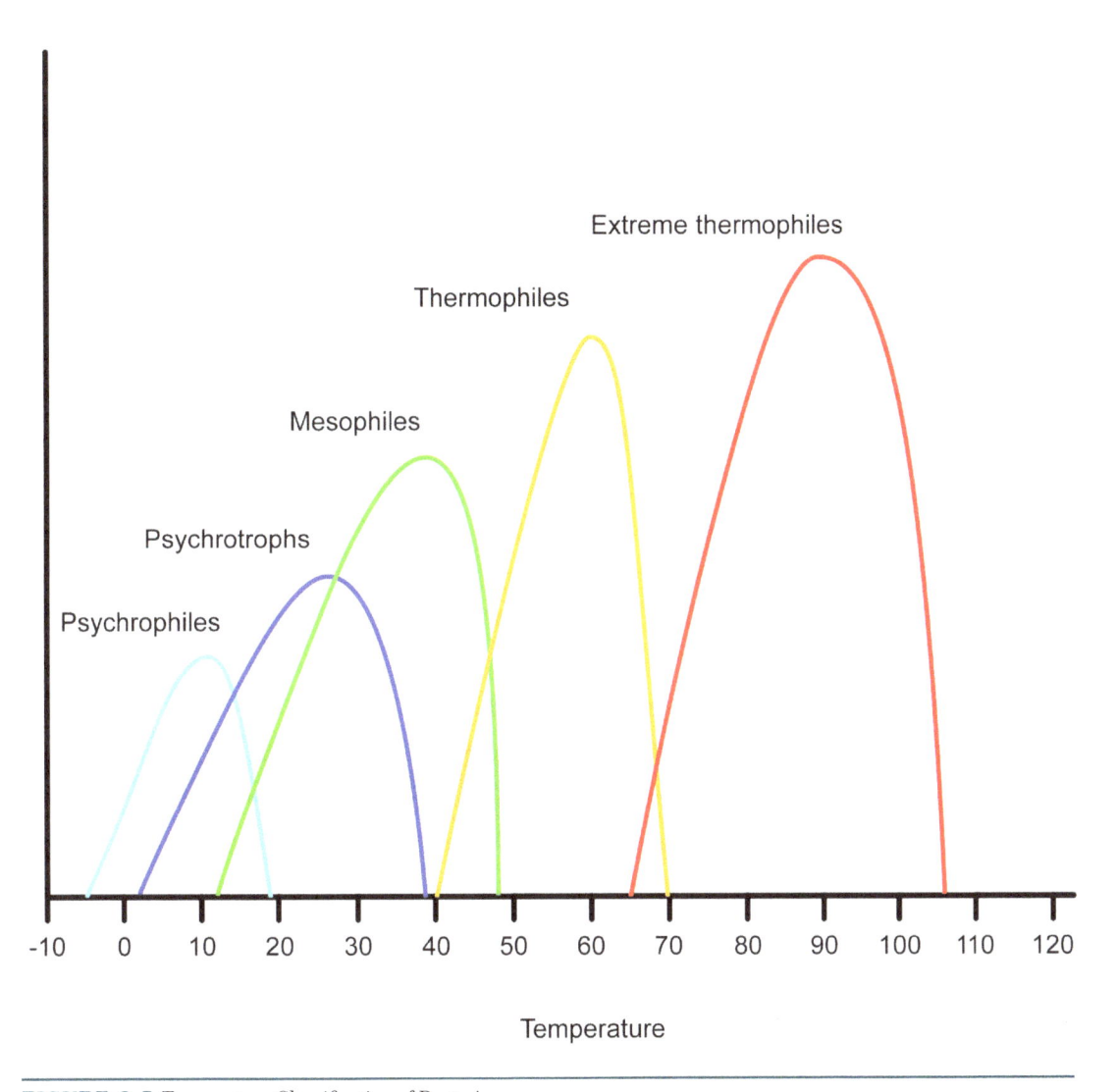

FIGURE 2.5 Temperature Classification of Bacteria

Exercise 2-3

R & Q

Organism	4 °C	22 °C	37 °C	55 °C
Janthinobacterium sp.				
Staphylococcus epidermidis				
Geobacillus stearothermophilus				

Looking at Figure 2.5 "Temperature Classification of Bacteria," describe which class each of the microbes you and your group of four tested falls into.

- *Janthinobacterium* sp.

- *S. epidermidis:*

- *G. stearothermophilus:*

Do some research and record the natural habitats you found for each of these bacteria species.

_____
_____
_____

Do these habitats make sense in regard to your temperature classification of these bacterial species?

_____
_____
_____

Can any of them grow and divide if placed in hot springs (85°C)? Explain your answer.

_____
_____
_____

Exercise 2-4

Isolating and Characterizing Bacteria from a Mixed Culture

Learning Objectives

To become familiar with pure culture techniques.
To increase understanding of colony and cell morphologies.

As you will see in this exercise, it is essential to work with pure cultures when studying bacterial characteristics.

You will once again perform the three-phase streak plate method; however, in contrast to the previous exercise, here you are provided with a mixed culture of two different bacterial species. You will use the three-phase streak technique to progressively dilute the mixed bacterial culture so that, at the end of the streak procedure, cells are spread across the surface so thinly that individual cells are isolated from each of the two species. After growth, this will give rise to single isolated colonies of the two different bacterial species.

When a bacterial colony is well isolated on the agar, it is considered to consist of cells of only one species. This is because all cells within the colony are regarded as offspring of the single bacterial cell that was separated from the other cells when performing the three-phase streak. By performing an additional streak of cells from the isolated colony, a pure culture plate will be generated (since it contains only one type of organism).

Day 1

Materials

- Saline suspension of:
  - Bacterial mixture 1
  - Bacterial mixture 2
  - Bacterial mixture 3
- TSA plates (4)
- Inoculating loop
- Bunsen burner

Work in groups of four.

Procedure

1. Each student in the group of four labels a TSA plate with all required information, including the respective number of the culture mixture to be streaked. Two students in each group of four will streak mixtures 1 and 2 respectively, and two students will both streak plates using mixture 3.
2. Perform the three-phase streak, using aseptic technique, to obtain single colonies of the mixed culture.
3. Incubate the plates streaked with mixtures 1 and 2 at 37°C. Tape closed the two plates of mixture 3 and incubate the plates at 37°C and room temperature (22°C), respectively.

Day 2

Materials

- TSA plates streaked in the previous lab period
- TSA plates (4)
- Inoculating loop
- Bunsen burner

Work in groups of four.

Procedure

1. Collect the three-phase streak plates that you streaked on Day 1. Do not remove the tape from the plates of Mixture 3 that were incubated at 37°C and 22°C. These plates are for observation only.
2. Examine all four plates in your group for isolated colonies. Confirm the presence of two distinct colony morphologies on each plate and that no contaminants are present.
3. In the *R & Q* section, using Box 3 and Figure 2.6 "Colony Morphology," describe the appearance of the two colony types on your plate, along with the remaining three plates of your group.

Recall that the purpose of the three-phase streak plate technique is to produce a pure culture. This is accomplished by diluting the original inoculum in such a way that the individual bacterial cells are separated from one another. After growth, the individual separated cells will form colonies, and these colonies are the ones we will use to generate pure culture plates.

4. Use a tiny amount of cells (i.e., corresponding to the size of the head of a tiny pin) of a separated colony from the Mix 1 and Mix 2 plates streaked on Day 1 to make a fresh three-phase streak plate. Do not streak any colonies from the Mix 3 plates that are closed with tape.

Exercise 2-4

5. Incubate the plates overnight at 37°C.

> **Box 3 Colony Morphology and Physical Characteristics**
>
> - **Color (Pigmentation):** Color or the absence of color
>
> - **Texture and consistency:** Rough or smooth; wrinkled; shiny or dull; dry or moist
>
> - **Type of margin or edge**: entire/regular; undulating/wavy; lobed; or filamentous
>
> - **Type of elevation:** cells are raised (elevated) above the surface of the agar; flat (not elevated); convex; or umbonate (only center of colony raised)
>
> - **Opacity:** Transparent; translucent (allow some light to penetrate); or opaque (colonies appear dense and allow no light to penetrate the cells)

Exercise 2-4

CONSISTENCY

TRANSPARENT TRANSPARENT   TRANSLUCENT TRANSLUCENT   OPAQUE

MARGIN

SMOOTH   UNDULATING   LOBED

IRREGULAR   CILIATE   FILAMENTOUS

ELEVATION

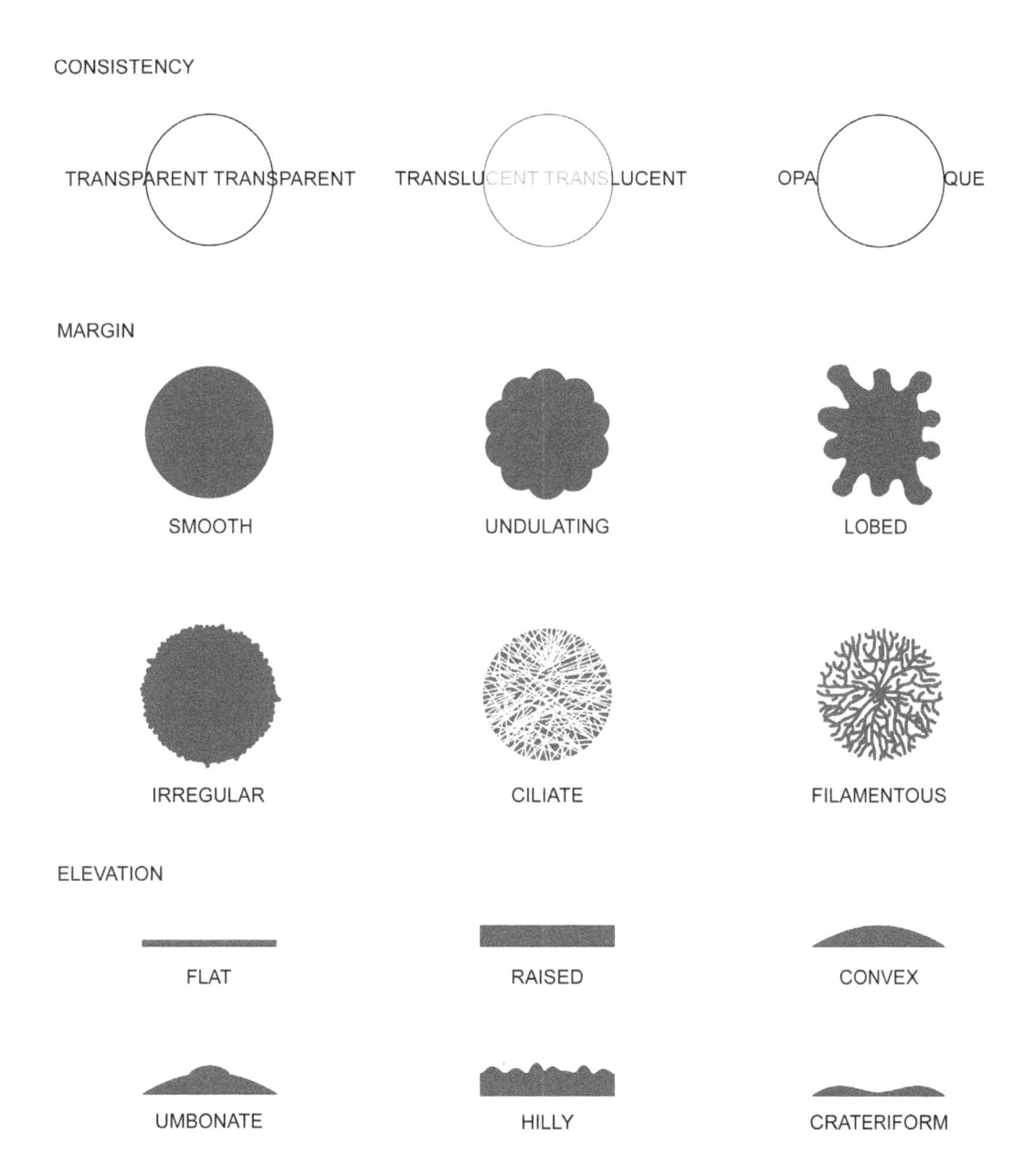

FLAT   RAISED   CONVEX

UMBONATE   HILLY   CRATERIFORM

FIGURE 2.6 Colony Morphology

Exercise 2-4

Mix	Organism	Colony Morphology	Gram Reaction and Cellular Morphology
Mix 1	*Escherichia coli*	*E. coli* produces **off-white colonies, translucent, shiny and moist** in appearance; their **surfaces** tend to be **smooth** and the **edges** of the colonies are usually **entire** when the colonies are small, but tend to be more **undulating** when colonies are larger or the culture is older (although overall, the colonies of a pure *E. coli* culture plate are expected to have the same colony morphology). *E. coli* also has a distinct aroma that you may recognize over time.	Gram negative bacilli
	Bacillus subtilis	*B. subtilis* produces rather **large, opaque, white-colored, irregular** colonies that appear **dry, dull and rough**.	Gram positive bacilli
Mix 2	*Streptococcus salivarius*	*Streptococcus salivarius* produces **opaque, small, off-white** colonies that are **smooth, shiny** and **convex** in appearance. The **edges** of the colonies are **entire**.	Gram positive cocci
	Enterobacter aerogenes	*Enterobacter aerogenes* produces **larger off-white** colonies that are **translucent** and **moist** in appearance; the edges of these colonies are **slightly undulating**; these colonies also appear **raised** above the surface of the agar.	Gram negative bacilli
Mix 3 at 37 °C	*Serratia marcescens*	*S. marcescens* produces **creamy colored colonies**. These colonies have **regular edges, fairly smooth surfaces**, and may be somewhat **raised** above the surface of the agar; they should also be **shiny** in appearance. The centers of the colonies tend to appear somewhat denser than the edges.	Gram negative bacilli
	Staphylococcus epidermidis	*S. epidermidis* produces **shiny** colonies that are **opaque, white** in color, and have **smooth, regular edges**; this organism is the **smaller** of the two colony types in the mixture.	Gram positive cocci
Mix 3 at 22 °C	*Serratia marcescens*	*S. marcescens* produces **reddish-orange colored colonies**. These colonies have **regular edges, fairly smooth surfaces**, and may be somewhat **raised** above the surface of the agar; they should also be **shiny** in appearance. The centers of the colonies tend to appear somewhat denser than the edges.	Gram negative bacilli
	Staphylococcus epidermidis	*S. epidermidis* produces **shiny** colonies that are **opaque, white** in color, and have **smooth, regular edges**; this organism is the **smaller** of the two colony types in the mixture.	Gram positive cocci

Exercise 2-4

Day 3

Materials

- Pure culture plates generated in previous lab period
- Crystal violet
- Gram's iodine
- Acetone-alcohol solution
- Safranin
- Bibulous paper
- Inoculating loop
- Bunsen burner
- Slide
- Brightfield microscope

Work individually.

Procedure

Divide the plates containing pure cultures of Mixes 1 and 2 amoung your group of 4. Use the following procedure to Gram stain the colony types that are present on your plates.

Exercise 2-4

Use the loop to add a small drop of water to a labeled microscope slide

Use a sterilized loop to take a small sample of culture and mix the sample into the drop of water creating a thin smear on the slide

When the smear has air dried completely, heat fix the slide by holding it with a clothespin and passing it over the flame 2-3 times

Cover the smear with crystal violet and allow it to remain on the smear for 60 seconds

After 60 seconds has elapsed, throughly rinse the slide with distilled water

Cover the slide with Gram's iodine and allow it to remain on the smear for 60 seconds

After 60 seconds has elapsed, throughly rinse the slide with distilled water

Briefly rinse the slide with acetone-alcohol for 2-3 seconds

Immediately rinse the slide with distilled water

Completely cover the smear with safranin and allow it to remain on the smear for 90 seconds

After 90 seconds has elapsed, throughly rinse the slide with distilled water

Blot the slide dry using Bibulous Paper

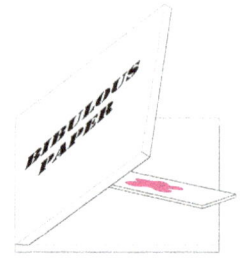

FIGURE 2.7 Gram stain

Exercise 2-4

R & Q

Day 2

Describe the morphology of the colonies you isolated.

_____
_____
_____

Describe the morphologies of the colonies isolated by your group of four lab partners.

_____
_____
_____

Comment on the microbial diversity that you observed on the four plates.

_____
_____
_____

Describe anything noticeable in regards to incubation temperatures for mixture 3.

_____
_____
_____

Colony morphology of a bacterium can be a first step in the identification process of a bacterial species. Some organisms are so distinct in their colony characteristics that, using these characteristics alone, their identities can be narrowed down to the genus level with relative certainty.

Are you able to identify the bacterial species on your plates by the characteristics you have observed so far?

_____
_____
_____

Exercise 2-4

Day 3

Describe and draw your observation of the bacterial strains after Gram staining in the area below.

Gram Reaction: _____

Cellular Morphology: _____

Cellular Arrangement: _____

Total Magnification: _____

Gram Reaction: _____

Cellular Morphology: _____

Cellular Arrangement: _____

Total Magnification: _____

Are you able to identify the bacterial species on your plates by the characteristics you observed after Gram staining?

_____

_____

Exercise 2-5

Dilution and Enumeration Using Spread Plate Technique

Learning Objectives

To learn how to perform a dilution series.
To learn how to enumerate cells.
To learn how to calculate the concentration of cells in a given culture.

The concentration of cells in a culture (i.e., the number of cells in a given volume of culture) can be determined in a number of different ways. Two of the three ways described below account for the number of cells in a culture regardless of viability, whereas the third accounts for only viable cells in the culture. This latter method is called the Total Viable Count and is discussed in detail first.

The Total Viable Count. This method allows a direct quantification of the number of living cells in the culture. A **serial dilution** (i.e., a step-by-step dilution) is prepared from a given culture, and the diluted samples are plated on nutrient-containing agar plates in such a way that colonies can be counted after incubation of the plates. Since the dilution factors of each dilution are known and the number of colonies on the corresponding plates can be counted, the concentration of viable cells in the original culture can be calculated. It is important to note that each colony represents one single cell that has undergone successive divisions and grown up as a visible colony. However, since the chance is that two or more cells may have given rise to a single colony instead of just a single cell, we calculate the **cell concentration** in the original culture as colony forming units per ml (**CFU/ml**).

Thus, the **enumeration** of a given microbial culture can be calculated as follows:

$$\frac{\text{Number of CFU}}{\text{Volume Plated} \times \text{Total Dilution}} = \text{CFU} / \text{ml}$$

Spread plate (or pour plate) methods are used for the Total Viable Count procedure. A **countable plate** contains between thirty and three hundred colonies. Plates that contain more than three hundred colonies or less than thirty colonies are not counted and therefore not used for calculation of CFU/ml of the original culture.

Exercise 2-5

The Petroff-Hausser counting chamber. This is a counting chamber consisting of a lined slide that is constructed so that the lined area matches a defined volume. The number of bacteria in this defined, small-lined area is counted using the compound brightfield microscope, and a provided formula is used to estimate the number of cells in the larger original sample. This procedure accounts for all cells in the culture, not only those cells that are alive.

Optical density OD. Cell numbers in a bacterial culture can be determined using a spectrophotometer. The spectrophotometer measures (in nanometers, or nm) the amount of light of a specified wavelength that passes through a sample of a bacterial culture. This method uses the assumption that the amount of light absorbed by the bacterial culture is proportional to the concentration of the bacterial cells in the culture. Typically, 600 nm is used for the optical density (OD_{600}) readings of the bacterial cell cultures. A sample of uninoculated growth medium (blank) is placed in a cuvette and inserted into the spectrophotometer. This reading is set to zero. Subsequently, a sample of the bacterial culture that has been grown in a similar medium is inserted into the spectrophotometer. The optical density is read and recorded. This procedure is repeated for all cell cultures for which the determination of the cell numbers is needed. The approximate cells/ml of the cultures can be determined using the assumption that OD_{600} of 1 corresponds to approximately 1×10^9 cell/ml of the culture.

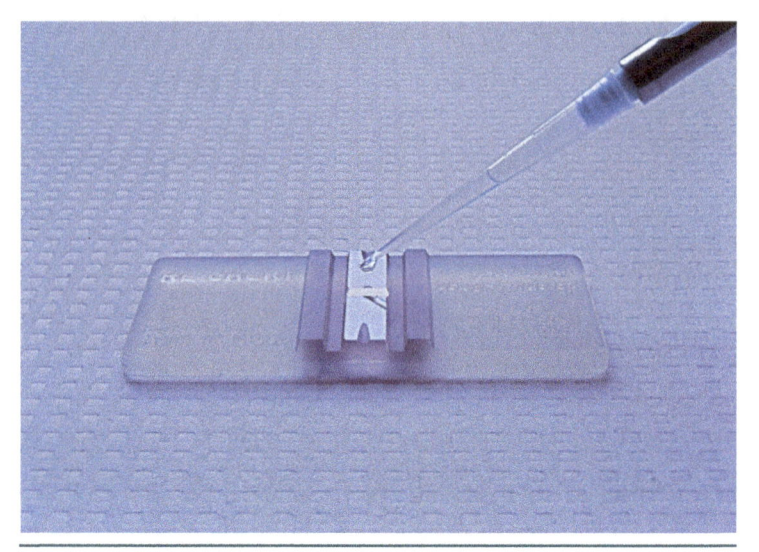

FIGURE 2.8 Petroff-Hausser counting chamber

Source: Copyright © Todd (CC BY-SA 2.0) at https://commons.wikimedia.org/wiki/File:Hemocytometer.jpg.

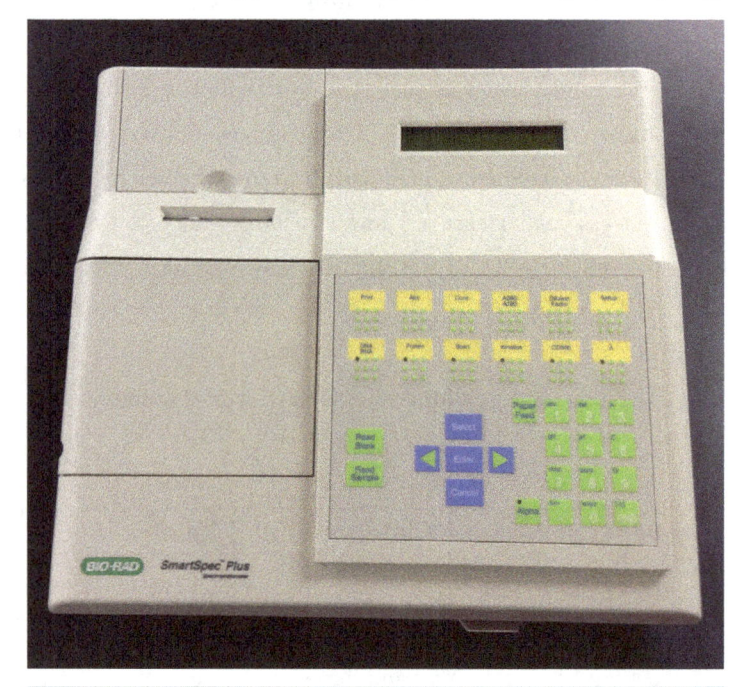

FIGURE 2.9 Spectrophotometer

Exercise 2-5

In this exercise, we will use the Total Viable Count method to enumerate cells in a culture of unknown cell concentration. We will prepare a dilution series and then spread samples of the dilutions onto TSA plates. We will use the spread plate techniques described below, incubate the samples at an appropriate temperature, and subsequently count the colonies present on the plates.

Occasionally, the pour plate technique is used in place of the **spread plate** technique. When performing the the pour plate technique, instead of spreading the cell on the surface of the agar plate, the diluted sample is mixed directly with the melted agar medium and poured into the petri dish or, alternatively, mixed with the melted agar directly in the petri dish. We will perform pour plate technique later when studying microbial organisms in food samples (Module 3).

Before we start diluting the culture, look at the calculation below, which shows how to determine the number of cells in an original culture. Complete the question that follows.

Four different dilutions were plated in duplicate (two spread plates per dilution). After incubation, the numbers of colonies on the plates originating from 0.1 ml of the cultures were:

Too high to count (10^{-3} total dilution)
389 and 435 (10^{-4} total dilution)
56 and 47 (10^{-5} total dilution)
15 and 23 (10^{-6} total dilution).

Similar to Figure 2.10, "Dilution Series", draw the tubes and plates used for the serial dilution. Indicate 1) how many ml of the dilutions were used for making the spread plates and 2) the individual and total dilutions.

Show drawing here:

Show how to calculate the concentration of colony-forming units per ml (cells/ml) in the original culture. Average the number of colonies from the plates created in doublets (two spread plate per dilution) to get the final CFU/ ml. Check your result with your TA before continuing with the exercise.

Colony-forming units per ml (cells/ml) in the original culture:

Practice using micropipettes or serological pipettes (refer to videos on how to use micropipettes and serological pipettes) before continuing this exercise.

Exercise 2-5

Day 1

Materials

- TSB culture of *E.coli*
- TSB broth tube
- Inoculating loop
- Bunsen burner

Work in groups of four.

Procedure

1. Ignite the Bunsen burner.
2. Aseptically remove a small amount of cells from the TSB culture to the TSB broth tube. Revisit the aseptic technique procedures to refresh your knowledge of this procedure.
3. Incubate the TSB culture tube at 37°C for twenty-four hours.

Day 2

Materials

- TSB broth tube inoculated in previous lab
- Tubes with 9.9 ml saline (2)
- Tubes with 4.5 ml saline (3)
- TSA plates (4)
- Spreader
- Beaker with alcohol
- Bunsen burner

Work in groups of four.

Exercise 2-5

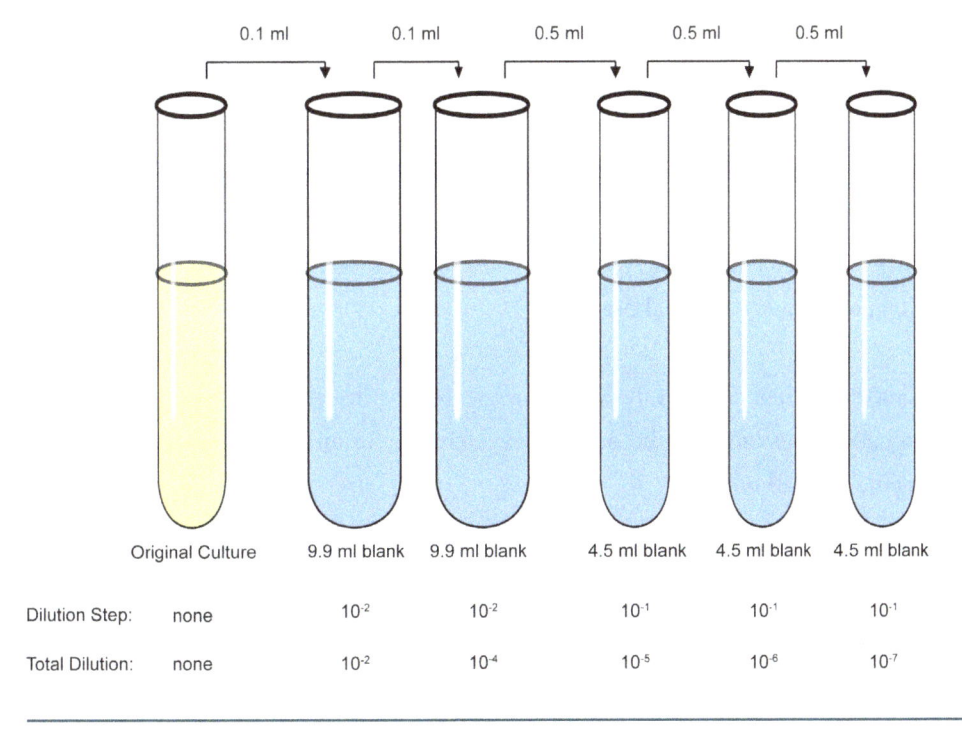

Procedure

4. Label all the tubes that will be used for the serial dilution with the total dilution factor as indicated below in Figure 2.10, "Dilution series."

   Tube 0: undiluted culture
   Tube 1: 10^{-2} (total dilution factor)
   Tube 2: 10^{-4}
   Tube 3: 10^{-5}
   Tube 4: 10^{-6}
   Tube 5: 10^{-7}

FIGURE 2.10 Dilution series

Exercise 2-5

5. Label the four TSA plates with the corresponding dilution factor and ml plated.

    Plate 1: 0.1 ml culture added of undiluted (original) culture
    Plate 2: 0.1 ml, 10^{-5} (total dilution factor)
    Plate 3: 0.1, 10^{-6}
    Plate 4: 0.1, 10^{-7}

6. Arrange all labeled tubes according to the total dilution factor, starting with the undiluted tubes, then the 10^{-2}, and ending with 10^{-7}.
7. Light the Bunsen burner.

Dilute the original culture as follows using aseptic technique:

8. Vortex the original (undiluted) tube, which is the first tube that will be used to withdraw a sample from. Light the Bunsen burner.

9. Using a micropipettes with tip attached or a serological pipette, aseptically transfer 0.1 ml of the undiluted *E. coli* culture to the 9.9 ml saline tube labeled 10^{-2} using the procedure described in steps 7–11.

See on-line movies for more on using micropipettes or serological pipettes. Online movies are available on how to use micropipettes and serological pipettes.

10. While holding the original culture tube at a 45° angle, remove its cap with the two or three free fingers of the same hand that is holding the micropipettes/pipette. To minimize the risk of contamination, point the cap down at all times.
11. Flame the lip of the culture tube by passing it through the flame of the Bunsen burner.
12. Remove the desired volume of culture with the micropipettes/serological pipette.
13. Flame the lip of the culture tube before you replace the cap.
14. Place the culture tube back in the test tube rack.
15. Vortex the 10^{-2} diluted culture tube. Using a micropipettes with a new tip attached (or a new serological pipette), aseptically transfer 0.1 ml of the 10^{-2} diluted *E. coli* culture to the 9.9 ml saline tube labeled 10^{-4}, as described in steps 7–11.

Similarly, complete dilutions 10^{-5}, 10^{-6}, and 10^{-7} aseptically, making sure to vortex tubes prior to transfers and ensuring that the correct volume is transferred from and to the appropriate tubes. Each group of four will be plating cells from the original culture as well as cells from each of the three most dilute cultures (Figure 2.10, "Dilution series"). Cells transferred from one or more of these cultures should give rise to at least one countable plate (30–300 colonies per plate).

16. Using an ethanol-sterilized glass/metal spreader, follow steps 14–20 to evenly spread 0.1 ml of each inoculum onto the appropriate labeled plate.
17. Vortex the tube containing the original culture.
18. Remove the cap as in step 7. Flame the lip of the culture tube by passing it through the open flame a few times.
19. Aseptically transfer a sample of culture onto the center of the corresponding plate.
20. Sterilize the metal or glass spreader by dipping it into a jar of alcohol. Tap off the excess alcohol from the spreader and quickly pass it through the flame only one time. Do not hold the spreader in the flame.
21. When the alcohol has burned off, cool the spreader by touching it to the inside of the lid of the plate for five seconds.
22. Gently drag the sterile spreader across the surface of the plate, spreading the sample across the entire surface of the plate.
23. Put the lid on the plate and flame the spreader as in step 17.
24. Invert the plate when the liquid has been thoroughly absorbed by the agar, and incubate the plate at 37°C for 1–2 days.

Caution: Alcohol is flammable, so use caution when working with alcohol near an open flame!

Day 3

Materials

- Four TSA spread plates, inoculated and incubated in previous lab

Work in groups of four.

Exercise 2-5

Procedure

1. Count the cells on each of the four plates and calculate the number of colony-forming units (CFU/ml) of the original culture. Record your answers in the *R & Q* section.

R&Q

Total dilution used	Volume Plated (ml)	CFU/plate
Original culture	0.1	
10^{-5}	0.1	
10^{-6}	0.1	
10^{-7}	0.1	

CFU/ml of original culture_____

Show your calculation:

Explain why it is important to vortex the sample before withdrawing samples.

_____
_____
_____

Explain which of the three methods described in the introduction accounts for viability of the cell and why the other methods do not account for viable cells.

_____
_____
_____

What does CFU stand for?

_____

Explain why we use the CFU/ml and not a cells/ml measure.

_____
_____
_____

Exercise 2-5

Explain what a countable plate is.
_____

How many cells does a visible colony consist of:

Assume that one cell gives rise to a visible colony after 10 hours of growth on a TSA plate and that the generation time (the time in which one cell divides to become two cells) is twenty minutes.

number of cells in the visible colony = $N0 \times 2^n$

N0 = number of cells before cell division starts
n = the number of divisions

Estimate the number of divisions and how many cells are in this visible colony:
_____

Do you think that all cells in the colony will grow and divide at the same rate?
_____

Explain your answer.
_____
_____
_____

Describe all the steps you need to take if you spill bacterial culture on the bench.
_____
_____
_____

STAINING BACTERIAL CELLS FOR MICROSCOPY

We saw in Module 1 that microbial cells look relatively transparent when observed with the compound brightfield microscope. Therefore, it is often necessary to stain bacterial organisms. Staining enhances the resolution and contrast and provides clear images of cellular features such as cell morphologies and arrangements. Visualizing physical characteristics of the bacterial cells (like **endospores**, **capsules**, and **flagella**) and studying fundamental differences in the cell wall structure also take advantage of staining procedures. Furthermore, staining bacterial cells is frequently used to identify species or to distinguish them from each other.

> **Box 4 First Simple Stains**
>
> Robert Koch (together with Louis Pasteur) was not only the first to isolate and grow pure cultures of bacteria; he also invented the first staining techniques to be used when observing microbes under the microscope. He developed these staining techniques using recently invented industrial dyes. Initially, he used methyl violet to provide evidence for and identify the germ that caused septicaemia (blood poisoning). He also used methyl violet, among other stains, to prove that the dreaded disease anthrax was caused by infection of the bacterial organism *Bacillus anthracis*. Later on, Koch included the much-improved stain methylene blue, which was invented by his friend, the German physician, scientist, and Nobel Prize laureate **Paul Ehrlich (1854–1915)**. He used methylene blue in his discoveries of the bacterial species that cause tuberculosis and cholera: *Mycobacterium tuberculosis* and *Vibrio cholerae*, respectively.

Dyes for Staining Bacteria

Stain	Basic Dyes	Acidic Dyes
Simple	Crystal violet Methylene blue	
Differential	Crystal violet Safranin Malachite green	Acid fuchsin

Today, a variety of different biological dyes is used to stain bacteria. Typically, basic dyes are used in staining bacterial cells. Basic dyes are salts composed of a positively charged ion (cation), which carries the dye (the chromophore), and a negatively charged ion (anion), often a chloride ion. The reason why bacteria have a strong affinity for basic dyes is because their cell surfaces have an overall negative charge. Other negatively charged cellular components, like nucleic acid, can also be stained with basic dyes. Examples of basic dyes (cationic dyes) that are commonly used for microscopy of bacterial cells are methylene blue, crystal violet, safranin, and malachite green (Table "Dyes for staining bacteria").

If the color is carried by the negative ion, the dye is called an **acidic dye**. Acidic dyes are most commonly used as background staining. This means they are dyes that stain everything on the slide but the cells. Such stains are called negative stains, as opposed to the basic dyes, which are positive stains. Acidic dyes cannot enter the cells as readily as basic dyes, since they are repelled by the overall negative charge of the bacterial cell surface. An example of an acidic dye is acid fuchsin (Table "Dyes for staining bacteria").

The staining methods are generally classified into two different groups: the **simple stain**, where one basic dye is applied to the specimen and all cells are colored in a similar fashion in a nonspecific way; and the **differential stain**, which often uses more than one dye, as well as other chemicals, to successfully stain structural and cellular components of bacterial cells (Table "Dyes for Staining Bacteria."). The differential stain is suitable for distinguishing between two distinct cell types and to classify bacteria according to cell-wall composition and other structural features, such as capsules, endospores, or flagella (Table "Dyes for staining bacteria"). Simple stain methods are mostly used to determine the size, shape, and arrangement of the bacterial cells. however these features are also visible after performing differential stains.

Box 5 Gram Stains

One of the most widely used and recognized differential stains is the Gram stain, which was developed in 1884 by the Danish physician and bacteriologist **Hans Christian Gram** (1853–1938). The Gram stain is based on differences in the structure and composition of the bacterial cell walls, and it groups the microbes into two classes: Gram-positive cells, which retain the dye and stain purple, and Gram-negative cells, which will lose the dye but are stained pink by the counterstain applied during the final step of the procedure (Figure 2.7 "Gram stain"). The Gram-positive and Gram-negative bacteria differ from each other with respect to the thickness of the peptidoglycan layer of their cell walls, with the Gram-positive bacterial cell having a much thicker peptidoglycan layer than the Gram-negative bacterial cell. The Gram-negative cell wall also comprises an outer membrane, which is positioned outside the peptidoglycan layer (Figure 2.11 "Gram-positive and Gram-negative cell walls").

Hans Christian Gram initially worked on developing the stain in order to visualize bacteria in infected lung tissues from patients who had died of pneumonia. He found that his stain could differentiate between the two bacterial strains causing lung infections: *Streptococcus pneumoniae* (Gram-positive) and *Klebsiella pneumonia* (Gram-negative). Today, the Gram stain is still an indispensable tool in medical microbiology, and the procedure is used for the fast, preliminary identification and classification of unknown bacteria in clinical specimens.

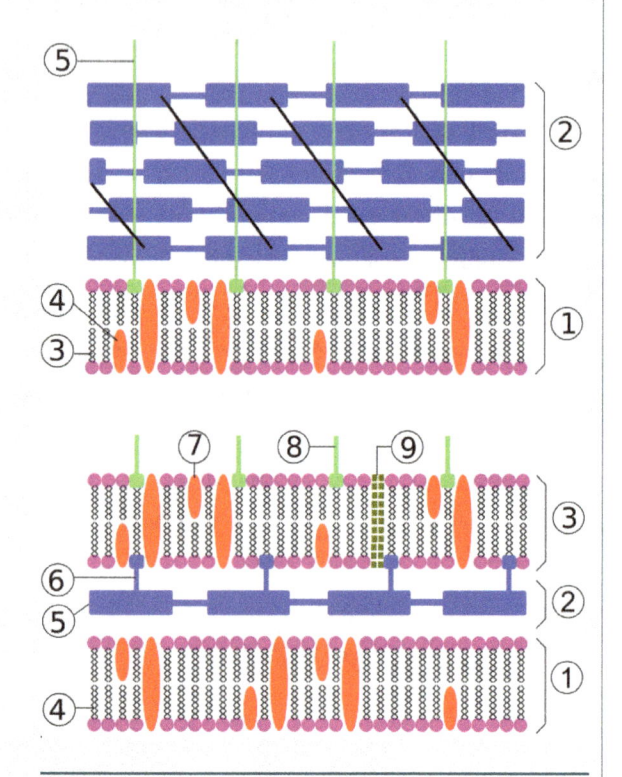

FIGURE 2.11 Gram-positive and Gram-negative cell walls Top: Gram-positive cell wall. 1-cytoplasmic membrane, 2-peptidoglycan, 3-phospholipid, 4-protein, 5-lipoteichoic acid. Bottom: Gram-negative cell wall. 1-inner membrane, 2-periplasmic space, 3-outer membrane, 4-phospolipid, 5-peptidoglycan, 6-lipoprotein, 7-protein, 8-LPS, 9-porins.

Source: Copyright © Franciscosp2 (CC by 3.0) at https://commons.wikimedia.org/wiki/File:Bacteria_cell_wall2.svg.

Once a pure microbial culture is obtained, it is ready for further examination. Aside from revealing properties of the bacterial cell walls (Gram-positive or -negative or acid-fast bacteria), other structural and cellular characteristics of bacterial cells can also be identified by employing different staining procedures, followed by microscopy. Such features include cell morphologies (shape and size) and arrangements, the presence of capsules or flagella, and whether an organism is an endospore-forming organism. These staining techniques will be covered in this section, starting with the simple stain (used to visualize cell morphologies and arrangements) and followed by the differential stains.

Box 6 Research Reveals New Insight into the Steps of Gram Stain

Originally, it was believed that the crystal violet dye (Figure 2.7 "Gram stain")—which forms larger complexes (precipitates) with the mordant iodine—would readily cross the three cell barriers (the outer membrane [OM], the peptidoglycan mesh [PM], and the cytosolic membrane [CM]), resulting in an accumulation of the dye–mordant precipitate in the PM and cytosol of the cells. The decolorizing step would then cause the thicker peptidoglycan layer of the **Gram-positive cell wall** to dehydrate and shrink (closing pores in the cell wall) and prevent the crystal violet–iodine precipitates from leaving the cells via the cell membrane. Due to the much thinner peptidoglycan layer of the Gram-negative cells and the effects of the decolorizing step on the OM, this would result in disruption of the PM, and the crystal violet–iodine precipitates would easily wash away.

Although this stain was developed more than one hundred years ago, research is still ongoing to better understand the molecular mechanisms of the individual steps in the Gram-staining technique. In regards to this, a new, extensive study (published in 2015) provides evidence for the fact that the crystal violet dye cannot cross the cytoplasmic membrane, as was originally believed. Thus, the dye and mordant do not accumulate freely in the PM and cytosol of the cells; rather, they diffuse slowly through the PM, where they accumulate as a precipitate. During the decolorizing step, the crystal violet–iodine precipitate is easily washed away from the Gram-negative cells but is retained by the mostly intact PM of the Gram-positive cells. The conclusion of this work: the stability of the PM decides whether the stain is retained or lost during the decolorization step.

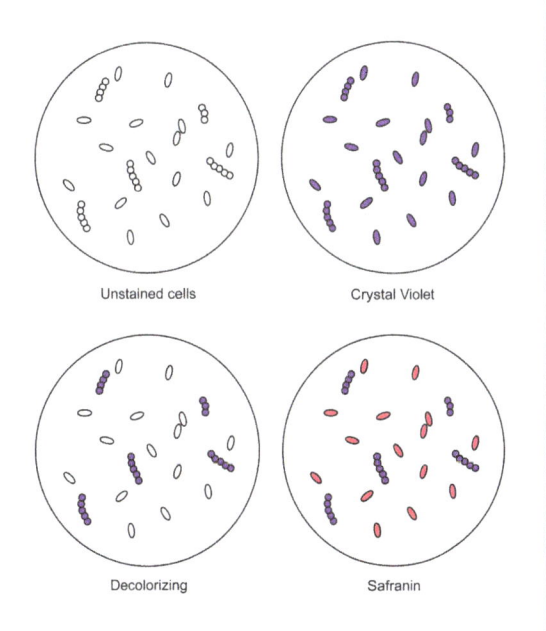

Unstained cells

Crystal Violet

Decolorizing

Safranin

Reference
Wilhelm, Michael J., Joel B. Sheffield, Mohammad Sharifian Gh., Yajing Wu, Christian Spahr, Grazia Gonella, Bolei Xu, and Hai-Lung Dai. "Gram's Stain Does Not Cross the Bacterial Cytoplasmic Membrane." ACS Chemical Biology 10 (2015): 1711–17. doi: 10.1021/acschembio.5b00042.

Basic and Practical Microbiology Lab Manual

Box 7 Bacterial Morphologies and Arrangements

Bacteria display a vast variety of cell morphologies and arrangements. However, the majority of bacteria exhibit one of three major cellular morphological types below:

- Coccus (plural cocci): spherical shape (coccus means berry)
- Bacillus (plural bacilli): rodlike shape (bacillus means staff or rod)

Bacili   Cocci   Spirilli

Spiral bacteria include morphologies as:
    vibrio(s)—a comma shape
    spirillum (plural spirilla)—a rigid, wavelike shape
    spirochete(s)—a corkscrew or helical shape

Bacteria also exhibit distinct cell arrangements resulting from their patterns of reproduction.
If bacteria divide in one plane, they are found as either:
    single cells
    in pairs (indicated by the prefix diplo-)
    in chains (indicated by the prefix strepto-)

Bacilli, cocci, and spiral bacteria all produce such arrangements.

Certain cocci can also divide in two or three planes; this ability gives rise to unique arrangement patterns such as:
    clusters (staphylo):
    groups of four (tetra)
    packets of eight (sarcinae)

Certain genera have been named according to their specific cellular characteristics: *Staphylococcus epidermidis* is a coccus that, after cell division, displays a staphylo arrangement.

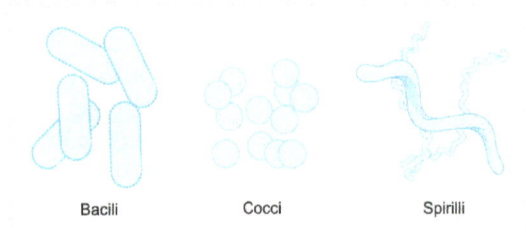

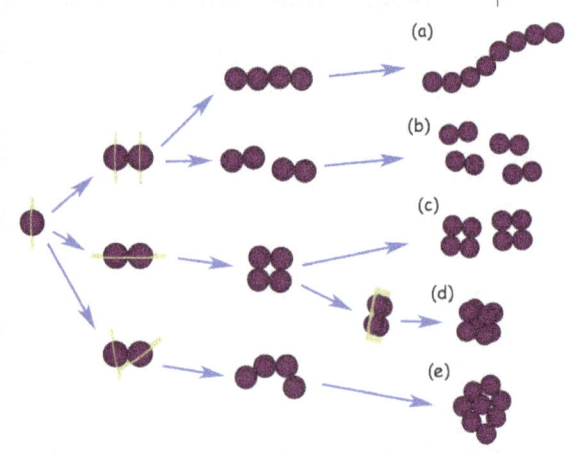

FIGURE 2.12 Bacterial Morphologies and Arrangements (a) streptococcus, divide along same plane. (b) diplococcus, make pairs of two cocci after division. (c) tetrad, divide along two planes regularly. (d) sarcina, divide along three planes regularly. (e) staphylococcus, divide along planes irregularly.

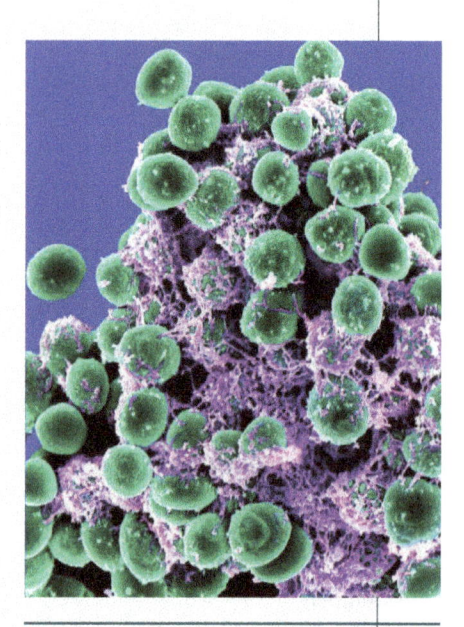

FIGURE 2.13 *Staphylococcus epidermidis*

Source: WPClipart, http://www.wpclipart.com/medical/anatomy/cells/bacili/cocci/spirilli.png.html. Copyright in the Public Domain.
Source: Copyright © Y tambe (CC BY-SA 3.0) at https://commons.wikimedia.org/wiki/File:Cocci_arrangement.png.
Source: National Institute of Allergy and Infectious Diseases (CC by 2.0) at https://commons.wikimedia.org/wiki/File:Staphylococcus_epidermidis_Bacteria_(5613984108).jpg.

Exercise 2-6

Simple Stain: Crystal Violet

Learning Objectives

To understand the principles behind the simple stain.

To practice aseptic technique while preparing samples for microscopic viewing.

To get acquainted with cellular morphology and arrangements.

We will first use the crystal violet stain to become accustomed to the staining technique and to learn to determine cellular characteristics such as cell morphology and arrangement.

Materials

- TSB culture of *S. epidermidis* (1)
- TSB culture of *E. coli* (1)
- Bunsen burner
- Inoculating loop
- Distilled water
- Microscope slide
- Staining rack
- Compound brightfield microscope
- Immersion oil
- Crystal violet
- Distilled water
- Bibulous paper

Work in pairs.

Use a sterilized loop to aseptically remove a sample of culture.

Transfer the culture to a microscope slide and spread out the dropplet to create a thin smear on the slide.

When the smear has air dried completely, heat fix the slide by holding it with a clothespin and passing it over the flame 2-3 times

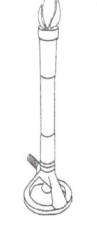

Cover the smear with crystal violet and allow it to remain on the smear for 60 seconds

After 60 seconds has elapsed, throughly rinse the slide with distilled water

Blot the slide dry using Bibulous Paper

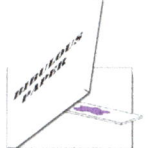

FIGURE 2.14 Crystal violet stain

Procedure

2. Use a wax pencil to divide a slide into two equal sections. Label one section of the slide "EC" for *Escherichia coli* and the other "SE" for *Staphylococcus epidermidis*.
3. Ignite the Bunsen burner.
4. Flame the inoculating loop and let it cool.
5. Aseptically, remove a tiny amount of the *E. coli* cells from the TSB culture and make a smear of the cells on the correct section of the slide.
6. Repeat steps 3–5 to make a smear of *S. epidermidis*.
7. Distribute the cells of the two organisms over a larger area to minimize the drying time. Allow the smear to air-dry completely.
8. Flame the loop and set aside.
9. When the smear has air-dried completely, fix the cells to the slide by passing it quickly above the flame of the Bunsen burner three times. When cells have been properly heat fixed, they are ready to be stained.
10. Cover the entire smear with the crystal violet and allow the dye to stain the cells for sixty seconds.
11. Rinse the slide thoroughly with distilled water.
12. Use the bibulous paper to blot the slide dry.
13. Observe the stained specimen under the compound brightfield microscope. Start with the 10X and then the 40X objectives before progressing to the 100X (oil-immersion) objectives.
14. Draw the appearance of each organism and describe your observations regarding the shape, size, and arrangements of the *E. coli* and *S. epidermidis* cells in the *R & Q* section. Use **Box 7** as a source of information about cell characteristics of bacterial organisms.
15. After completing your observations of each of the two organisms, rotate the 4X objective into position and remove the slide. Discard your used slide in the red biohazard container found at your bench.

Exercise 2-6

R & Q

Bacterial Cell Morphology and Cellular Arrangement

○

Organism: _____

Cellular Morphology: _____

Cellular Arrangement: _____

Total Magnification: _____

○

Organism: _____

Cellular Morphology: _____

Cellular Arrangement: _____

Total Magnification: _____

Exercise 2-6

Describe what you think the outcome would be if the cells were heat fixed for too long or too short a time.

Describe what you think may happen to the cells if they are stained too long or if too little water was used to rinse the slide.

Can motility be examined by microscopic observations of stained cells? Explain your answer.

Differential Stain: Gram Stain

Learning Objectives

To understand the principles behind the Gram stain.
To be able to perform Gram stains and to interpret the results.

We will practice the Gram-staining method to get used to a differential staining technique and to learn to differentiate Gram-positive cells from Gram-negative cells.

Before you start to stain *E. coli* and *S. epidermidis*, use Figure 2.15, "Gram Stain" to compare the color development of each step of the procedure for Gram-positive and Gram-negative cells.

Explain each step of the procedure, including the color development of the Gram-positive cells, to your lab partner.

Next, your lab partner will explain each step of the procedure, including color development, to you.

Materials

- TSB culture of *S. epidermidis*
- TSB culture of *E. coli*
- Inoculating loop
- Microscope slide
- Staining rack
- Vortexer
- Bunsen burner
- Compound brightfield microscope
- Immersion oil
- Crystal violet
- Gram's iodine
- Acetone-alcohol solution
- Safranin
- Distilled water
- Bibulous paper

Work in pairs.

86　Exercise 2-7

Use a sterilized loop to aseptically remove a sample of culture.

Transfer the culture to a microscope slide and spread out the dropplet to create a thin smear on the slide.

When the smear has air dried completely, heat fix the slide by holding it with a clothespin and passing it over the flame 2-3 times

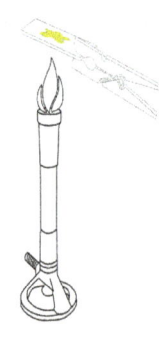

Cover the smear with crystal violet and allow it to remain on the smear for 60 seconds

After 60 seconds has elapsed, throughly rinse the slide with distilled water

Cover the slide with Gram's iodine and allow it to remain on the smear for 60 seconds

FIGURE 2.15A Gram stain (part 1)

Exercise 2-7   87

After 60 seconds has elapsed, throughly rinse the slide with distilled water

Briefly rinse the slide with acetone-alcohol for 2-3 seconds

Immediately rinse the slide with distilled water

Completely cover the smear with safranin and allow it to remain on the smear for 90 seconds

After 90 seconds has elapsed, throughly rinse the slide with distilled water

Blot the slide dry using Bibulous Paper

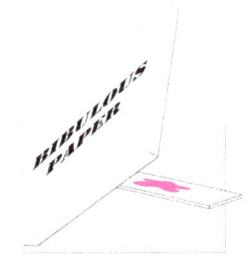

FIGURE 2.15b Gram stain (part 2)

Exercise 2-7

Procedure

1. Use the wax pencil to divide a microscope slide into two equal sections. Label the sections according to the cultures you will be staining.
2. Use the loop to perform the smear according to the directions in Figure 2.15, "Gram stain".
3. Allow the smears to air dry completely.
4. Heat fix the cells and place the slide on the staining rack.
5. Cover the entire smear with the crystal violet and allow the dye to stain the cells for sixty seconds.
6. Rinse the slide thoroughly with distilled water.
7. Cover the smear with Gram's Iodine and leave for sixty seconds.
8. Rinse the slide thoroughly with distilled water.
9. Briefly rinse the slide with acetone-alcohol for 2–3 seconds, and immediately rinse the slide thoroughly with water to completely remove the decolorizing solution.
10. Cover the smear in safranin for ninety seconds.
11. Thoroughly rinse the slide with water and use the bibulous paper to dry the slide.
12. Use the brightfield microscope to observe the stained specimen. Start with the 10X and then the 40X objectives before progressing to the 100X (oil-immersion) objective.
13. Draw the appearance of each organism and describe your observations of the *E. coli* and *S. epidermidis* cells in the *R & Q* section. Describe the Gram reaction, and confirm the cell morphology and arrangement of each species. Use **Box 7** as a source of information about cell characteristics of bacterial organisms.
14. After completing your observations of each of the two organisms, rotate the 4X objective into position and remove the slide. Discard your used slide in the red biohazard container located on your bench.

Exercise 2-7

Examining Gram-stained Smears

Gram Reaction: _____

Cellular Morphology: _____

Cellular Arrangement: _____

Total Magnification: _____

Gram Reaction: _____

Cellular Morphology: _____

Cellular Arrangement: _____

Total Magnification: _____

Which step in the Gram-stain procedure can be referred to as the true differential step? Explain your answer.

_____
_____

Explain the purpose of adding Gram's iodine in the Gram-stain procedure.

_____
_____

Exercise 2-7

Explain why Gram-negative cells stain pink and not purple.

_____
_____
_____

Describe the challenges you may encounter when Gram staining a culture that turns out not to be a pure culture. Explain which steps you will take to ensure that a pure culture will be obtained.

_____
_____
_____

If both Gram-positive-stained and Gram-negative-stained cells are visible in the smear, explain the steps you will take to make sure that a given bacterial strain is pure and is a Gram variable and not a mixed culture.

_____
_____
_____

Suggest differences between the lung tissues infected with *Streptococcus pneumoniae* and *Klebsiella pneumonia*, respectively, that Hans Christian Gram would have observed using his own developed Gram stain.

_____
_____
_____

Acid-fast Stain

Learning Objectives

To understand the chemical procedure of the acid-fast stain.
To be able to distinguish between acid-fast and non-acid-fast organisms.

There is a small group of bacteria that cannot efficiently take up the dye when Gram-stained. This is due to the presence of a waxy layer on the surface of their cell walls. This additional layer consists of complex waxy lipids (predominantly mycolic acids) and comprises about 60% of the cell wall (Figure 2.15 "Acid fast cell wall"). Although the bacteria are Gram-positive, this waxy lipid layer prevents the uptake of basic dyes; however, harsher staining methods (the Ziehl-Neelsen or Kinyoun's staining procedures—also known as the acid-fast-staining procedures) can stain these bacteria. In contrast to bacteria that stain negative with the Kinyoun's procedure, the acid-fast bacteria retain the dye during the treatment with the acid-alcohol decolorizing agent; hence the name acid-fast bacteria.

Below we will use Kinyoun's staining method to stain an acid-fast-positive and an acid-fast-negative strain.

Examples of acid-fast bacteria are those belonging to the genus *Mycobacterium*. Some of these bacterial species are found in soil, and others are pathogens; an example of a pathogen species is *Mycobacterium tuberculosis*, the causative agent of tuberculosis (TB).

The bacterial species of the genera *Nocardia* are mycelial bacteria (hyphal morphology) and are present in soil, too. Bacteria belonging to this genus are also found among the natural oral microflora. *Nocardia* species can be **opportunistic pathogens** (affecting mostly immunocompromised humans), with *Nocardia*

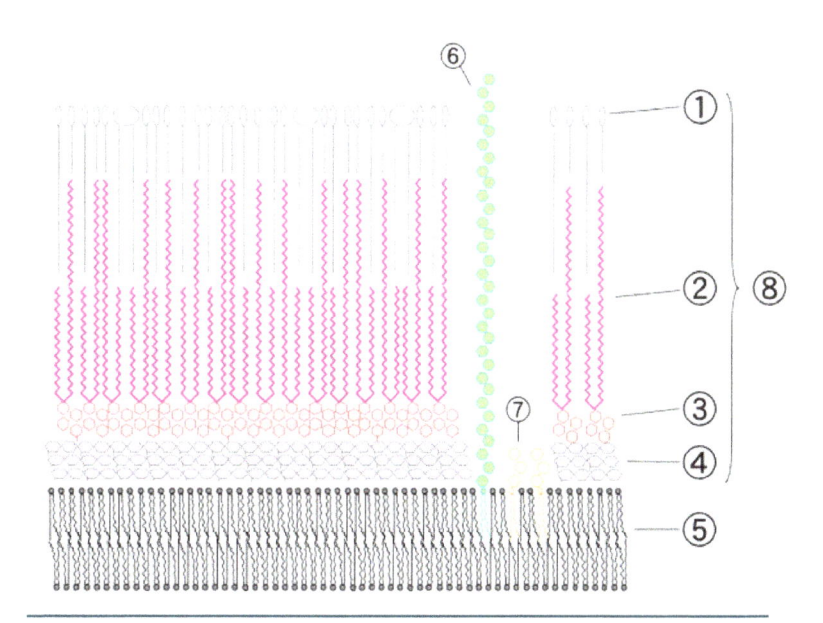

FIGURE 2.16 Acid fast cell wall
Schematic diagram of Mycobacterial cell wall.
1. outer lipids, 2. mycolic acid, 3. polysaccharides (arabinogalactan), 4. peptidoglycan, 5. plasma membrane, 6. lipoarabinomannan (LAM), 7. phosphatidylinositol mannoside, 8. cell wall skeleton

Copyright © Y tambe (CC BY-SA 3.0) at https://commons.wikimedia.org/wiki/File:Mycobacterial_cell_wall_diagram.png.

Exercise 2-8

asteroides responsible for causing Nocardiosis, an infectious disease affecting the lungs. *Nocardia* infections can spread to the other parts of the body, such as the brain or the skin.

Materials

- Prepared slide

or

- TSB culture of *Mycobacterium smegmatis*
- TSB culture of *S. epidermidis*
- Inoculation loop
- Bunsen burner
- Microscope slide
- Gloves
- Bibulous paper
- Compound brightfield microscope
- Immersion oil
- Carbolfuchsin (includes mordants Triton-x and phenol)
- Hydrochloric acids-alcohol solution
- Methylene blue
- Distilled water

Work in pairs.

Procedure

1. Use the wax pencil to divide a microscope slide into two equal sections. Label the sections according to the cultures you will be staining.

Use the loop to add a drop of serum albumin or egg albumin to a labeled microscope slide

Use a sterilized loop to take a small sample of culture and mix the sample into the drop of albumin creating a thin smear on the slide

When the smear has air dried completely, heat fix the slide by holding it with a clothespin and passing it over the flame 2-3 times or more

Cover the smear with Kinyoun's carbolfuchsin and allow it to set for 5-10 minutes. Add fresh carbolfuchsin, if the slide begins to dry

Hold the slide at an angle and gently rinse it with acid-alcohol until no more color runs off from the smear

Gently rinse the slide with water and place it back on the staining rack

FIGURE 2.17 Acid fast stain procedure

2. Prepare smears using the two cultures and allow them to dry completely before heat fixing. Due to the large content of lipids, *M. smegmatis* may need a bit more heat fixing before attaching properly to the slide.
3. Heat fix the smear and place the slide on a staining rack.
4. Cover the smear with Kinyoun's carbolfuchsin stain and allow it to set for 5–10 minutes. Add fresh carbolfuchsin if the slide begins to dry.
5. Hold the slide at an angle and gently rinse it with acid-alcohol until no more color runs off from the smear.
6. Gently rinse the slide with water and place it back on the staining rack.
7. Cover the smear with methylene blue and counterstain this slide for about ninety seconds before rinsing it with water and blotting it dry with bibulous paper.
8. Observe the stained cells under the compound brightfield microscope and record your observations in *R & Q*.

   Note: Due to the coat of mycolic acid on the surface of mycobacteria, these microbes do not attach well to the microscope slides. To help the lipid-rich cells better adhere to the slide, serum albumin or egg albumin can be mixed with the cells on the slide prior to heat fixing.

Completely cover the smear with methylene blue and allow it to remain on the slide for 90 seconds

After 90 seconds has elapsed, gently rinse the slide with distilled water

Blot the slide dry using Bibulous Paper

FIGURE 2.17 Acid fast stain procedure, cont.

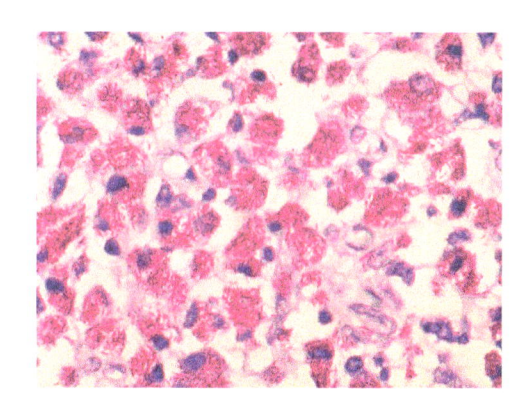

FIGURE 2.18 *Mycobacterium avium*-intracellulare infection of lymph node in patient with AIDS. Ziehl-Neelsen stain (acid-fast stain). Histopathology of lymph node shows tremendous numbers of acid-fast bacilli within plump histiocytes

Edwin P. Ewing, Jr., https://commons.wikimedia.org/wiki/File:Mycobacterium_avium-intracellulare_01.png. Centers for Disease Control and Prevention, 1983. Copyright in the Public Domain.

Exercise 2-8

R & Q

Examining Acid-fast Staining

Description: _____

_____

Specimen: _____

Total Magnification: _____

Exercise 2-8

Use Figure 2.16 "Acid-fast cell wall" to name the layers of an acid-fast cell wall. Briefly compare the acid-fast cell wall with those of the Gram-positive and -negative cells.

_____
_____
_____

Explain why acid-fast bacteria do not readily take up dyes like those used in Gram staining do.

_____
_____
_____

Describe your observations of the clinical sample in Figure 2.18.

_____
_____
_____

Capsule Stain

Learning Objectives

To understand the various functions of capsules.
To become familiar with the procedure of capsule staining.
To recognize why the capsule stain is a negative stain.

Some bacteria contain capsules or slime layers (gel-like coatings surrounding the bacteria). Capsules and slime layers are large structures consisting mostly of polysaccharides that are situated on the surface of the bacteria. In contrast to slime layers, which appear diffuse and irregular, capsules appear more distinct. The presence of some capsules and slime layers enables the bacteria to easier attach to specific surfaces (e.g., rocks, teeth, or other bacteria) and can facilitate the formation of biofilm as the bacteria grow.

Some capsule-containing bacteria are pathogens, such as *Streptococcus pneumonia* (which can cause pneumonia) and *Bordetella pertussis* (the causative agent of whooping cough). The presence of capsules increases the pathogenesis of a given microbe. This is because the capsules can protect the microbial organisms from the host's immune system by hindering the process by which the host's defense system engulfs and destroys the bacteria. Thus, the capsules can contribute to the bacteria's virulence (the ability of the bacteria to invade a host tissue and cause disease).

Materials

- Agar slant of *B. megaterium*
- Inoculation loop
- Bunsen burner
- Microscope slide
- Gloves
- Compound brightfield microscope
- Immersion oil
- Congo red
- Maneval's solution
- Distilled water

Work in pairs.

Exercise 2-9

97

Add one drop of Congo Red near the end of the slide

Aseptically, use the loop to remove a small sample of culture and mix it into the drop of Congo Red

Use a second microscope slide to spread the mixture over the surface of the first slide

Allow the slide to air dry

Cover the slide with Maneval's solution and leave on for 2 minutes

Rinse both sides of the slide with water

Allow the slide to air dry

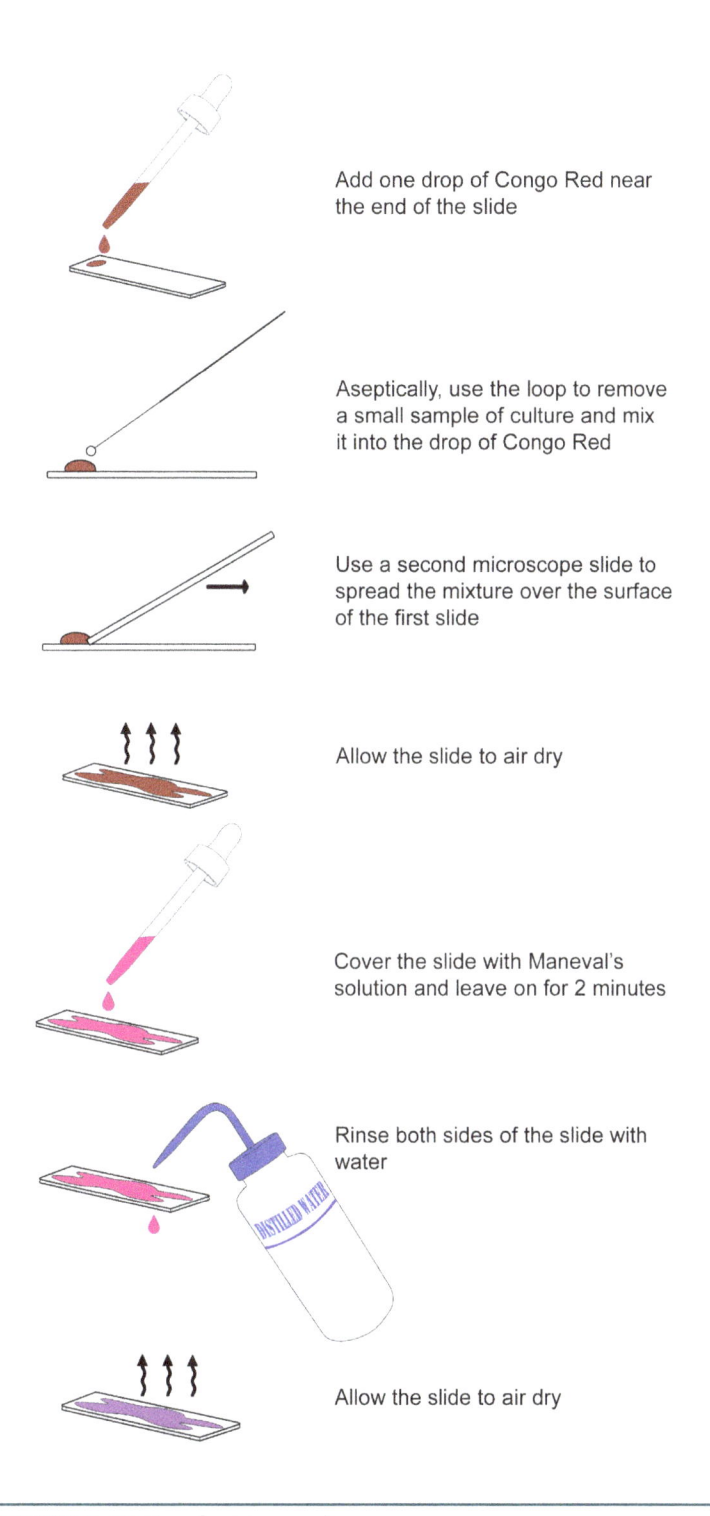

FIGURE 2.19 Capsule stain procedure

Exercise 2-9

Procedure

Caution: Wear gloves throughout all the steps of this procedure.

1. Label a microscope slide "BM" for *Bacillus megaterium*.
2. Add one drop of Congo red close to the end of the slide.
3. Flame the loop.
4. Aseptically, remove a small amount of *B. megaterium* cells from the slant and mix the cells with the drop of Congo red.
5. Spread the suspension over the surface of the slide by gently pushing a clean microscope slide at a 45° angle into the Congo red cell mixture until the suspension reaches its edge. Then slowly draw the clean slide in the opposite direction until the suspension is spread evenly over the entire slide (Figure "Capsule stain").

   Note: The cell suspension should not be spread too thinly, since a thicker layer of color improves the contrast and the appearance of the capsules.

6. Allow the slide to air-dry.

   Note: When performing the capsule stain, we do not heat fix cells to the slide. Exposure to heat causes capsules to dry out and may distort, destroy, or cause the capsules to shrink.

7. Add Maneval's solution so it covers the smear. Leave the solution on the slide for two minutes.
8. Rinse the slide thoroughly with water and air-dry the slide.

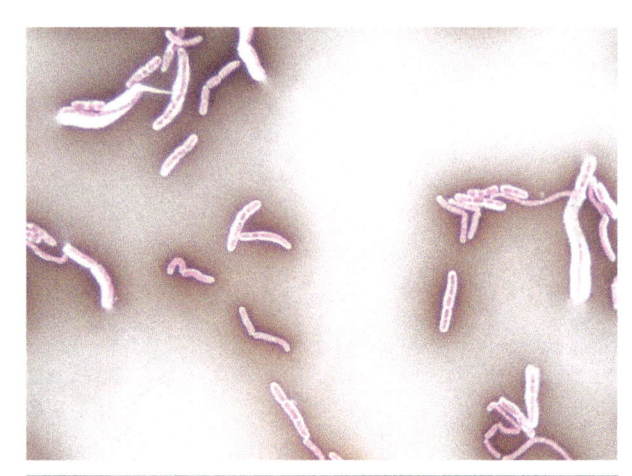

Capsule stain of *B. megaterium*.

   Note: Since the cells are not heat fixed, it is important to *not* blot the slide dry with bibulous paper.

9. Use the oil-immersion objective to observe the smear.

R & Q

Draw and describe your observations of the stained smear of *B. megaterium*.

Include the color of the background, the bacterial cells, and the appearance of the capsule in your description.

Description: _____

_____

Specimen: _____

Total Magnification: _____

Exercise 2-9 99

Exercise 2-9

Do some research and suggest how bacterial capsules can contribute to the virulence of pathogenic bacteria.

The presence of capsules can facilitate the formation of biofilms. Do some research and define biofilm. Give a brief description of how biofilm is formed.

Observation of Endospores—Crystal Violet Stain

Learning Objectives

To learn about endospore formation.
To microscopically distinguish between vegetative cells and endospores.

Most cells that are actively growing and metabolizing (vegetative cells) will eventually stop growing and die if they encounter environmental stress, such as nutritional depletion, high temperatures, radiation, or toxic compounds. However, vegetative cells of endospore-forming bacteria, such as *Bacillus* and *Clostridium*, are able to survive such stressors. This is due to the fact that endospore-forming cells, upon stress, initiate a process called sporulation. The sporulation process results in the formation of specialized structures called endospores, which are metabolically inactive and are extremely resistant structures.

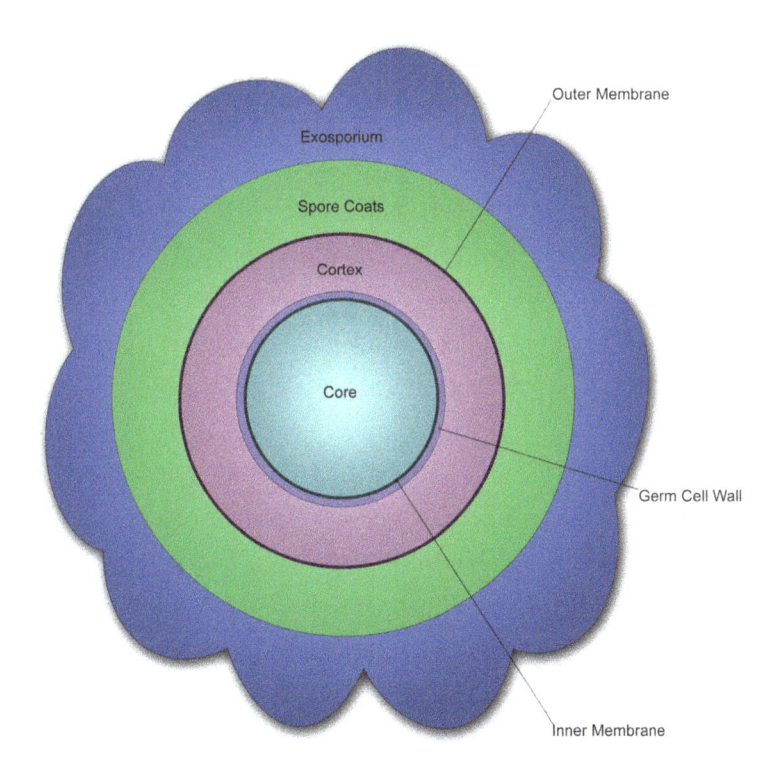

FIGURE 2.20 Endospore structure

A vegetative cell can produce only one endospore. The endospore can form at the poles of the vegetative cell (terminal endospore), in the middle (central endospore), or in between the poles and the middle of the vegetative cell (subterminal endospore). When maturated, the endospore detaches from the vegetative cell and become a free endospore.

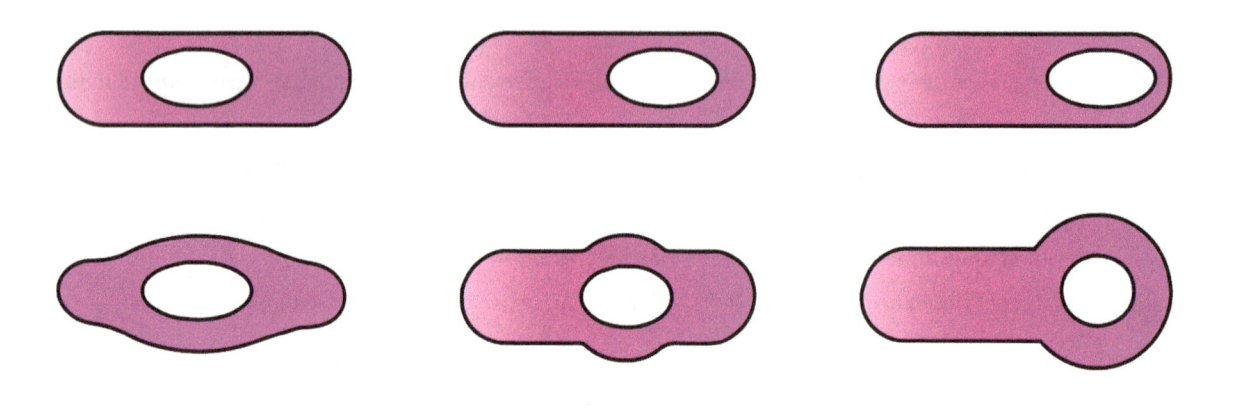

FIGURE 2.21 Terminal, central and subterminal endospores

Free endospores germinate (return to the vegetative state) as the harsh environmental conditions are removed, with each endospore giving rise to one vegetative cell.

Note: For some microorganisms, **spore** formation is a reproductive process, not to be confused with the endospore formation described here, which is a survival mechanism.

Several major clinical implications arise from studying the group of endospore-forming bacteria. Members of the genus Bacillus are the causative agents of the disease anthrax (*Bacillus anthracis*). Certain strains of *Bacillus cereus* can cause foodborne illness, whereas others are important for producing antibiotics. In the genus *Clostridium* are three unsafe pathogens: 1) *Clostridium botulinum* responsible for botulism and can cause severe and sometimes fatal food poisoning; 2) *Clostridium tetani* causes tetanus; and 3) *Clostridium perfringens*, known for causing the deadly disease gas gangrene as well as food poisoning.

Exercise 2-10

In this exercise, you will observe endospores produced by an environmentally stressed, nonpathogenic bacterium (*Bacillus subtilis*) and compare it with *B. subtilis* cells that have not experienced environmental stress (vegetative cells).

You will observe endospores using two different methods:

The first method will use a simple stain with a basic dye. If spore-forming bacteria are stained with the dye crystal violet, vegetative cells will take up the stain but endospores will remain unstained. Observing endospores in this way is another example of a negative stain.

> **Note:** Cells that have not yet completed sporulation should show clear, unstained oval endospores inside purple vegetative cells. Free endospores will be visible as unstained oval bodies, and vegetative cells that did not sporulate will appear as purple rods.

The second method (the Schaeffer-Fulton stain) is named after the two microbiologists who developed the endospore-staining procedure in the 1930s. Since the endospores show resistance to taking up dye, heat is involved. It is a differential stain that ends up staining endospores green (malachite green) and vegetative cells pink or red (safranin).

> **Note:** It is worthwhile to mention that you can also view endospores of unstained cells by making a wet mount and using a phase microscope. Because endospores and vegetative cells have different densities, light refracts differently as it passes through the cell structures. Therefore, the endospores will appear bright inside or outside the darker vegetative cells. Your lab instructor may ask you to view endospores in this way instead of proceeding to the Schaeffer-Fulton stain.

Each pair of students will prepare a stained slide of *Bacillus subtilis*. One pair performs the crystal violet stain, and the other pair performs the endospore stain (Exercise 2-11). Alternatively, a wet mount of unstained cells can be prepared if you also wish to view unstained endospores under the phase contrast microscope.

Exercise 2-10

Materials

B. subtilis agar slant

- Inoculating loop
- Microscope slide
- Staining rack
- Inoculating loop
- Bunsen burner
- Compound brightfield microscope
- Phase contract microscope
- Immersion oil
- Crystal violet
- Distilled water
- Bibulous paper

Work in groups of four.

Procedure

1. Label one microscope slide
2. Prepare smear.
3. Stain smear with crystal violet
4. Observe endospores and vegetative cells under the compound brightfield microscope.

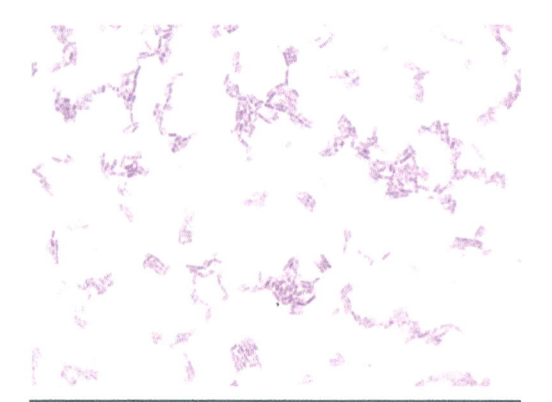

Simple stain of *B. subtilis*.

Use the loop to add a small drop of water to a labeled microscope slide

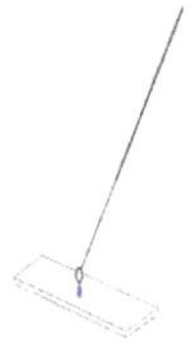

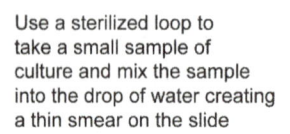

Use a sterilized loop to take a small sample of culture and mix the sample into the drop of water creating a thin smear on the slide

When the smear has air dried completely, heat fix the slide by holding it with a clothespin and passing it over the flame 2-3 times

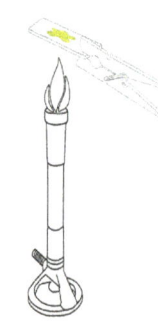

Cover the smear with crystal violet and allow it to remain on the smear for 60 seconds

After 60 seconds has elapsed, throughly rinse the slide with distilled water

Blot the slide dry using Bibulous Paper

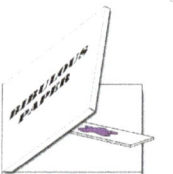

R & Q

Draw and describe your observations of the crystal-violet-stained smear. Identify the free spores, endospores, and vegetative cells in your illustration.

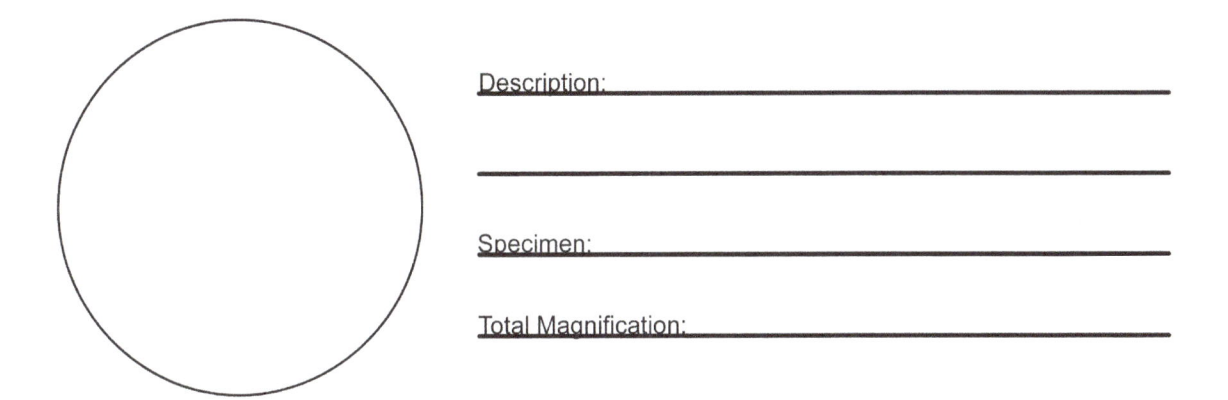

Description: _____

_____

Specimen: _____

Total Magnification: _____

Optional:

Prepare a wet mount by mixing cells in a drop water on the slide using a loop.
Describe and draw your observations of endospores and vegetative cells using the phase contrast microscope. Include free endospores, endospores, and vegetative cells.

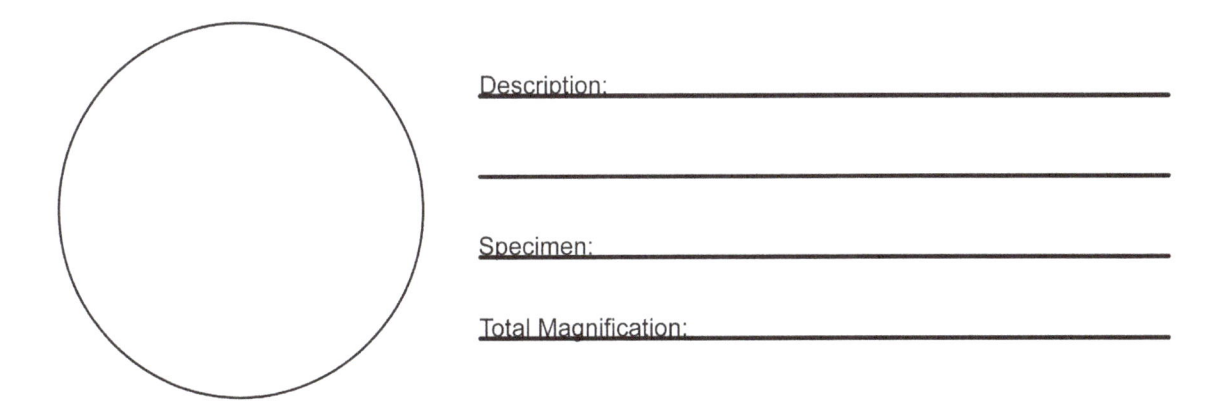

Description: _____

_____

Specimen: _____

Total Magnification: _____

Exercise 2-11

The Endospore Stain

Objective

To understand the principle behind the endospore stain.

Materials

- *B. subtilis* agar slant
- Inoculating loop
- Microscope slide
- Staining rack
- Bunsen burner
- Fume hood
- Heating apparatus/incubator
- Forceps
- Compound brightfield microscope
- Immersion oil
- Eye protection
- Gloves
- Malachite green
- Safranin
- Distilled water
- Bibulous paper
- Work in groups of four

Procedure

1. Use the wax pencil to label the microscope slide.
2. Use the loop, water, and cells to perform the smear.
3. Heat fix the cells and place the slide on the staining rack.
4. Place slide in slide container filled with malachite green and stain for 10 min.
5. Rinse thoroughly with water to decolorize the smear.
6. Cover the smear in safranin for sixty seconds.
7. Thoroughly rinse the slide with water and use the bibulous paper to dry the slide.
8. Use the compound brightfield microscope to observe the stained specimen. Start with the 10X and then the 40X objectives before progressing to the 100X (oil-immersion) objective.

Endospore stain of *B. subtilis*

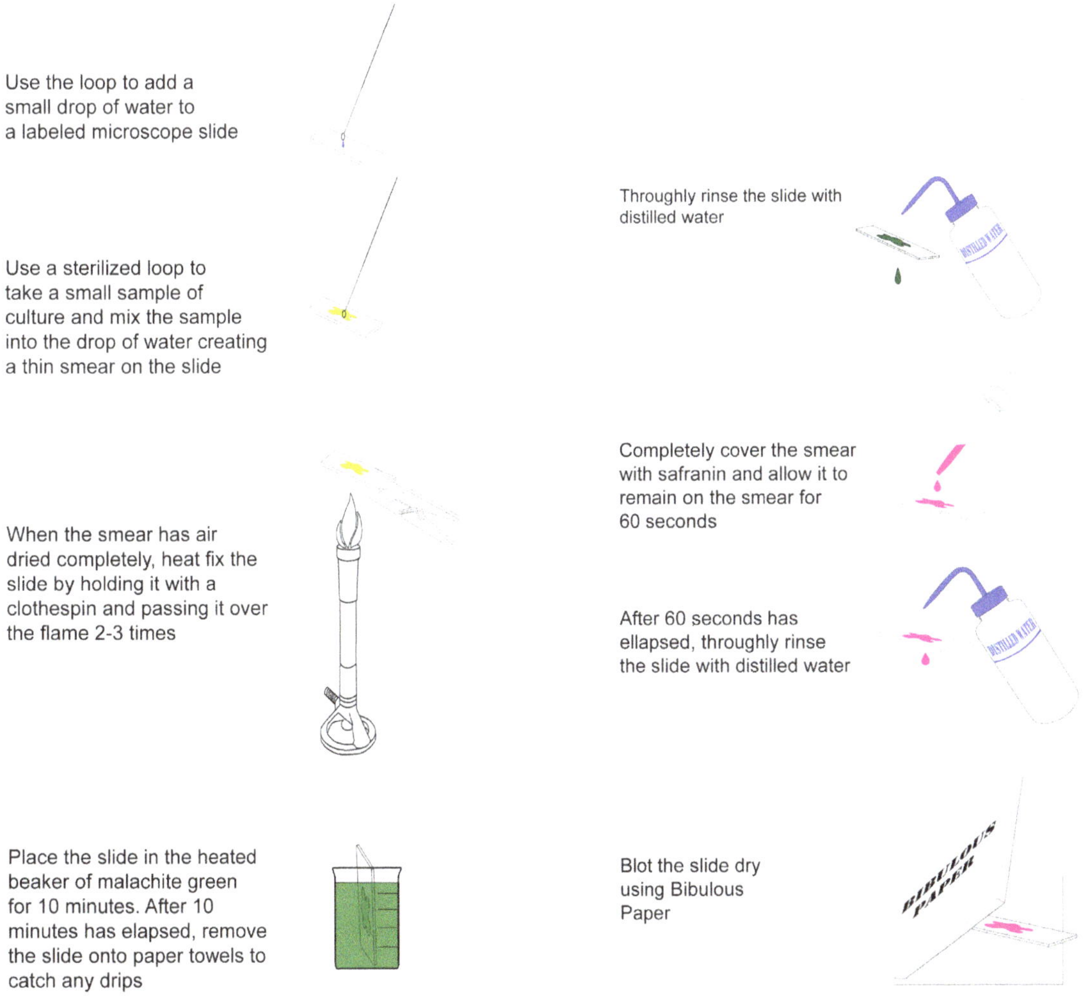

Use the loop to add a small drop of water to a labeled microscope slide

Use a sterilized loop to take a small sample of culture and mix the sample into the drop of water creating a thin smear on the slide

When the smear has air dried completely, heat fix the slide by holding it with a clothespin and passing it over the flame 2-3 times

Place the slide in the heated beaker of malachite green for 10 minutes. After 10 minutes has elapsed, remove the slide onto paper towels to catch any drips

Throughly rinse the slide with distilled water

Completely cover the smear with safranin and allow it to remain on the smear for 60 seconds

After 60 seconds has ellapsed, throughly rinse the slide with distilled water

Blot the slide dry using Bibulous Paper

Exercise 2-11

R & Q

Draw and describe your observations of the endospore stain. Identify free spores, endospores and vegetative cells.

Description: _____

_____

Specimen: _____

Total Magnification: _____

Explain why you think that heat is used in the endospore stain.

_____
_____
_____

Suggest three ways to environmentally stress *B. subtilis*. Does the amount of time (minutes, hours, or days) the cells are stressed matter for the successful production of endospores?

_____
_____
_____

Do endospores contain chromosomes? Explain your answer.

_____
_____
_____

Describe why bacteria benefit from producing endospores.

_____
_____
_____

The Flagella Stain

Learning Objectives

To get acquainted with motility and flagella.
To understand the principle behind the flagella stain.

Flagella are very tiny structures used by certain microbes to move around in their environment. The helical-shaped bacterial flagella (which predominantly consist of the protein flagellin) provide locomotion by rotating in a clockwise or counterclockwise direction.

In Module 1, we used the phase contrast microscope to view bacteria with flagella propel themselves through their environment. Occasionally, it is possible to view the bacterial flagella without staining but, due to their small size, it is often necessary to apply a dye to see these structures. Stains used to view the flagella structures coat the entire flagella to a size that is more easily visible under the microscope. Since some of these dyes can be toxic, in this exercise we will view slides that have already been stained. The prepared slides contain bacterial species such as *E. coli*, *P. vulgaris*, and *Spirillum volutans*, all of which contain flagella that extend out from the cells.

Materials

- Prepared slide of *P. vulgaris*
- Prepared slide of *Spirillum volutans*
- Compound brightfield microscope

Work in pairs.

Procedure

1. View the prepared slides with the 100X objectives.

Exercise 2-12

R & Q

Draw and describe your observations. Include detailed illustrations of the flagella.

Description: _____

_____

Specimen: _____

Total Magnification: _____

Description: _____

_____

Specimen: _____

Total Magnification: _____

The Microbes Around Us

ENVIRONMENTAL MICROBIOLOGY

Microbes are everywhere: in the air, the soil, the water, and our food, as well as around, on, and inside our bodies. However, in order to maintain their growth they strictly dependent on nutrient sources (i.e. the availability of carbon and energy sources). Many microorganisms can produce their own "food"/nutrients from inorganic carbon and energy sources (chemoautotropic organisms); others depend on the environment to provide nutrients (chemoheterotropic organisms); and some organisms rely on the absorption of light to obtain energy (photoautotrophs and photoheterotrophs organisms; see Figure 3.3 "Nutritional Classification of Bacteria"). Due to their diversity, microbial species can be found in almost any type of habitat on Earth. This is why we say that microbes are ubiquitous, which means that they appear to be present everywhere. Furthermore, bacteria fall into a group of highly diverse microorganisms, as you will see throughout this course.

The number of bacteria in the world is enormous: five million trillion trillion is the number estimated in 1998 by microbiologist William B. Whitman and his research team at the University of Georgia (Box 1). Of those, only around sixteen thousand species have been further described in detail and catalogued (Box 2).

Box 1 Microbes are Everywhere

Although bacterial cells are invisible to us, they are present everywhere in our environment. Researching several representative microbial habitats, Dr. Whitman and his research team set out to directly assess the number of the earth's prokaryote organisms and to find their most populated locations. Their studies revealed that most of the prokaryotes reside in open ocean, the soil, and terrestrial and oceanic subsurfaces (see Whitman 1998 below). They documented that the upper 200 meters of an open ocean contain 5×10^5 (500,000) prokaryotic cells/ml water, but below 200 meters, the number would decrease tenfold to 5×10^4 (50,000) cells/ml water. When analyzing up to 10 cm of the sediment, they recorded 4.8×10^8 (or 480 billion) prokaryotic cells. Similarly, the team recorded the number of prokaryotes in various ecosystems and found the following: in tropical rain forests, 17×10^{12} prokaryotes/m²; in savanna, 15×10^{12}/m²; and in swamps and marshes, 2×10^{12}/m². Prokaryotes also populate animals, and although the number of bacteria living on or inside animals is high, this number, compared to the total number of the earth's prokaryotes, is quite low.

Most of animal-associated prokaryotes are found on the skin and in the gastrointestinal tract; the number of prokaryotes on human skin is found to be 10^3–10^4 (or 1,000 to 10,000) cells/cm², with more prokaryotes populating the groin (10^6 cells/cm²). The overall number of prokaryotes on the skin of a human being is 3×10^8. A lot more prokaryotic cells are found in the intestines of humans (3.2×10^{11} cells/ml). The symbiotic relationship between animals and prokaryotes is mostly mutualistic, and for human beings the presence of bacteria has important nutritional and heath benefits (Module 6).

You can further explore Dr. Whitman and his coworkers' work about the number of prokaryotes on Earth, as well as the microbes' contributions to the earth's content of carbon, nitrogen, and phosphorus, in the references listed below.

Reference
Whitman, William B., David C. Coleman, and William J. Wiebe. "Prokaryotes: The Unseen Majority." Proceedings of the National Academy of Sciences of the United States of America 95, no. 12 (1998): 6578–83.

You can read more about numbers in this brief editorial review: "Microbiology by the numbers." Nature Reviews Microbiology 9 (September 2011): 628. doi:10.1038/nrmicro2644.

Box 2 Classifying Prokaryotes

Almost sixteen thousand prokaryotes, which include bacteria and archaea, are categorized and included in the LPSN (List of Prokaryotic Names with Standing in Nomenclature). This is a list of prokaryotic organisms stating their correct names, synonyms, and other characteristics of the organisms.

The names given to prokaryotes are strictly regulated. Rules and regulations exist for how to properly name the organisms. The rules apply to both organisms already known and those newly discovered. Naming an organism is not trivial, and information that can be retrieved about the organisms in the LPSN includes the taxonomic range, phylum, kingdom, division, and domain, followed by the rank of class, subclass, order, suborder, tribe, subtribe, family, subfamily, genus, subgenus, species, and subspecies. Included in the work to categorize bacterial organisms (or to identify two organisms as the same species) is the examination of their genetic material. Comparison of genes with conserved DNA sequences (sequences that essentially have not changed throughout evolution), such as the 16S ribosomal RNA (rRNA) gene sequence, is typically used in this process.

Although the prokaryotic classification and cataloguing of information seems vast, such taxonomy–related information is indispensable for almost any microbiological work, whether it is 1) working in the research lab with well-known prokaryotics to gain more understating of certain cellular pathways; 2) exploring and gaining more knowledge about new prokaryotic species important for our environment, such as those found in microbial ecosystems; or 3) working in hospital settings identifying bacterial species from patients with infectious diseases so proper diagnosis and treatment can be achieved.

The list of prokaryotes grows quickly and has recently increased by approximately eight hundred new names annually (see Nucleic Acids Research below).

Phylogenetic Tree of Life

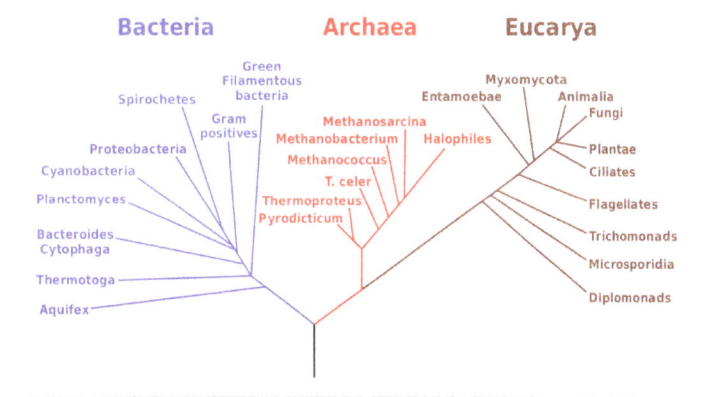

A phylogenetic tree of living things with scientific names, based on RNA data and proposed by Carl Woese, showing the separation of bacteria, archaea, and eukaryotes. Trees constructed with other genes are generally similar, although they may place some early-branching groups very differently, thanks to long branch attraction. The exact relationships of the three domains are still being debated, as is the position of the root of the tree. It has also been suggested that due to lateral gene transfer, a tree may not be the best representation of the genetic relationships of all organisms. For instance some genetic evidence suggests that eukaryotes evolved from the union of some bacteria and archaea (one becoming an organelle and the other the main cell).

Reference

"Parte AC, LPSN—List of Prokaryotic Names with Standing in Nomenclature." Nucleic Acids Research 42 (Database issue) (January 2014): D613–16. doi:10.1093/nar/gkt1111.

You can explore the website of LPSN by following this link: **http://www.bacterio.net**.

FIGURE 3.1 *Diaemus youngi*

Besides thriving at temperatures that are suitable to us, certain bacterial organisms are found living in places with extreme temperatures or under other challenging environmental conditions. Such places include hot springs and glaciers (Box 3 and Box 4), or caves where bacteria can live as microbial communities or inside cave-residing animals, such as bats (Figure 3.1). Again other bacteria live on or inside us skin, our mouth, our teeth, and our intestines (Box 1). Some require oxygen to live; others do not or cannot live in the present of oxygen; some thrive in the salty environment of our skin; and others benefit from the nutrients we eat. Whereas this module emphasizes the aspect of microbes in the environment, Module 6 will focus on the impact of microbes on human health.

Bacteria settling on surfaces tend to "stick" together, and as they grow, more bacteria attach, resulting in the formation of thin, complex layers of bacteria called biofilm. Biofilm may consist of only one bacterial species, but often it is made of a variety of different species, including other microbes

Box 3 Bacteria Inhabiting Ice

Certain microbes thrive in the earth's cryosphere, whether in sea ice, mountain glaciers, ice sheets in Greenland, or icy realms in the Arctic and Antarctica polar oceans. Bacterial species are the most abundant among microorganisms found in sea ice, and they are found throughout the ice, regardless of the depth. Other microbes found in ice include archaea, algae, and fungi, such as the genera *Aspergillus* and *Penicillium*. Viruses have also been reported to be present in ice.

The population of bacteria in ice varies with the season as well as the location within the ice, and it has been reported that the number of bacteria in the ice ranges from 10^3 (1,000) cells/ml to 10^7 (10 million) cells /ml. Most of the bacteria living in the cryosphere fall into the group of heterotrophs (see Figure 3.3), with much fewer falling into the group of phototrophs. Green nonsulfur bacteria, purple sulfur bacteria, and cyanobacteria are among the bacterial organisms found in sea ice. It is interesting that several types of the same bacterial species found living in ice located at one pole of earth are also found living at the other pole.

Most of the bacteria in the ice live as single-cell organisms (planktonic bacteria), but they also engage in important mutual relationships with other microorganisms that are also part of the sea-ice ecosystem.

FIGURE 3.2 Mountain glaciers

You can read more about bacteria in the sea ice and glaciers here:
Boetius, A., Alexandre M. Anesio, Jody W. Deming, Jill A. Mikucki, and Josephine Z. Rapp. "Microbial Ecology of the Cryosphere: Sea Ice and Glacial Habitats." Nature Reviews Microbiology 13 (2015): 677–90.

Copyright © Gcarter2 (CC BY-SA 2.5) at https://commons.wikimedia.org/wiki/File%3ADiaemus_youngi.jpg.
U.S. National Oceanic and Atmospheric Administration, https://commons.wikimedia.org/wiki/File%3ASea_ice_terrain.jpg. Copyright in the Public Domain.

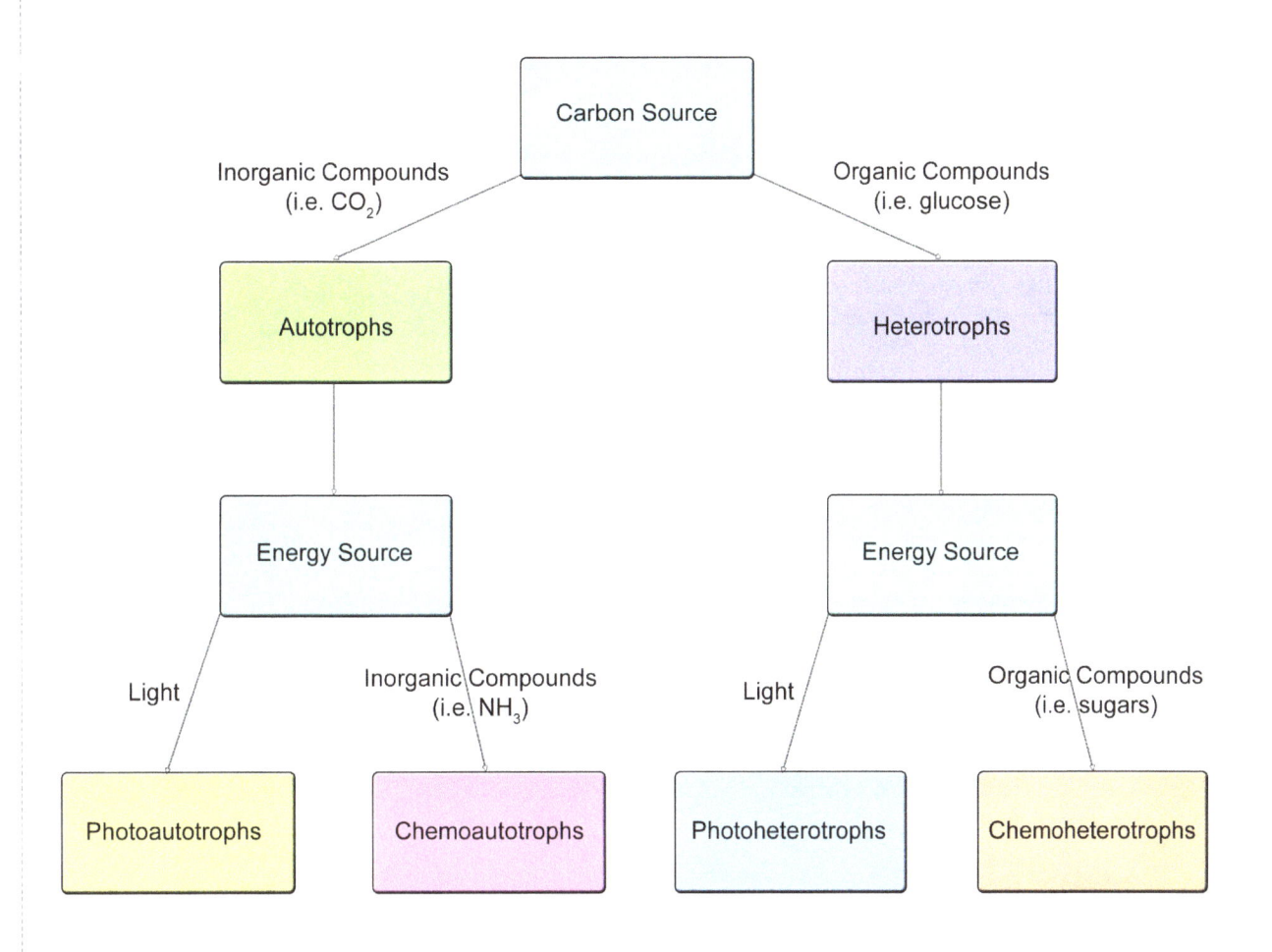

FIGURE 3.3 Nutritional Classification of Bacteria
Note: Chemotrophic organisms further divide into two classes depending on which molecules they use as electron donors; thus a chemolithotroph organism oxidizes inorganic molecules, and a chemoorganotroph oxidizes organic molecules.

Box 4 Bacteria Inhabiting Hot Springs

In 1966, Dr. Thomas Brock, a microbiologist at the University of Wisconsin, first discovered and isolated bacteria able to thrive in environments with boiling-hot temperatures (Brock 1967 and 1997). Dr. Brock's interest in studying microbes in their natural environment had led him to explore hot springs in Yellowstone National Park, and there he isolated the extreme thermophile bacteria *Thermus aquaticus*. Soon after the discovery of *T. aquaticus* and other thermophilic bacteria, these organisms became of much importance due to their heat-stable proteins. As a consequence, one of the most indispensable techniques was invented: the polymerase chain reaction, or PCR. PCR is a laboratory procedure that employs a heat-stable enzyme (DNA polymerase), DNA and other components, and a thermal cycler to copy and amplify specific strands of DNA (Brock 1967). Today, PCR is still an important technique in many research labs, and it is an indispensable procedure used by the biotechnology industry, by criminologists, and for medical diagnoses. Dr. Kary B. Mullis, who invented PCR, received a Nobel Prize in Chemistry for his work in 1993.

Microbes growing in other hot springs worldwide, as well as in fumaroles, such as those found in Hawaii, are still subject for intense research. However, another different kind of project that has been undertaken is the one in Iceland, where a research team has set out to examine the effect of the microbial changes in natural thermal bathing pools, including assessing the risk of infections by opportunistic pathogens deposited in the pools by bathing guests (Thorolfsdottir 2013).

FIGURE 3.4 Hot spring in Iceland. Courtesy of George Allen.

References

Brock, T.D. "Life at High Temperatures." Science *158 (1967)*: 1012–19.
Brock, T.D. "The Value of Basic Research: Discovery of Thermus aquaticus and Other Extreme Thermophiles." Genetics *146 (1997)*: 1207–10.
Thorolfsdottir, Berglind O.T. and Viggo T. Marteinsson. "Microbiological Analysis in Three Diverse Natural Geothermal Bathing Pools in Iceland." International Journal of Environmental Research and Public Health *10, no. 3 (2013)*: 1085–99. doi:10.3390/ijerph10031085

You can read more about Dr. Kary Mullis here: http://www.karymullis.com/pcr.shtml.

such as fungi. Besides the microbes, the established biofilm consist of a dense matrix of polysaccharides, proteins, DNA and inorganic components, and channels for transportation of nutrients. Living together as a community, the microbes use signals to communicate with each other (a phenomenon called quorum sensing), make collective decisions, and stay attached to each other as long as food is plentiful. However, as food (nutrients) becomes limited, the single-celled microbes (planktonic cells) will detach from the biofilm and move away in order to find another nutrient-rich location in which to settle. Biofilm can be found in nature (e.g., rocks in the water),

FIGURE 3.5 Biofilm

in human beings (e.g., on teeth), or as biofilm infections, acquired either in association with medical devices (catheters and prostheses) or independently of such devices (e.g., chronic lung infections in patients suffering from cystic fibrosis). Due to the dense structure of biofilms, it is difficult to destroy these compact layers of microbes, and bacteria contained within biofilm often show resistance to antibiotics and are known for escaping the host's immune defenses. Both Gram-positive (e.g., *Staphylococcus aureus*) and Gram-negative (*Escherichia coli* and *Pseudomonas aeruginosa*) bacteria, as well as the fungus *Candida albicans*, are often seen in biofilm infections.

The isolation and identification of bacteria from environmental samples (such as soil, water, or even dental plaques) can be a difficult task for scientists. When isolated from one another, only about 1% (or even less) of the bacterial organisms are able to readily grow as isolated colonies in or on the media we typically use in the laboratory. The difficulty in growing the organisms in the laboratory comes from the fact that many of the bacteria require special, unique nutrients and growth conditions and, if at all possible, it can take months or even years to find the right circumstances that keep just a single, newly isolated microbial organism alive (Azvolinsky 2015). Therefore, many bacterial organisms are never characterized due to the difficulties in culturing them on growth media and keeping them alive as isolated cultures. Thus, the amount of research that can be performed with a given newly isolated bacterial species depends on the degree of complications in culturing the species after removing from it from its natural habitat.

Reference

Azvolinsky, A. "Lost Colonies: Next-generation Sequencing Has Identified Scores of New Microorganisms, but Getting Even Abundant Bacterial Species to Grow in the Lab Has Proven Challenging." *The Scientist*. October 1, 2015. http://www.thescientist.com/?articles.view/articleNo/44098/title/Lost-Colonies/.

Exercise 3-1

Sampling the Environment

Learning Objective

To become familiar with the diversity and ubiquity of microbes in our environment.

In this exercise, we will sample the laboratory environment on a TSA plate, and after growth, we will be viewing and describing the colonies that appeared.

Day 1

Materials

- TSA plate
- Tube of sterile water
- Sterile swab

Work in pairs.

Procedure

1. Label your TSA plates.
2. Select an area to test for the presence of microbes (e.g., doorknob, faucet, bench, book, shoe, floor, or other item). Do not sample your skin, mouth, etc. Label the plate with your chosen source.
3. Bring the plate, the tube of sterile water, and a swab to your chosen source. Aseptically open the package containing the swab as shown in Figure 3.6 "Sampling the environment."

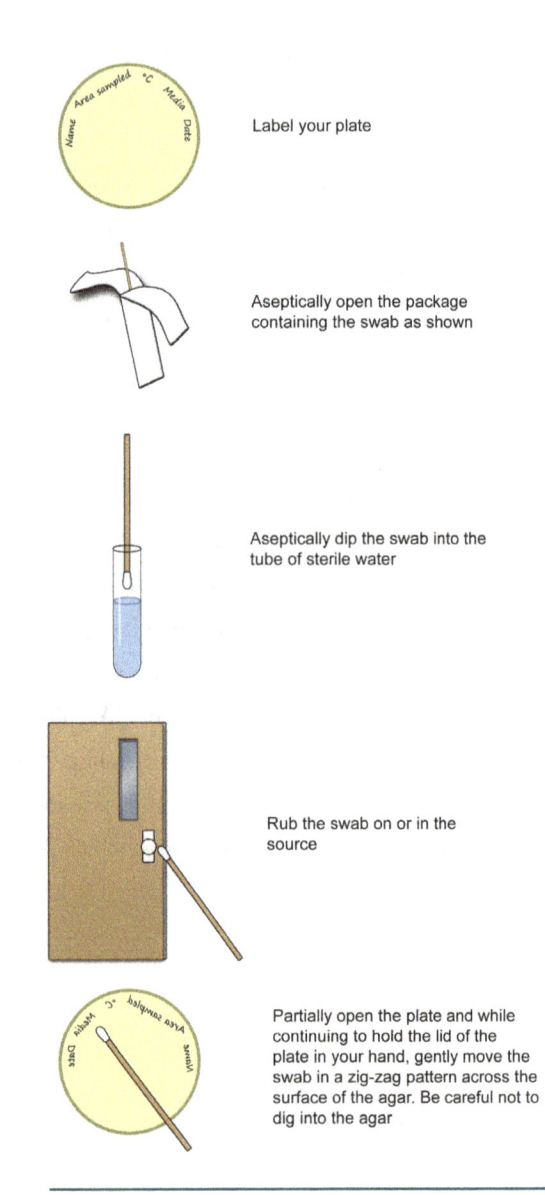

Label your plate

Aseptically open the package containing the swab as shown

Aseptically dip the swab into the tube of sterile water

Rub the swab on or in the source

Partially open the plate and while continuing to hold the lid of the plate in your hand, gently move the swab in a zig-zag pattern across the surface of the agar. Be careful not to dig into the agar

FIGURE 3.6 Sampling the environment

Exercise 3-1

4. Dip the swab into the tube of sterile water and rub the swab on or in the source.
5. Partially open the TSA plate and, while continuing to hold the lid of the plate in your hand, gently move the swab in a zigzag pattern across the entire surface of the agar. Be careful not to dig into the agar.
6. When done, tape this plate shut with masking tape.
7. Discard the swab in the biohazard container.
8. Invert the plate prior to incubation at 30°C for 48 hours.

Day 2

Materials

- TSA plate inoculated on Day 1.

Procedure

1. Do not open the TSA plate when viewing and describing the colonies.

Exercise 3-1

R&Q

Use Table "Colony Morphologies" in Module 2, Exercise 2-4 to describe four well-isolated colonies present on the plate. Include whether the microbes are bacteria or fungi/hyphal fungi.

_____
_____
_____

Explain why specifically a TSA plate was used to sample the environment and why incubation at 30°C was an ideal temperature for incubation.

_____
_____
_____

Why do you think that we do not want to open the plate with the environmental sample when viewing the colony morphology?

_____
_____
_____

Explain why you think that some bacteria prefer growing at colder but not warmer temperatures, like in soil as opposed to inside the human body.

_____
_____
_____

Suggest other ways of taking advantage of heat-stable proteins isolated from extreme thermophiles.

_____
_____
_____

Exercise 3-1

Refer to Figure 3.3 Nutritional Clasification of Bacteria and explain why you think fewer phototrophs exist in ice.

_____
_____
_____

Considering temperature, mention which groups of microbes you are most likely to find in sea ice, hot springs, and inside humans.

_____
_____
_____

Exercise 3-2

Biofilm Formation Using Pond Water Sample

Learning Objective

To gain knowledge about biofilm.

We will be performing a very simple experiment that shows how easily biofilm forms on a surface if biofilm-forming bacteria are present. We will use a water source (pond water/hay infusion) and a glass slide, which will be stained to view the formed biofilm.

Day 1

Materials

- Glass slides (2)
- Pond water (hay infusion)
- Beaker

Work in groups of four.

Procedure

1. Label your two slides with your group number.
2. Place the two clean slides in the beaker with pond water (hay infusion) so the area you labeled on the slides stays dry.
3. Let the slides sit undisturbed in the pond water for 5–7 days at room temperature.

Day 2

Materials

- Beaker with pond water (hay infusion) and slides
- Gram-stain solutions
- Staining rack
- Forceps
- Beaker with water

Work in groups of four.

1. Collect the slides from the pond water using a pair of forceps, and dip the slides in provided large beaker with water.
2. Inspect the slides. Are they cloudy, indicating that biofilm formed? Record your observation in the *R & Q* section.
3. Completely dry off one side of the slides with a paper towel or Kimwipes, removing the biofilm from that side of the slide.
4. Place one slide on the staining rack.
5. Gram stain one slide (Do not heat fix). refer to Module 2, Exercise 2-7 for Gram stain procedure.
6. Carefully dry of the second slide with a paper towel and add a coverslip. Use a compound brighttfield microscope to observe the slide at 400X total magnification.
7. Optional: To increase the contrast, view the slide prepared in step 6 with the phase contrast microscope. Use both the darkfield and phase contrast settings.

Exercise 3-2

R & Q

Describe and draw your observations of the unstained slide viewed using the brightfield microscope. Include a description of the types of microorganisms you see.

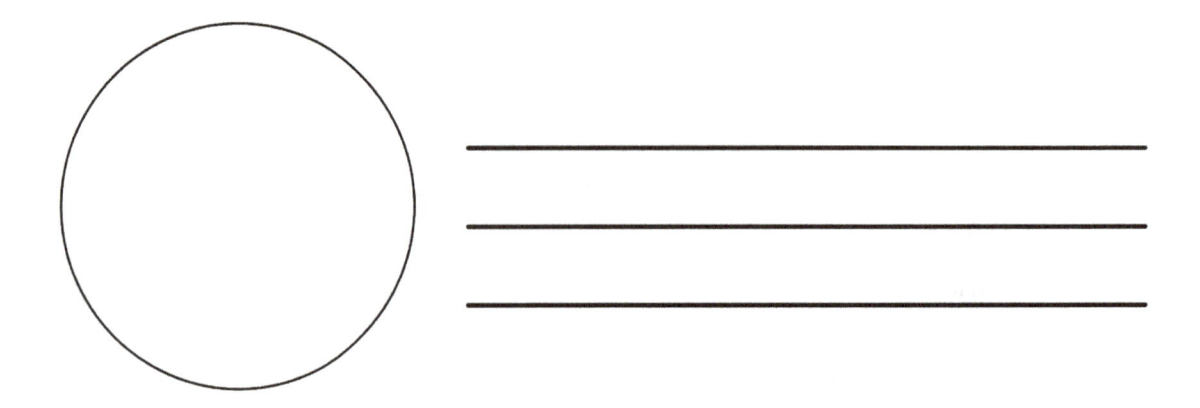

Optional: Describe and draw your observations of the unstained slide that you viewed with the phase contrast microscope using darkfield and phase contrast settings.

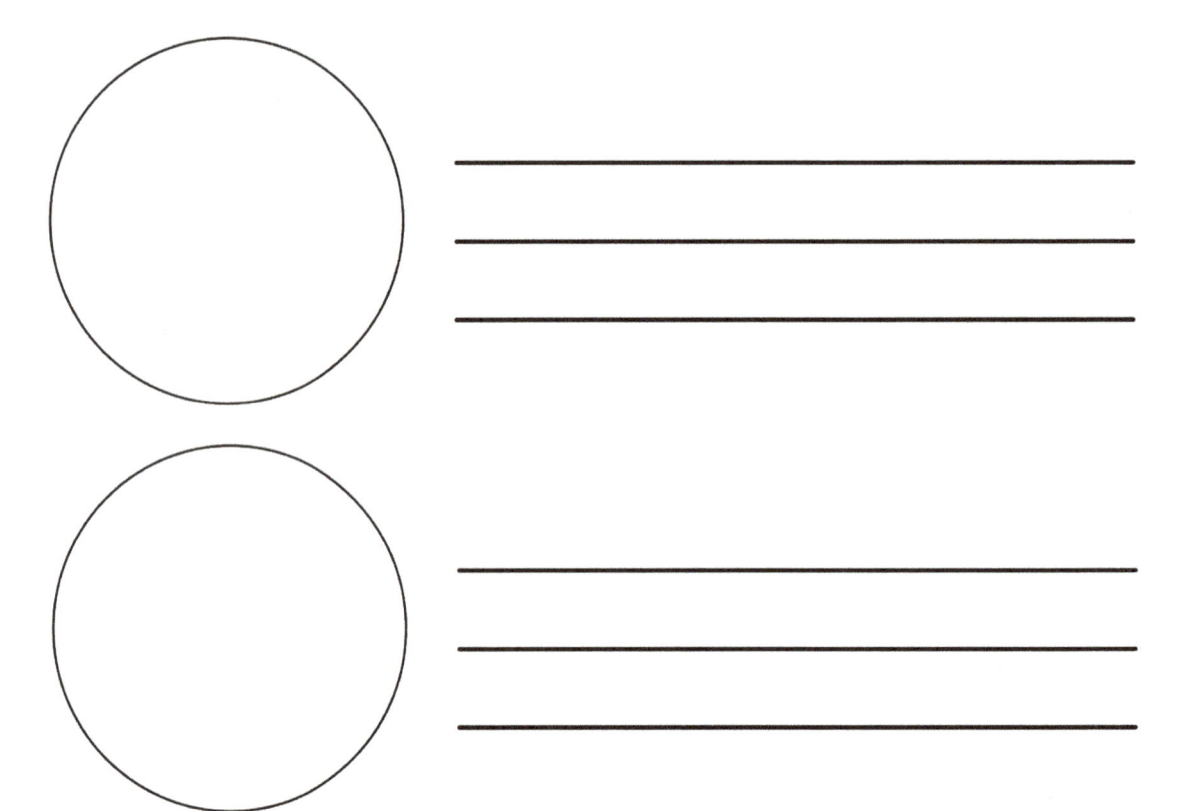

Exercise 3-2

Describe and draw your observations of the Gram-stained slide that you viewed using the brightfield microscope.

Are both Gram-positive and Gram-negative bacteria present in the biofilm? In what ratio?

Why is it not necessary to heat fix when staining the biofilm on the slide?

Exercise 3-3

Isolation of Biofilm-Forming Bacteria from Soil

Learning Objectives

To gain knowledge about biofilm-forming microbes.
To further understand the effects of biofilm on our environments.

In this exercise, you will isolate two bacterial species from a simulated soil sample. The soil sample only contains two live bacteria species that have been deliberately added to a sterile sample of soil. You will isolate and identify the bacteria by microscopic observation of the unstained and stained microbes. Thereafter, you will culture the isolated bacterial organisms and investigate whether any of them are able to form biofilm.

Day 1

Materials

- Simulated soil sample containing *Pseudomonas fluorescens* and *Micrococcus luteus*
- TSB tube
- TSA plate
- Inoculating loop

Work in groups of four.

Procedure

1. Aseptically add a small amount of soil to TSB medium. Gently mix the sample to suspend the soil bacteria by rolling the tube between the palms of your hands.

Aseptically add a small amount of soil to 5ml TSB medium. Gently mix the sample to suspend the soil bacteria

Let the sample sit undisturbed for 30 min on the bench. The soil should settle on the bottom of the tube

Aseptically use the loop to remove a sample from the upper layer of the soil sample tube

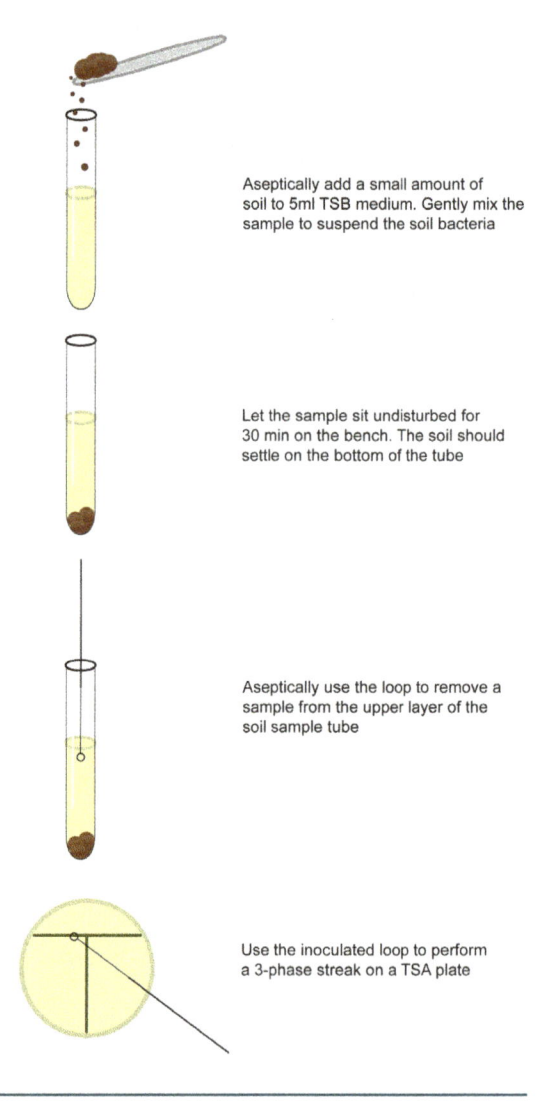

Use the inoculated loop to perform a 3-phase streak on a TSA plate

FIGURE 3.7 Soil Sample Procedure

2. Let the sample sit undisturbed for 30 minutes on the bench. The soil should settle on the bottom of the tube.
3. Light the Bunsen burner.
4. Flame the inoculating loop.
5. Inoculate a TSA plate with a sample from the upper layer of the soil-sample tube and perform a three-phase streak.
6. Incubate plates at 30°C for 2 – 4 days.

Note: If you were to collect your own soil sample and wanted to isolate *P. fluorescens*, you would have to enrich/select for the bacterium first. The reason for this is that other bacteria in the soil are abundant compared to *P. fluorescens*. Therefore, it would be more difficult to find *P. fluorescens* colonies among colonies of the other species. Since we are working with a prepared soil sample, we do not have to enrich for *P. fluorescens*; it is added to the soil sample in sufficient amounts.

Day 2

Materials

- TSA plate streaked on Day 1
- TSA plates (2)
- Gram-stain solutions

Work in groups of four.

Procedure

1. Observe the colonies on the plate from Day 1. Use Box 3 and Figure 2.6 in Module 2, Exercise 2-4 ("Colony Morphology") to describe colony characteristics of the two isolated bacterial species present on the plate. Write your answer in the *R & Q* section.
2. Pick a well-isolated colony of each of the two species and restreak each one on TSA plates to produce pure culture plates.
3. Incubate the two plates at 30°C for 2 – 4 days.
4. Use cells from the same colonies to perform Gram stains. Refer to Module 2, Exercise 2-4 for procedure.
5. Describe the Gram reaction and identify your organisms in the *R & Q* section.

Exercise 3-3

Day 3

Materials

- TSA plates (2) streaked on Day 2
- TSB 5 ml tubes (2)

Work in groups of four.

Procedure

1. Inoculate 5 ml of TSB medium with a tiny amount of cells from one organism.
2. Repeat step 1 for the other organism.
3. Incubate the two tubes for 2 – 4 days at 30°C.

Day 4

Materials

- TSB cultures inoculated on Day 3
- TSB 4.5ml tubes (2)
- 96-well Microtiter plate
- P200 micropipettes and tips
- P1000 micropipettes and tips

Work in groups of four.

Procedure

1. Collect the two TSB tubes inoculated on Day 3.
2. Dilute each of the cultures 10X by adding 0.5 ml culture to 4.5 ml TSB.
3. Add 100 µl of the diluted cultures to five wells each of a 96-well Microtiter plate. Record which wells your group used and which culture the wells contain.
4. Incubate the plate at room temperature for 4-7 days.

Day 5

Materials

- Microtitter plate with incubated cultures
- Crystal violet
- Distilled water
- Dropper

Work in groups of four

Procedure

1. Remove the media by gently shaking the media out of the well into the provided liquid waste bin (to collect the media for autoclaving).
2. Carefully rinse the wells with distilled water using a dropper and collect the water in the liquid waste bin as in step 1. Tap the plate on a paper towel to remove the remaining water from the wells. Discard the paper towel in the biohazard bin.
3. Add drops of the crystal violet solution to fill each well and stain for 10–12 minutes. If biofilm has formed on the sides and bottom of the wells, it will be stained by the crystal violet.
4. Collect the crystal violet solution in the liquid waste bin, and rinse the wells three times with water, as in step 2 above.
5. Place the plate upside down on a paper towel to dry. Let the wells dry for 15–30 minutes.
6. Record your observations in the *R & Q* section.

Exercise 3-3

R & Q

Day 2

Describe the colony morphology of the two bacteria species on the plate. Refer to Box 3 and Figure 2.6 in Module 2, Exercise 2-4.

_____
_____
_____

Record your Gram-stain and colony morphology observations in the Table below. Which organism is which?

_____
_____
_____

Day 5

Record your observations regarding biofilm formation in the Table below. Did both, one, or none of the bacterial species form biofilm?

Organism	Colony Morphology	Gram Reaction	Presence of Biofilm
Organism 1			
Organism 2			

Describe and discuss three advantages of bacteria growing in biofilm, compared to planktonic cells (single living cells).

_____
_____
_____

FOOD MICROBIOLOGY

You have already learned that microbes are everywhere, and that includes the food and beverages we consume. When talking about food and microbes, two processes come to mind: the constructive process, in which microbial organisms are added on purpose and used to produce certain food items, and the destructive process, in which microbes, if present, can cause spoilage of the food.

Many food products are nutritionally rich and easily provide favorable growth environments for a variety of both harmless and harmful microbes. Thus, the microbial growth may be either constructive or destructive, and this will depend in part on the types of microbes present and their by-products.

Box 5 Microbes in Food and Beverages

The end result of a constructive microbial-associated process in food production is a desirable food or beverage item. Such processes often involve fermentation; examples are bread, cheese, yogurt, soy sauce, tofu, vinegar, and sauerkraut, as well as beverages such as beer and wine. Bacterial strains are also involved in the production of food additives and nutritional additives.

The end result of a destructive microbial-related process that occurs in food or certain beverages is spoilage; examples are the breakdown of food products into less desirable forms, as well as the growth of organisms that can cause food poisoning. A few examples of food-borne pathogens are *Salmonella, E. coli, Clostridium botulinum, Listeria monocytogenes,* and *Staphylococcus aureus*.

Occasionally, the line between constructive and destructive processes in food is blurred (e.g., in the case of the production of vinegar/wine from grape juice fermentation). If the purpose of the fermentation was to produce vinegar, the process would be considered constructive. However, if the goal was to produce wine, vinegar production would definitely be considered destructive.

Recall the work of Louis Pasteur and how he discovered that contaminating bacteria caused the spoilage of beer and wine produced in Europe. He furthered this work by showing that heating the beer and wine was sufficient to destroy or lower the number of damaging microbes, thereby preventing spoilage of the beverage. Today, pasteurization is still an essential process that is commonly used by the dairy and food industries to control the growth of unwanted microbes.

Jon Sullivan, https://commons.wikimedia.org/wiki/File:Beer_and_bread.jpg. Copyright in the Public Domain.

In this section of module 3, you will have an opportunity to observe some of the constructive and destructive effects of microbes in food and beverages. We will examine and compare a variety of beverages and/or food samples by inoculating samples onto agar plates and incubating at the desirable temperatures.

However, in order to view microbes originating from solid food on agar plates, it is necessary to produce a suspension of the items. A suspension of solid food samples is commonly made in a blender or by using a stomacher, an apparatus that homogenizes food samples by using physical action, similar to the human stomach. As the suspension is produced, the microbes present in the food sample are released, typically into an isotonic solution to ensure that the microbes are kept intact. If necessary, the suspension can then be diluted to provide a countable number of microbes when spread onto agar plates and incubated.

In the exercises to follow, we will be looking at samples that have been preserved in different ways: either fresh out of the refrigerator or stored for longer under unfavorable conditions and temperatures. The individual samples will either be plated directly onto agar medium or diluted prior to plating. In most cases, spread plates will be produced to view the microbes in the food and beverage samples, with one exception: the juice samples, which will be inoculated using the pour plate technique, a plating technique often used in food microbiology. We will also calculate the original concentration of microbes in some of the food or beverage samples and use these numbers to evaluate methods for sustaining food quality.

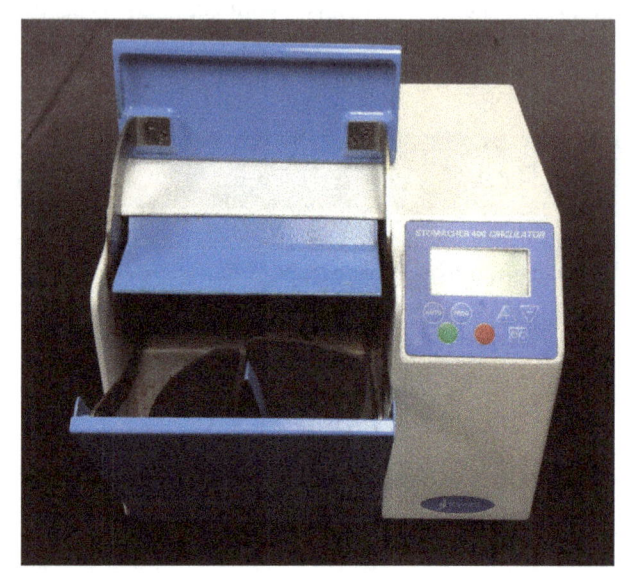

FIGURE 3.8 Stomacher open

In the two following exercises, we will analyze microbial content in food and beverage products such as meat, cheese, milk, and juice.

Exercise 3-4

Examination of microbes in milk and juice

Learning Objectives

To acknowledge the role of microbes in the preparation of food.
To differentiate between constructive and destructive properties of microbes in food.
To enumerate microorganisms in food samples.
To become familiar with the pour plate method.

Day 1

Materials

- Four demo milk samples for observation (share with entire class)
- Assigned milk sample
- Assigned juice sample
- TSA plate
- Liquefied PDA pH 5.6 +/− 0.2
- Empty petri dish
- P1000 micropipettes with tips or 1 ml serological pipettes (8)
- Sterile swabs

Work in groups of four.

Procedure

Food Sample	Procedure
Milk	Use a swab to zig-zag streak sample onto a TSA plate
Juice	Use pour plate technique

Milk samples
The purpose of this part of the exercise is to look at how microbes affect milk, as well as how to control the growth of microbes in milk.

Exercise 3-4

Milk demo samples

1. Examine the provided demo milk sample.
   a. Pasteurized milk stored at 4°C for one week
   b. Pasteurized milk stored at room temperature for four days
   c. Autoclaved milk
   d. Fresh buttermilk
2. Record your observations in the *R & Q* section.

Milk hands-on samples

1. Label a TSA plate according to your assigned milk product.
   a. Pasteurized milk stored at 4°C for one week
   b. Pasteurized milk stored at room temperature for four days
   c. Autoclaved milk
   d. Fresh buttermilk
2. Use a sterile swab to inoculate your assigned milk sample onto the TSA plate. Streak a broad zigzag pattern across the entire surface of the plate.
3. Incubate the TSA plate 37°C for 24–48 hours.

Juice samples

Besides examining juice samples for bacterial and yeast microbial organisms (microbes), the purpose of looking at juice samples is also to evaluate ways of preserving the beverage.

1. Label an empty petri dish according to your assigned juice product.
   a. Processed/filtered juice
   b. Juice from frozen concentrate
   c. Fresh-squeezed juice
2. With a P1000 micropipettes or 1 ml serological pipette, add 0.5 ml of the juice sample to the bottom of the empty petri dish.
3. Add liquefied Potato Dextrose Agar (PDA), kept at 45°C to prevent the agar from solidifying. Immediately, gently swirl the petri dish so the juice sample mixes with the warm PDA medium (Figure 3.10 "Pour Plate").

   Note: To prevent the PDA from solidifying in the tube, do not remove the tube from the water bath until just before adding the medium to the petri dish.
4. Invert the plate when the agar has solidified.
5. Incubate the PDA plates at 30°C for 48–96 hours.

Exercise 3-4   135

Use a p1000 micropipettor or a 1 ml serological pipette to add 0.5 ml of the juice sample to the bottom of an empty petri dish

Pour liquefied Potato Dextrose Agar (PDA), kept at 45°C to prevent the agar from solidifying. Immediately, gently swirl the plate, so the juice sample mixes with the warm PDA medium

Allow the agar to solidify. When it has solidified, invert the plate and incubate it

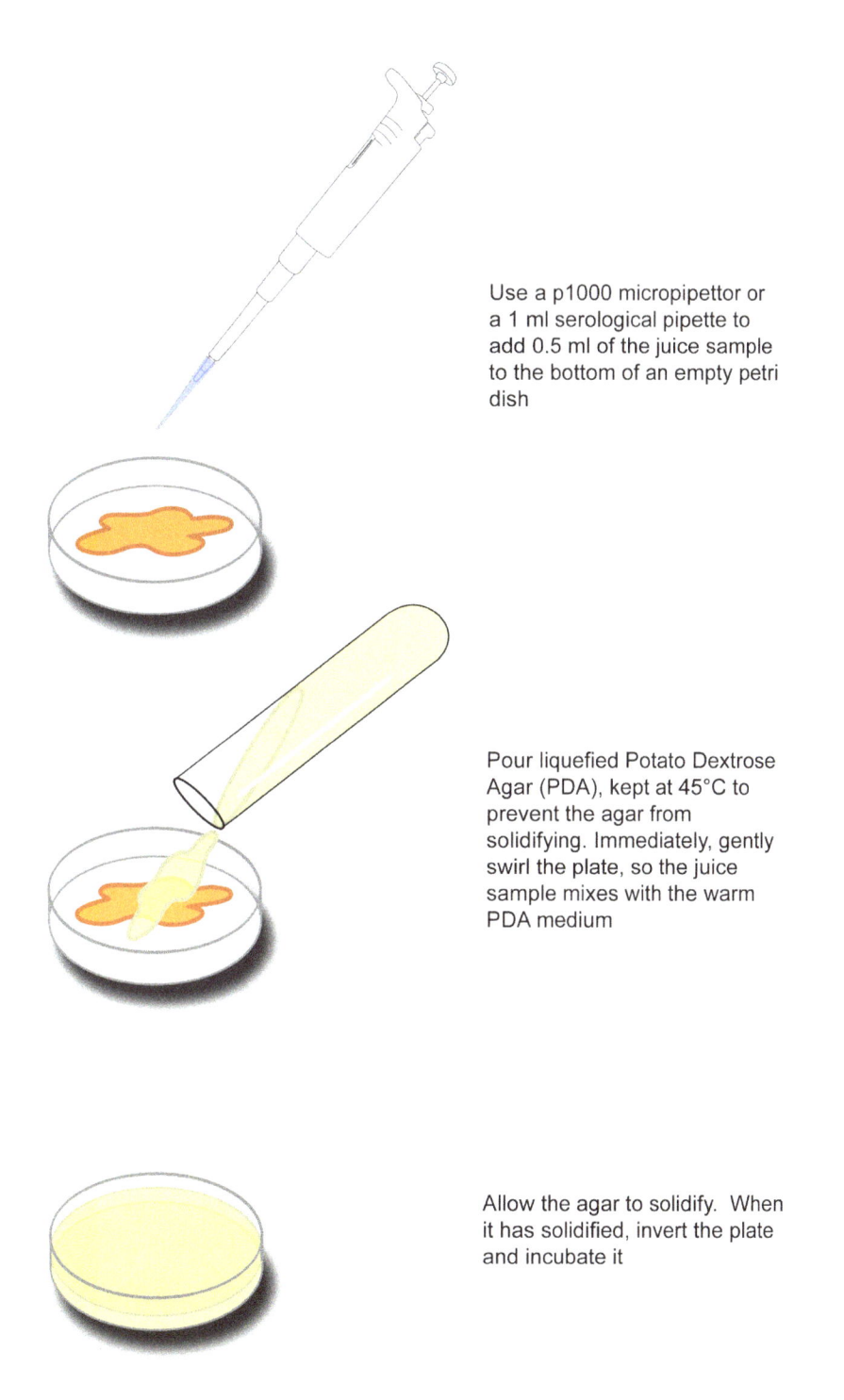

FIGURE 3.9 Pour plate technique

Day 2

Materials

Plates containing milk and juice samples inoculated during previous lab period.

Procedure

1. Record your observations of the milk and juice samples in the *R & Q* section.

R & Q

Day 1

Milk demo samples:

Pasteurized milk stored for one week at 4°C:

Texture? _____

Color? _____

Odor? _____

Pasteurized milk stored for four days at room temperature:

Texture? _____

Color? _____

Odor? _____

Autoclaved milk:

Texture? _____

Color? _____

Odor? _____

Fresh buttermilk:

Texture? _____

Color? _____

Odor? _____

Exercise 3-4

Day 2

Milk hands-on samples:

Milk Product	Growth on TSA? (yes or no)	Sterile? (yes or no)	Constructive or Destructive process?
Pasteurized Milk Stored 1 week at 4°C			
Pasteurized Milk Stored 4 days at Room Temperature			
Autoclaved Milk Stored 4 days at Room Temperature			
Buttermilk (Fresh)			

What do you expect the microbial content to be in fresh pasteurized milk?

_____
_____
_____

Correlate your observation of the demo milk samples and the milk samples your group of four plated. Comment on the microbial content and if constructive and destructive processes occurred.

_____
_____
_____

Describe the effect of storage temperature on the microbial content in pasteurized milk.

_____
_____
_____

Originally, buttermilk was the sour liquid left after butter was produced from whole milk. Today, it is typically produced by adding selected bacterial cultures to milk and incubating the mixture until it sours.

Exercise 3-4

The solids that form as a result of this process are broken up into fine particles to generate the thickened consistency of the final product. Was any growth observed from the buttermilk sample? Is this result logical?

_____
_____
_____

Juice samples

Juice Sample	Growth	Constructive or Destructive process?
Juice (Processed/Filtered)		
Juice (from Frozen Concentrate)		
Juice (Fresh Squeezed)		

Do bacteria and yeast appear to be present in any of the samples? Explain the observations that led you to this answer.

_____
_____
_____

Filtering can be quite effective in removing microbes from suspension. How does the filtered-juice sample compare to the frozen and freshly squeezed juices?

_____
_____
_____

Explain why a given beverage product may be frozen for storage rather than filtered.

_____
_____
_____

Exercise 3-5

Examination of microbes in meat and cheese

Learning Objectives

To acknowledge the role of microbes in the preparation of food.
To differentiate the constructive and destructive properties of microbes in food.
To enumerate microorganisms in food samples.

Day 1

Materials

- Assigned cheese sample
- Assigned meat sample
- 4.5 ml blanks of peptone water (5)
- 9.9 ml blank of peptone water
- P200 micropipettes with tips or 1 ml serological pipettes.
- P1000 micropipettes with tips or 1 ml serological pipettes
- TSA plates (3)
- PDA plates pH 5.6 +/− 0.2, (3)
- EMB agar plate
- Glass or metal spreader
- Alcohol jar

Work in groups of four.

Procedure

Food Sample	Procedure Summary
Meat	Dilute sample and plate dilutions on TSA plates. Use the loop to 3-phase streak the original sample onto an EMB plate
Cheese	Dilute sample and plate dilutions on PDA plates

Exercise 3-5

Cheese samples

Cheese is made from milk and can only be produced with the help of microbes. We will use homogenized cheese to observe some of the types of microbes that are used to generate cheese, and we will calculate colony-forming units per gram of cheese.

The suspensions used in this exercise were prepared using the stomacher: a 10x dilution of a given cheese sample was prepared by placing 10 g of cheese into 90 ml of **peptone water** (a minimal growth media), and the mixture was stomached for two minutes.

2. Prepare and label tubes for a serial dilution of the cheese suspension according to Figure 3.10 "Serial Dilution Cheese."
    a. Bleu cheese
    b. Brie cheese
3. Perform the serial dilution using P1000 and P200 micropipettes or the appropriate serological pipettes.

    Note: Remember to change tips or pipettes in order to avoid carrying over cells that will give you inaccurate colony counts, vortex well between each dilution to properly resuspend the cells.

	0.1 ml	0.5 ml	0.5 ml
	Original Culture	9.9 ml blank	4.5 ml blank	4.5 ml blank
Dilution Step:	10^{-1}	10^{-2}	10^{-1}	10^{-1}
Total Dilution:	10^{-1}	10^{-3}	10^{-4}	10^{-5}

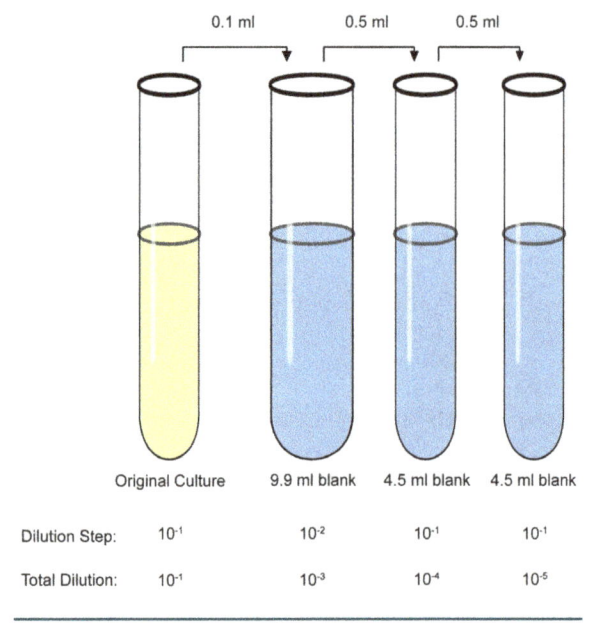

FIGURE 3.10 Serial Dilution Cheeese

You have now obtained three subsequent dilutions, with the most dilute suspension representing a total dilution of 10^{-5} relative to the original sample of cheese.

4. Label one PDA plate for each of the three cheese dilutions that you prepared.

    Make sure to include the type of cheese, as well as the dilution used and the volume of inoculums that you are going to spread on each plate:

    > 0.1 ml of a 10^{-3} dilution
    > 0.1 ml, 10^{-4}
    > 0.1 ml, 10^{-5}

5. Use a bent glass or metal spreader to spread 0.1 ml of the respective dilutions onto each plate.

   CAUTION: Alcohol is flammable. Use caution when working with alcohol near an open flame!

6. Incubate the PDA plates at 30°C for 48–96 hours.

Beef samples

The purpose of this exercise is to examine the microbial content of fresh meat and stored meat before and after cooking. Potential fecal contamination in freshly ground meat, which is determined by the presence of *E. coli* in the meat sample, will also be analyzed.

The suspensions used in this exercise were prepared using the stomacher: a 10x dilution of a given meat sample was prepared by placing 10 g of meat into 90 ml of **peptone water** (a minimal growth media), and the mixture was stomached for two minutes.

7. Prepare and label tubes for a series dilution of the meat suspension according to Figure 3.11 "Meat Dilution Series."
   a. Fresh ground beef
   b. Ground beef stored at 4°C for three days
   c. Ground beef that was stored at 4°C for three days and then cooked by microwaving for 4–6 minutes at full power in an 800W microwave oven.
8. Perform the serial dilution using P1000 and P200 micropipettes or 1 ml serological pipettes.

   Note: Remember to change tips or pipettes appropriately in order to avoid carrying over cells that will give you inaccurate colony counts, vortex well between each dilution to properly resuspend the cells.

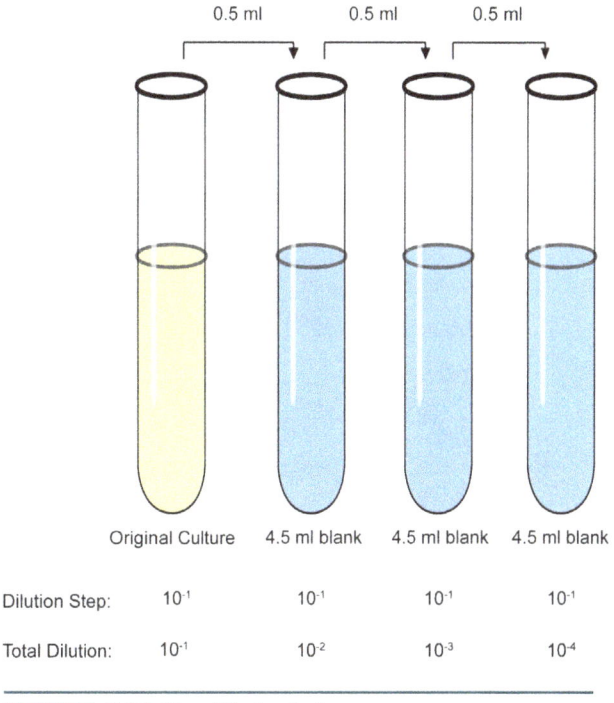

	Original Culture	4.5 ml blank	4.5 ml blank	4.5 ml blank
Dilution Step:	10^{-1}	10^{-1}	10^{-1}	10^{-1}
Total Dilution:	10^{-1}	10^{-2}	10^{-3}	10^{-4}

FIGURE 3.11 Meat Dilution Series

Exercise 3-5

Label one TSA plate for each of the three meat dilutions that you prepared.

> Make sure to include the type of beef, as well as the dilution used and the volume of inoculums that you are going to spread on each plate:
>
> 0.1 ml of a 10^{-2} dilution
>
> 0.1 ml, 10^{-3}
>
> 0.1 ml, 10^{-4}

9. Use a glass or metal spreader to spread 0.1 ml of the respective dilutions onto each plate.

   CAUTION: Alcohol is flammable. Use caution when working with alcohol near an open flame!

10. Incubate the TSA plates at 37°C for 24–48 hours.

Due to the methods used to produce ground meat, fecal bacteria, such as *E. coli*, may contaminate the end product. We will test our ground-meat sample for the presence of *E. coli* contamination by plating samples onto EMB (the selective-differential agar medium Eosin Methylene Blue) plates. EMB plates are used to specifically test for the presence of *E. coli*, a lactose fermenter that utilizes the mixed-acid pathway (module 4), and whose **coliform** colonies have a metallic green sheen when grown in this medium (Figure 3.12 *E. coli* on EMB).

1. Label one EMB plate for spreading a sample of the original meat suspension.
2. Use a glass or metal spreader to spread 0.1 ml of the original suspension of meat onto the EMB agar.
3. Incubate the EMB plate at 37°C for 24–48 hours.

Day 2

Materials

Plates containing cheese and meat samples inoculated during previous lab period.

FIGURE 3.12 EMB plate three-phase streaked with a pure culture of *E. coli*.

Exercise 3-5

Procedure

1. Record your observations and calculate CFU/g cheese and meat.

R & Q

Cheese Product	Growth? (yes or no)	Appearance of growth: bacterial or fungal?	Constructive or Destructive process?
Bleu Cheese			
Brie Cheese			

Choose one set of cheese plates and calculate CFU/g cheese.

Use the formula below to calculate the concentration of microbial colony-forming units (CFU)/g in the original cheese sample.

$$\frac{\text{Number of CFU}}{\text{Volume Plated} \times \text{Total Dilution}} = \text{CFU} / \text{g}$$

In the table provided below, record the class observations and conclusions regarding growth on these plates.

Total Dilution Used	Volume Plated (ml)	Bacterial/Yeast Colonies per Plate	Hyphal Fungi Colonies per Plate
10^{-3}	0.1		
10^{-4}	0.1		
10^{-5}	0.1		

Exercise 3-5

Discuss whether any of the colonies produced from the two cheese samples appear to be bacterial or fungal in nature. Explain how you would confirm this.

_____
_____
_____

Why do you think it is important to keep the PDA plates at pH 5.6? Hint: The pH of most other media used here (i.e. TSA) is around 7, so think about pH optima of different microbes.

_____
_____
_____

Exercise 3-5

Meat Sample	Growth (in cfu/g?)	Constructive or Destructive process?
Fresh Ground Beef		
Ground Beef Stored at 4°C for 3 days		
Ground Beef Stored at 4°C for 3 days, then Cooked		

Choose one set of meat plates (except cooked) to use to calculate CFU/g.

Calculate the number of colony-forming units (CFU)/g in the original meat sample.

$$\frac{\text{Number of CFU}}{\text{Volume Plated} \times \text{Total Dilution}} = \text{CFU} / \text{g}$$

In the table provided below, record the class observations and conclusions regarding growth on these plates.

Total Dilution Used	Volume Plated (ml)	Bacterial Colonies per Plate
10^{-2}	0.1	
10^{-3}	0.1	
10^{-4}	0.1	

Describe how the bacterial diversity compares among the three different food sources on the TSA.

_____
_____
_____

Exercise 3-5

Refer to Box 3 in Module 2 ("Colony Morphology") to describe colony morphology of four well-isolated colonies on one plate. Discuss whether they could be beneficial or harmful microbes.

What can you conclude about storing uncooked meats in the refrigerator?

Describe how the growth on the TSA plates compares to the growth on the EMB plates.

Is *E. coli* present in the original suspension of the ground beef? If so, what does that imply about fecal contamination?

Regarding food poisoning in general, do some research and answer the following question: if all potential pathogens are killed in a contaminated food item by heating/cooking, will it be safe to eat, or could the food still be poisonous to eat? Explain you answer.

Exercise 3-6

Procedure

1. Describe the consistency and smell of your yogurt product and record this information in the table in the *R & Q* section.
2. Measure the pH of your yogurt sample by dipping a pH indicator strip into the yogurt product.

    Remove excess yogurt from the pH indicator strip by sliding/tapping it on the top of the tube. Record the pH in the table.

    Note: This particular pH indicator strip measures pH ranging from two to nine. Use the color code displayed on the pH indicator strip box to determine the pH of your sample.

3. Measure diacetyl production in your yogurt product:

    Vigorously shake the tube containing the yogurt sample. Transfer 1 ml from the middle of the tube to a microfuge tube.

    With your lab instructor's assistance, place and balance the microfuge tubes in the bench centrifuge. Spin at maximum speed for three minutes.

    Transfer 0.5 ml of the supernatant (the upper liquid layer) to a new microfuge tube.

    Carefully add 0.5 ml of 40% KOH down the wall of the microfuge tube containing the supernatant.

    Allow the tube to stand at room temperature for 30–60 minutes. A pink layer will form in the presence of diacetyl in the yogurt sample. Record your results in the table.

4. Compare and record your results with the entire class.

    Note: again, do not eat the yogurt!

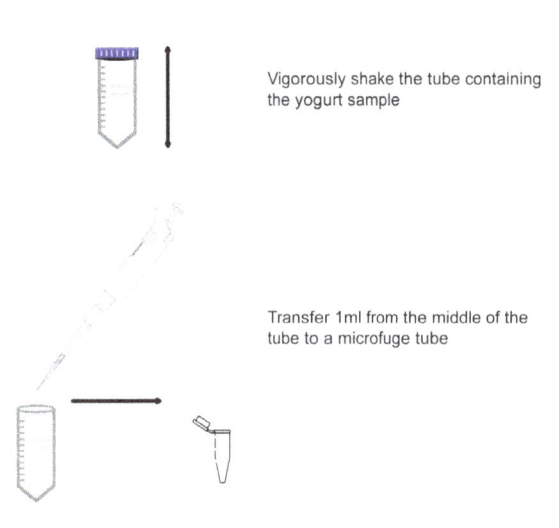

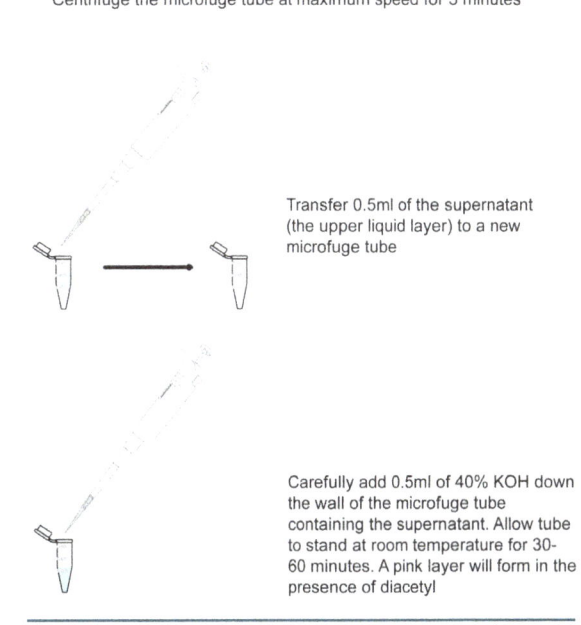

Vigorously shake the tube containing the yogurt sample

Transfer 1ml from the middle of the tube to a microfuge tube

Centrifuge the microfuge tube at maximum speed for 3 minutes

Transfer 0.5ml of the supernatant (the upper liquid layer) to a new microfuge tube

Carefully add 0.5ml of 40% KOH down the wall of the microfuge tube containing the supernatant. Allow tube to stand at room temperature for 30-60 minutes. A pink layer will form in the presence of diacetyl

FIGURE 3.13 Diacetyl Test

Exercise 3-6

R & Q

Yogurt	Yogurt Consistency	Yogurt Smell	Diacetyl Production	pH
Milk				
Milk + *S. thermophilus*				
Milk + *L. bulgaricus*				
Milk + *S. thermophilus* + *L. bulgaricus*				

Based on the results above, which batch(es) of yogurt production was (were) successful?
_____
_____
_____

Explain why yogurt production for some of the batches was unsuccessful.
_____
_____
_____

Describe why it is important to keep starter cultures sterile/pure prior to use in yogurt production.
_____
_____
_____

Bacterial Metabolism

METABOLIC DIVERSITY OF BACTERIA

Bacterial diversity is vast. In Modules 2 and 3, we already saw that bacteria differ with respect to cell morphology, cell wall composition, and whether they are able to produce endospores. We were also briefly introduced to the fact that they differ regarding their nutritional requirements and, referring to Figure 3.3 Nutritional Classification of Bacteria that bacteria differ with respect to carbon and energy sources to support their growth. In addition, we saw that bacteria vary regarding their optimum growth temperatures. These and other features, such as the ability to grow at different pH levels and in different salt concentrations, as well as their diverse metabolic capabilities, can all be used to group or categorize bacterial species.

Categorizing bacteria according to their metabolic proficiencies will be covered in this module. Further details about temperature, pH optima, and salt requirements (including how some of these characteristics can be used to control growth of bacteria) will be covered in Module 5.

	Carbohydrate Usage	Protein Usage	Aerobic Respiration	Anaerobic Respiration	Bile Salt and Crystal Violet Resistance	Irgasan Resistance
Phenol Red Mannitol Broth	x	x				
Phenol Red Glucose Broth	x	x				
Phenol Red Lactose Broth	x	x				
Kligler Iron Agar (KIA)	x	x				
MRVP	x					
Simmons Citrate Agar	x					
Tryptone Broth		x				
Gelatin Strip		x				
Catalase Test			x			
Cytochrome Oxidase Test			x			
Nitrate Broth				x		
GasPac Jar				x		
MacConkey Agar	x				x	
Starch Agar	x					
Pseudomonas Isolation Agar (PIA)						x

When talking about the **metabolism** of a certain bacterial species, we refer to all the biochemical reactions that take place within its cells. The biochemical reactions are carried out by specific enzymes. Some of the reactions are identical among different species, but others are highly specific. The exercises in this module focus on the vast metabolic diversity of bacteria.

Bacteria produce enzymes that enable them to oxidize a number of different energy sources in order to produce energy (ATP). In the exercises to follow, we will first highlight carbohydrate usage to create energy.

Chemoheterotrophic bacteria include the group of bacteria that are capable of using carbohydrates as carbon and energy sources. However, the ability to utilize (catabolize) a specific carbohydrate depends on whether a given bacterium produces the appropriate enzymes. Thus, not all heterotrophic bacteria are able to catabolize the same carbohydrates. The reason for this is that the bacterial species are not genetically identical; they do not carry an identical pool of genes, and therefore they do not produce exactly the same proteins and thus may not carry out exactly the same catabolic processes. Therefore, depending on which genes a given bacterial species expresses (and therefore which enzymes are being produced within the bacterial species), the bacterial species will differ with respect to which carbohydrates it can catabolize (compared to another bacterial species, which may express a different set of carbohydrate-catabolizing enzymes).

Although glucose is the main energy-generating carbohydrate, other carbohydrates such as lactose, mannitol, and starch can also be catabolized by bacteria if they possess the correct enzymes. Furthermore, protein, peptides, or amino acids can also be used to produce energy. We will demonstrate in the exercises below that not all bacteria will be able to catabolize this variety of carbohydrates.

The exercises to come will also provide insight into how the various biochemical tests work, including an understanding of the media used, how to perform the different biochemical tests, and how to interpret the results. You will learn to use the results to determine which biochemical pathways are taking place in the bacterial cells of your study.

This module also covers exercises that examine the presence of the enzymes cytochrome oxidase and catalase. Oxidases are produced by bacterial cells that use aerobic respiration to generate energy (ATP). In the process of aerobic respiration, the majority of ATP is generated as a result of the Krebs cycle and the oxidation-reduction reactions of electron-transport-chain components in the bacteria's cell membrane. Oxidases are essential enzymes for this process, since they catalyze the oxidation-reduction reactions. The end result of this series of oxidation-reduction reactions in aerobic respiration is the reduction of molecular oxygen and the generation of a proton gradient that is used by ATPase to produce ATP. The enzyme in the electron transport chain that catalyzes the oxidation of the last cytochrome in the system is the enzyme cytochrome oxidase.

Subsequently, oxygen, which serves as the final (terminal) electron acceptor, is reduced to water (H_2O), and occasionally, hydrogen peroxide (H_2O_2) is produced. Since hydrogen peroxide is a reactive oxygen species and toxic to the cells, enzymes like catalase and peroxidases rapidly degrade hydrogen peroxide to minimize damage to the bacterial cells. Catalase is found in almost all organisms exposed to oxygen. Catalase catalyzes the breakdown of hydrogen peroxide, producing water and oxygen.

To investigate if an organism uses aerobic respiration to create energy, we will examine bacterial species for the presence of cytochrome oxidase. We will continue the exercise to examine the cells for catalase production to see if the cells are able to convert the toxic hydrogen peroxide to water and oxygen.

In contrast to **aerobic** bacterial organisms, **obligate** (or strict) **anaerobe** bacteria cannot live in the presence of oxygen, and these bacteria generate ATP by anaerobic respiration or fermentation. However, some anaerobic bacteria are **aerotolerant**, which means that they do survive short exposures to oxygen, but they cannot grow and divide under such conditions. Other bacteria are **facultative anaerobes**, and such bacteria can live in both the presence and absence of oxygen. Facultative anaerobes can, when needed, switch among aerobic respiration, anaerobic respiration, and fermentation for generation of ATP. **Microaerophilic** bacteria do need oxygen to proliferate, but they can only survive in environments where the oxygen levels are low—much lower than the concentration of atmospheric oxygen levels.

To study the metabolic capabilities of bacteria to grow in the presence or absence of oxygen, we will take advantage of the GasPak anaerobic system. We will incubate bacteria inoculated on agar plates in the GasPak jars, which are chemically depleted of oxygen after adding the plates. This procedure works well if working with small batches of agar plates. However, other arrangements may be necessary for more extensive work on anaerobes (e.g., those in research labs studying obligate anaerobes). Later in this module, you will be informed about further details on such working arrangements, as well as how scientist years back created oxygen-free environments to study such organisms.

Above, we discussed how cells that respire aerobically use oxygen as the final electron acceptor, and we saw how we could examine cells for cytochrome oxidase and catalase activities. Anaerobes do not produce enzymes like catalase and peroxidase to eliminate the toxic end products (reactive oxygen species) from the oxidation-reduction reactions, and they do not use oxygen as the terminal electron acceptor. Thus, anaerobic respiring cells use other compounds (inorganic compounds) as terminal electron acceptors. Examples are sulfate (SO_4^{2-}), nitrate (NO_3^-) or sulfur (S). Compared to oxygen, these compounds do have lower reduction potential, and consequently less energy will be produced, which results in slower growth rate compared to the aerobic organisms.

In the related exercise in this module, we will focus on anaerobic respiration that uses nitrate as the final electron receptor. Nitrate reduction can occur via different biochemical pathways, depending on which enzymes are produced by the bacteria. The specific nitrate-reduction pathways generate different end products, which, through biochemical tests, we can reveal, distinguish, and thus use to verify the nitrate-reduction pathway used by the organism. The exercise outlines nitrate-reduction pathways and specifies that nitrate can be reduced to either 1) nitrite or ammonia, which usually is used by enteric facultative anaerobes, or 2) nitrogen gas (denitrification), which is commonly used by soil bacteria. We will test specific organisms for the ability to reduce nitrate by anaerobic respiration and investigate which pathway is used to reduce nitrogen by examining the end products of the reaction.

In the very end of this section, you will again be inoculating agar plates. In this exercise, we will expand our understanding of how agar media also can help us group or categorize bacteria according to their biochemical pathways. Such media are classified as **selective, differential,** and **selective-differential,** and they are also essential tools in categorizing and identifying unknown bacteria.

When you move through the exercises in this module, keep in mind that we will be using the knowledge gained here to provide ways of identifying unknown bacteria and to distinguish one bacterial species from another (Module 5 – "Identification of Unknown Bacteria").

CARBOHYDRATE USAGE

As we learned previously, carbohydrates can be used by chemoheterotrophic bacteria as carbon and energy sources to support growth. We also know that the ability to utilize a specific carbohydrate depends on whether a given bacterium produces the appropriate enzymes.

The following exercises will provide insight into which metabolic pathways different types of bacteria apply in order to catabolize carbohydrates. To determine whether a specific carbohydrate is used as a carbon and energy source by a bacterium, it is often necessary to check for the presence of various by-products that result from the oxidation of the particular carbohydrate. For example, pH indicators may be incorporated into a medium to detect metabolic acids produced as a result of the breakdown of a carbohydrate. Similarly, reagents may be added after incubation in order to identify if certain by-products have been formed upon utilization of a certain carbohydrate. **Box 1** will give you further information about the breakdown of carbohydrates examined in this section and which enzymes are involved.

Specifically, we will be inoculating different carbohydrate-containing media (phenol red carbohydrate broth) with various bacterial strains to test their catabolic capabilities. We will do that by directly examining the media for evidence of carbohydrate fermentation after growth in carbohydrate broth media. Thus, we will be monitoring pH changes and gas production after incubation of the inoculated glucose, lactose, and mannitol broth media. Note that the broth media contain Durham tubes to collect gas (bubbles) if produced (**Box 2**).

We will also be introduced to a different kind of medium, KIA (Kligler Iron Agar), which also examines the ability of the bacterial organisms to ferment the carbohydrates glucose and lactose. In contrast to phenol red carbohydrate broth, KIA medium can be used to test for the simultaneous use of glucose and lactose in a medium. KIA medium can also be used to detect if proteins included in the medium are used as an energy source instead of carbohydrates (**Box 3**).

Later in this exercise, we will be inoculating media to analyze which pathway certain bacteria use when fermenting glucose. The test that will be performed is the MRVP test (Methyl Red-Voges Proskauer test). After incubating the bacterial species in MRVP medium, a small aliquot of the media is used to test for certain by-products of the fermentation reaction. Depending on the results, it will be revealed whether a high amount of organic acids has been produced as a result of glucose fermentation (mixed-acids pathway) or a high amount of neutral by-products has been produced (butanediol pathway). (**Box 4**).

Finally, we will be testing bacteria for the ability to use citrate as the sole carbon source. Utilization of exogenous citrate requires the presence of certain proteins (permeases) to transport citrate from the medium into the bacterial cells. Only the organisms that produce the citrate-specific permeases show a positive result after growth in the medium Simmons Citrate Agar (**Box 5**).

Box 1 Carbohydrate Breakdown

Glucose is an abundant monosaccharide (simple sugar) that is easy to break down, and it is most often the carbohydrate used as an energy source by bacteria categorized as heterotrophs. Thus, heterotrophic bacteria typically produce the enzymes necessary to break down glucose.

Complex carbohydrates, such as disaccharides (sucrose and lactose) and polysaccharides (starch), are used less often as energy sources. This is because they consist of chains of two or more simple sugar molecules, and more enzymes are required for their degradation. In order for bacteria to catabolize such carbohydrates, they must produce enzymes that specifically cleave the bonds between each monosaccharide molecule. Further breakdown of the resulting simple sugars cannot take place before the bonds are cleaved and the monosaccharides are released.

Less common types of carbohydrates that some bacteria are able to use as energy and carbon are sugar alcohols (polyols). These are hydrogenated forms of carbohydrates. One example of a sugar alcohol is mannitol. The sugar monomer mannose is formed upon oxidation of mannitol.

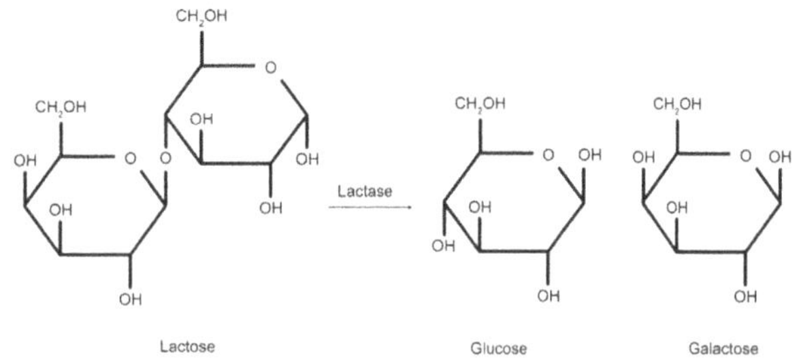

Generally, if an energy source is available that can be degraded using fewer enzymes, this source will typically be used before carbohydrates, which require more enzymes for their breakdown.

Bacteria that are able to use the disaccharide lactose (milk sugar) must produce the enzyme lactase. Lactase breaks down the glycosidic bond between the glucose and galactose monomers comprising the lactose molecule.

Figure legend starch breakdown: Degradation of starch requires the enzymatic activity of α-amylase to break the glycosidic bonds between the glucose monomers that make up this large polysaccharide.

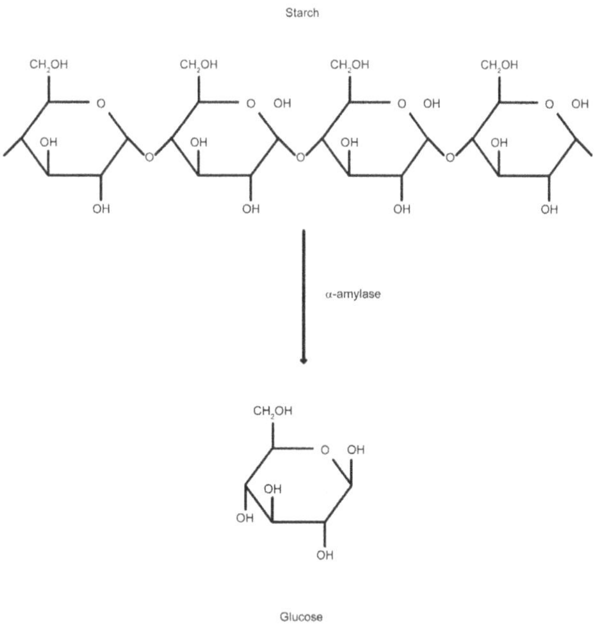

FIGURE 4.1 Lactose breakdown

FIGURE 4.2 Starch breakdown

Box 2 Interpretation of Results—Phenol Red Carbohydrate Broth Media

Fermentation of glucose, lactose, and mannitol

Bacteria can metabolize carbohydrates by aerobic respiration or, in the absence of oxygen, by fermentation (see Figure 4.4, "Aerobic Respiration or Fermentation"). Here we will focus on the ability of bacteria to ferment the sugars.

Phenol red broth media with a certain carbohydrate source added (glucose, lactose, or mannitol) will be inoculated with certain bacterial species. After incubation and fermentation of the sugars, the culture tubes will be examined for the presence of organic acid and gas production (see Figure 4.3, Phenol red carbohydrate broth results). The broth medium contains a pH indicator, phenol red, which turns yellow as the pH in the media drops to 6.4 or below. Therefore, the appearance of a yellow color in the broth medium indicates that the carbohydrate has been utilized.

If gas is produced after incubation, it will be trapped as a bubble in the Durham tube submersed in the carbohydrate-containing broth medium.

Other results:
If the phenol red carbohydrate broth remains red and clear following incubation, the inoculated organism could not utilize the specific carbohydrate and could not grow under the anaerobic condition.
If the medium becomes turbid (cloudy) but remains red, the organism can grow in the broth but uses peptone, the alternative energy source that is also present in the phenol red carbohydrate broth medium.

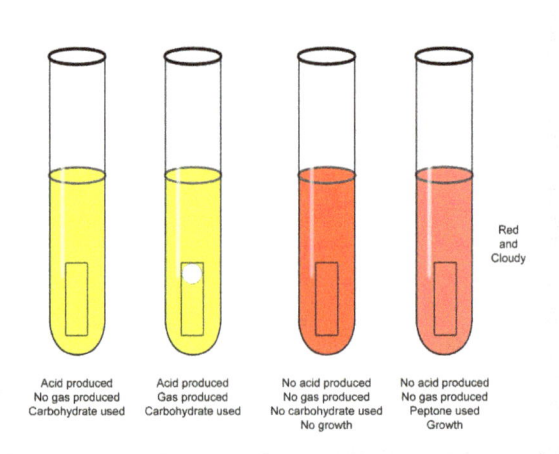

FIGURE 4.3 Phenol red carbohydrate broth results

Figure legend
- Acid (A) production: the broth medium turns yellow. The tested bacterium is able to ferment the carbohydrate present in the medium.
- Acid and gas (A+G) production: the broth turns yellow, and a gas bubble appears in the tube. The tested bacterium is able to ferment the carbohydrate present in the medium and gas is produced.
- No reaction (-): the broth medium remains clear with no color change; the tested bacterial species cannot utilize the carbohydrate added to the medium and does not grow under anaerobic conditions.
- Growth, but no acid production (-): the broth medium is turbid (cloudy), but color remains unchanged. The tested organism can grow in the medium, but instead of using the added carbohydrate as an energy source, the bacterium uses peptone (peptides and amino acids), which is also added to the medium. Refer to Exercise 4-2 for more on oxidation of proteins for energy production).

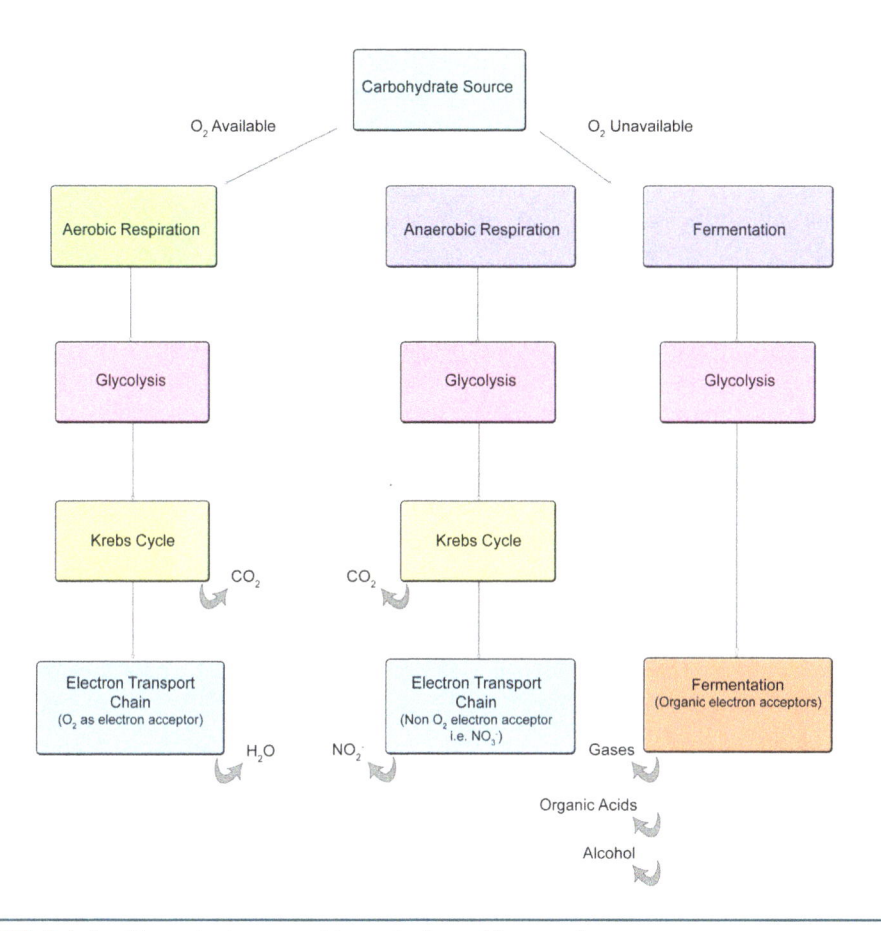

FIGURE 4.4 Aerobic respiration, anaerobic respiration and fermentation

---

Box 3 Interpretation of Results—KIA Medium

Fermentation of lactose and glucose and protein utilization

One advantage of the KIA (Kligler Iron Agar) medium is that it can be used to test for the simultaneous use of glucose and lactose. Furthermore, for organisms that are unable to catabolize lactose and glucose, peptone and proteins from the beef extract are present and can serve as alternative energy sources. Phenol red is used as the pH indicator.

Recall that lactose is a dimer made up of one glucose molecule and one galactose molecule. Thus, bacteria that are able to ferment lactose must also be able to ferment glucose. The amount of lactose available in the KIA medium is ten times greater than that of glucose. Therefore, organisms that are able to ferment both lactose and glucose generally have sufficient amounts of carbohydrates present to support growth throughout the incubation times we use in these labs. A KIA result of acid/acid (A/A) is generally indicative of both lactose and glucose utilization.

In the thinner, more oxygenated slant portion of the tube, there are fewer nutrients available. Therefore, organisms may begin to use peptone and other proteins provided by the added beef extract as a source of energy. The end products created from degradation of the proteins are alkaline (basic) and can cause a sufficient rise in pH, which turns the pH indicator in the media red. However, often the amount of acid produced from the lactose and glucose fermentation creates a low pH, which will prevent smaller amounts of alkaline products from changing the pH indicator to red. As a result, both the slant and butt of the tube will remain yellow throughout the incubation period.

Glucose is generally used quite readily by most microbes. However, bacteria that do not possess the enzyme lactase cannot break down lactose into glucose and galactose units. The relatively small amount of glucose available in KIA tends to be consumed rather quickly. The fermentation of this small amount of glucose by bacteria that are unable to use lactose results in significantly less acid production. This allows the pH to rise at the upper part of the slant when peptone and other proteins are used as energy source. The pH may be lower throughout the remaining tube, resulting in K/A.

Due to anaerobic conditions (and therefore slower growth rates in the butt portion of the tube), anaerobic degradation of proteins does not generally raise the pH sufficiently to cause a color change of the phenol red pH indicator. Therefore, the KIA medium in the butt portion of the tube may remain yellow or unchanged. When aerobes and facultative anaerobes are grown in this medium, their growth rates will be significantly higher in the slant portion of the tube, where they can respire aerobically and generate more energy.

Gas production resulting from either glucose or lactose utilization can be detected either by the presence of bubbles (usually seen between the medium and the tube) or as cracks/separations in the KIA medium.

If neither carbohydrate is utilized but the organism grows, that means the proteins present in the medium have been used as the sole source of energy. This gives rise to one of the two following results:

1. the slant and butt of the tube appear red due to basic end products produced by aerobic and anaerobic protein utilization (K/K); or
2. only the upper part of the slant appears red, indicating that protein is used only under aerobic conditions (K/no change).

The protein sources contained in the KIA medium originate from the added beef extract and peptones. When bacteria that produce the enzyme desulfhydrase are grown in KIA medium, the proteolytic action of the enzyme on sulfur-containing amino acids results in the production of a metabolic gas called hydrogen sulfide (H_2S). If hydrogen sulfide is produced within the KIA medium, it combines with the iron sulfate ($FeSO_4$) present in the medium and forms ferrous (iron) sulfide (FeS). Ferrous sulfide appears as a black precipitate in the butt portion of the tube.

$$H_2S + FeSO_4 = H_2SO_4 + FeS$$

The possible reactions in KIA include:
1. glucose fermentation, which appears as a red slant/yellow butt (K/A);
2. lactose and glucose fermentation, which produces a yellow slant/yellow butt (A/A);
3. protein utilization as the sole carbon source, which produces a red slant/red butt (K/K) or red slant/no change in the butt (K/no change);
4. carbon dioxide (CO_2) production, which is indicated by breaks in the agar medium; and
5. desulfhydrase activity, which is detected by the formation of a black precipitate (FeS) in the medium.

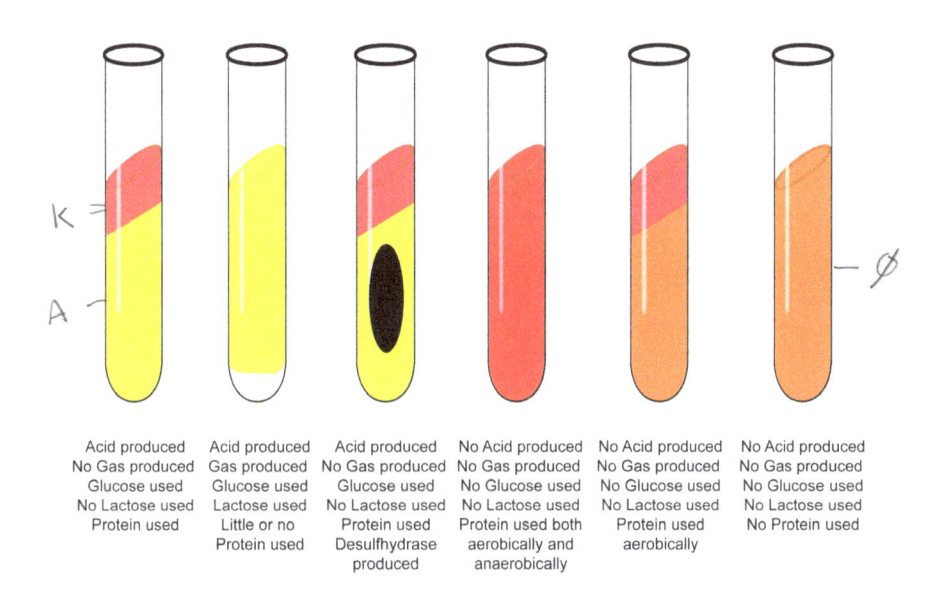

Acid produced	Acid produced	Acid produced	No Acid produced	No Acid produced	No Acid produced
No Gas produced	Gas produced	No Gas produced	No Gas produced	No Gas produced	No Gas produced
Glucose used	Glucose used	Glucose used	No Glucose used	No Glucose used	No Glucose used
No Lactose used	Lactose used	No Lactose used	No Lactose used	No Lactose used	No Lactose used
Protein used	Little or no Protein used	Protein used Desulfhydrase produced	Protein used both aerobically and anaerobically	Protein used aerobically	No Protein used

FIGURE 4.5 KIA results

Box 4 Interpretation of MR and VP Results

Glucose fermentation by enterics using either mixed-acid pathway or the butanediol pathway

MRVP medium is a glucose phosphate broth and is commonly used to identify the metabolic pathway used by enterics to ferment glucose. Two glucose-fermenting pathways, the mixed-acid pathway and the butanediol pathway, are distinguished from each other on the basis of the by-products produced. After incubating bacterial strains in MRVP medium, the cultures are split into two separate tubes, and the **MR** (methyl red) and **VP** (Voges Proskauer) tests are performed.

The **MR test** uses methyl red as a pH indicator to examine the relative amount of organic acids produced from glucose fermentation. Methyl red turns from yellow to red in the presence of high amounts of acid, at pH 4.2–4.3. A high amount of organic acids is usually produced by glucose fermenters that use the mixed-acid pathway.
If a bacterium tests negative for the mixed-acid pathway, the relative amount of acid is low, and the medium remains yellow or turns slightly orange.

FIGURE 4.6 MR results

Note: In our analysis, an orange color signifies a negative test. This is because the aim is to test if the pH has dropped to 4.3 or lower. The methyl red pH indicator changes from yellow to orange before it turns red at about pH 4.3.

The **VP test** examines if the butanediol pathway is used by a given bacterium to ferment glucose. This pathway produces higher amounts of neutral products compared to acidic products. The test employs α-naphthol and potassium hydroxide (KOH), specifically to examine if an intermediate, acetoin (or acetylmethylcarbinol), of the butanediol pathway is produced. If acetoin is produced as a result of the glucose breakdown, subsequent reactions with α-naphthol, potassium hydroxide (KOH), and oxygen results in the development of a pinkish color. Thus, the development of the pink color signifies a positive VP reaction. The color will appear after about 20 minutes, and oxygen is required for the reaction, so tubes have to be vortexed!

FIGURE 4.7 VP results

Note: Some organisms may produce combinations of positive MR and VP reactions (MR:pos/VP:neg, pos/pos, neg/pos, neg/neg), depending on the metabolic pathways that they use.

Box 5 Interpretation of Results—Simmons Citrate Agar Medium

Citrate as the only carbon source

Not all bacterial organisms produce a citrate–specific permease, so not all species are capable of using citrate as the sole carbon source (e.g., certain coliforms). However, bacterial species that can utilize citrate as the sole carbon source do produce permeases specific for importing citrate. Such bacterial organisms can be distinguished from those that do not utilize citrate by taking advantage of the medium Simmons Citrate Agar. In Simmons Citrate Agar, medium citric acid (citrate) is provided as the sole carbon source. When the organic acid is used as a carbon source by the bacterium, the reduction of acid and the production of alkaline by-products raise the pH in the medium. The rise of pH in the medium to above 7.6 turns the pH indicator, bromothymol blue, from green (pH 7) to blue (pH 7.6 and above).

Figure legend:
Citrate-positive organisms (+) can utilize citrate as the sole carbon source, and growth can be observed in the Simmons Citrate Agar slant after incubation. Due to the reduction of citric acid and the production of alkaline by-products (carbonates and bicarbonates) as citrate is catabolized, the pH of the medium rises. This results in the pH indicator turning the slant blue.

Citrate-negative organisms (-) cannot utilize citrate as the sole carbon source, and no growth (or only a trace of growth) can be observed in the Simmons Citrate Agar medium after incubation. The pH in the Simmons Citrate Agar slant remains unaltered and green in color, like the uninoculated slant.

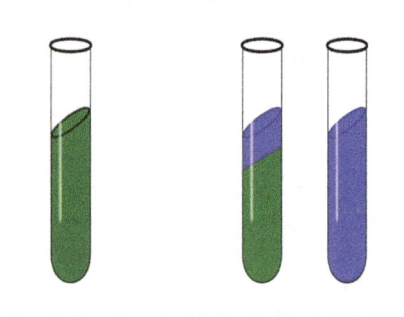

FIGURE 4.8 Simmons citrate

Note: MRVP, citrate, and indole tests are collectively called the IMViC tests.

Exercise 4-1

Carbohydrate utilization

Learning Objectives

To comprehend metabolic diversity of bacteria.

To recognize and name various carbohydrates and examine the utilization test media.

To learn how to apply and interpret the results of various carbohydrate- and protein-utilization tests.

Day 1

Materials

- TSB cultures of each of the following:
    - *H. alvei*
    - *E. coli*
    - *A. faecalis*
    - *E. aerogenes*
- Three tubes of one type of the following phenol red carbohydrate broths:
    - Glucose with Durham tubes (3)

    or
    - Lactose with Durham tubes (3)

    or
    - Mannitol with Durham tubes (3)
- Tubes of
    - Methyl Red-Voges Proskauer (MRVP) broth medium (2)
    - Simmons Citrate Agar (green agar slant) (2)
    - Kligler Iron Agar (KIA—orange-red agar slant) (3)

Work in groups of four.

Exercise 4-1

Procedure

Glucose Broth, Lactose Broth, or Mannitol Broth:

1. Use label tape and a Sharpie to label the assigned tubes of phenyl red carbohydrate broth, including the type of medium and the name of the organisms:

    Escherichia coli

    Hafnia alvei

    Alcaligenes faecalis

2. Vortex the three bacterial cultures.
3. Light the Bunsen burner.
4. Use the sterilized inoculating loop to inoculate the three carbohydrate broth tubes with one of the three cultures (one culture per tube). To mix the inoculum into the broth, roll the tubes between your hands.

    Note: Do not vortex the carbohydrate broth tubes, since this may introduce air into the Durham tube and give a false-positive result.

5. Place inoculated media tubes in racks or cups for incubation at 37°C for 24 hours.

MRVP Medium:

1. Use label tape and a Sharpie to label the two MRVP broth tubes, including the name of the organism you will be inoculating the medium with:

    Escherichia coli

    Enterobacter aerogenes

2. Vortex the two bacterial cultures.
3. Use a sterile loop to inoculate the two MRVP broth tubes with cells from each of the two cultures.
4. Place inoculated media tubes into the provided rack or cup for incubation.

Simmons Citrate Agar:

1. Use label tape and a Sharpie to label the two Simmons Citrate Agar tubes, including the name of the organism you will be inoculating this medium with:

    Escherichia coli

    Enterobacter aerogenes

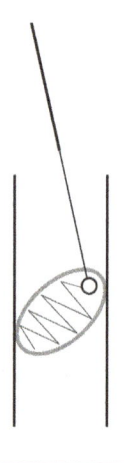

FIGURE 4.7 Inoculation Simon Citrate Agar Slant

Exercise 4-1

2. Vortex the two bacterial cultures.
3. Use the technique shown in Figure 4.7 "Inoculate Simon Citrate Agar Slant" to inoculate the surface of each Simmons Citrate Agar slant with the respective organisms.
4. Place inoculated media tubes into the provided rack or cup for incubation at 37°C for 24 hours.

Kligler Iron Agar—KIA:
1. Use label tape and a Sharpie to label the three KIA tubes, including the name of the organisms:

   Hafnia alvei

   Alcaligenes faecalis

   Escherichia coli

2. Vortex the three bacterial cultures.
3. Use the inoculating needle as shown in Figure "Streak and Stab Technique" to inoculate the three KIA tubes.
4. Place the inoculated media tubes into the provided rack or cup and incubate at 37°C for 24 hours.

Day 2

Materials

- Cultures inoculated in previous lab
- Small test tubes (4)
- P1000 micropipette and tips or 1 ml serological pipettes (2)
- Methyl red
- α-naphthol solution
- 40% KOH
- Gloves

Work in groups of four.

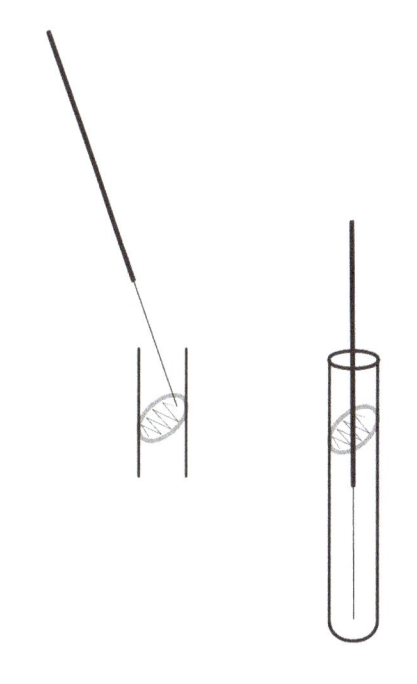

FIGURE 4.8 Streak and stab technique

Exercise 4-1

Procedure

CAUTION: Wear gloves when performing these tests.

MR and VP tests:

1. Use label tape and a Sharpie marker to label the four small test tubes, including the type of medium and the name of the organisms:

    MR *E. coli*
    MR *E. aerogenes*
    VP *E. coli*
    VP *E. aerogenes*

2. Vortex the MRVP culture tubes containing the cultures.

3. Use a P1000 micropipettes or a 1ml serological pipette to transfer 0.5 ml of the appropriate culture from the MRVP culture tubes into each of the small tubes (**Box 4**).

MR test:

1. Add three drops of methyl red to the small tube containing 0.5 ml of culture.
2. Observe for an immediate color change to red, indicating a positive result.

    Note: A red color indicates a positive MR test, and a yellow or orange color indicates a negative test.

Transfer 0.5 ml of culture from the MRVP tube into a small tube

Add three drops of methyl red to the small tube containing 0.5 ml of culture

Observe for an immediate color change. A red color indicates a positive MR test and a yellow or orange color indicates a negative test

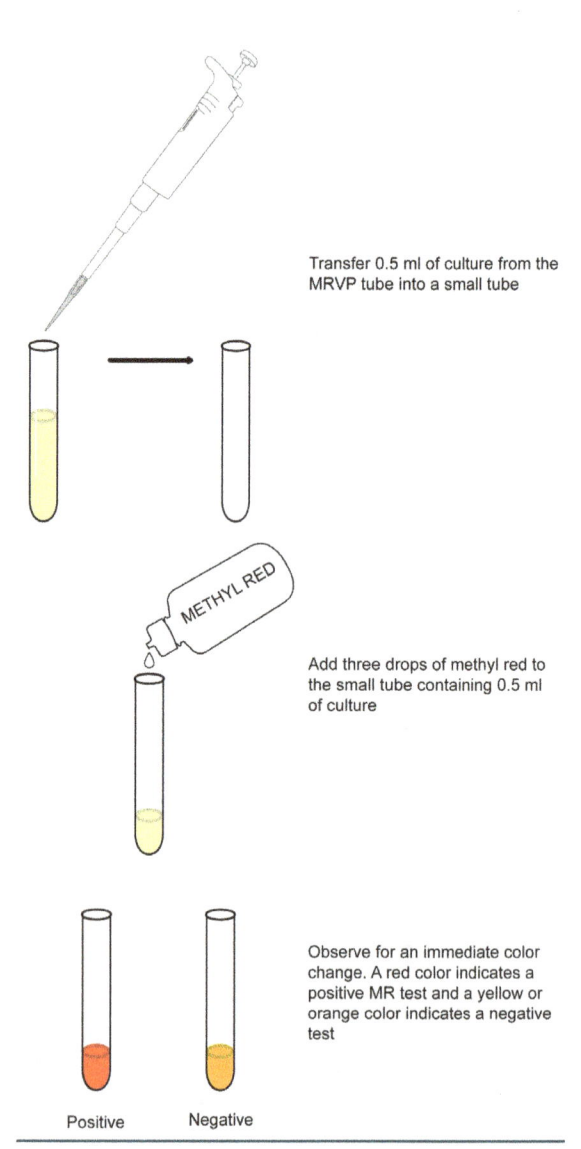

Positive   Negative

FIGURE 4.9 MR test procedure

VP test:

1. Add six drops of α-naphthol to each of the small tubes containing 0.5 ml of culture.
2. Add three drops of 40% KOH to each of the small tubes containing 0.5 ml of culture and α-naphthol.
3. Place caps on the tubes.
4. Vortex each of the small tubes well and allow the tubes to sit undisturbed on the bench for a minimum of 10-15 minutes.
5. Observe the tubes for the presence of a red ring at the top of the medium, indicating a positive result.
6. Record your observations in the *R & Q* section.
7. In the *R & Q* section, record your interpretation regarding the bacterial use of the mixed-acid pathway (MR+/-) or the butanediol pathway (VP+/-) to ferment glucose.

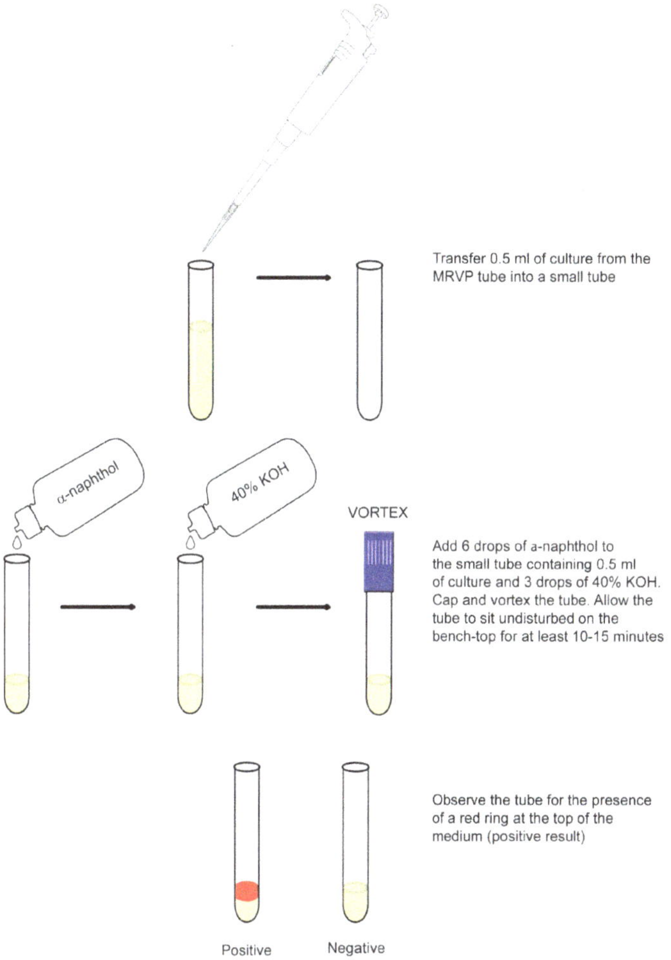

Phenol Red Glucose, Lactose, and Mannitol Broth:

1. Observe all tubes and record the results in the *R & Q* section.

KIA—Kligler Iron Agar:

1. In the *R & Q* section, record your observations of the slant and butt of the KIA tubes.
2. Interpret and record the results regarding carbohydrates utilization by the bacteria species tested.

Simmons Citrate Agar:

1. Record your observation and interpretation of the Simmons Citrate Agar tubes in the *R & Q* section.

FIGURE 4.10 VP test procedure

MRVP—Methyl Red–Voges-Proskauer Tests:

1. Record your observations in the *R & Q* section, and include if the organisms use the mixed-acid pathway (MR+/-) to ferment glucose or the butanediol pathway (VP+/-).

R & Q

Organism	Glucose Broth		Lactose Broth		Mannitol Broth	
	acid	gas	acid	gas	acid	gas
Hafnia alvei						
Alcaligenes faecalis						
Escherichia coli						

Note: Yellow color of the broth indicates a positive result for acid production. For the organisms used in this study, a red or orange color in the broth indicates a negative result. A bubble in the Durham tube indicates a positive result for gas production.

Organism	KIA	
	pH slant/butt	carbohydrates used
Hafnia alvei		
Alcaligenes faecalis		
Escherichia coli		

Organism	Simmons Citrate Agar	MRVP Broth	
		MR reaction	VP reaction
Escherichia coli			
Enterobacter aerogenes			

Exercise 4-1

169

Explain why bacteria will use glucose before lactose.

_____
_____
_____

Explain what the colors red and yellow reflect in the phenol red mannitol broth.

_____
_____
_____

Analyze the three KIA results.

_____
_____
_____

Explain how the MR and VP tests work, along with the result *MR:positive/VP:negative*.

_____
_____
_____

PROTEIN UTILIZATION

Respiration is an essential process for cells to gain energy that subsequently can be used to fuel cellular activity. Although glucose is the main energy–generating carbohydrate, microbes can also oxidize proteins in order to produce energy. This process is generally more complex than the oxidation of carbohydrates, mostly since proteins are structurally more complex than carbohydrates. In addition, not all proteins can readily enter bacterial cells.

Many proteins that are unable to cross cell membranes due to their size and structure need to be cleaved to smaller peptides (polypeptides) or amino acids in order to enter the cells. To facilitate this import process of proteins from the environment, bacteria produce enzymes called peptidases (proteases) that specifically break down proteins to produce small peptides or amino acids. Peptidases are produced inside the bacterial cells, but some of the peptidases are exported from the cells into the surrounding environment, where they become catalytically active. Peptidases that are exported to the environment are called **exoenzymes** or **extracellular enzymes**.

Once proteins outside the cells have been cleaved by the exported peptidases, the resulting peptides can readily be imported into the cells. Inside the cells, the peptides are further degraded by other peptidases that are residing within the cells. The intracellular peptidases are called **endoenzymes** or **intracellular enzymes**.

Adding proteins to the growth medium, which are unable to readily enter bacterial cells can be used to test for certain exoenzyme activities produced by bacterial organisms. In this lab period, you will examine the activity of the exoenzyme gelatinase. Gelatinase is a peptidase that hydrolyzes the

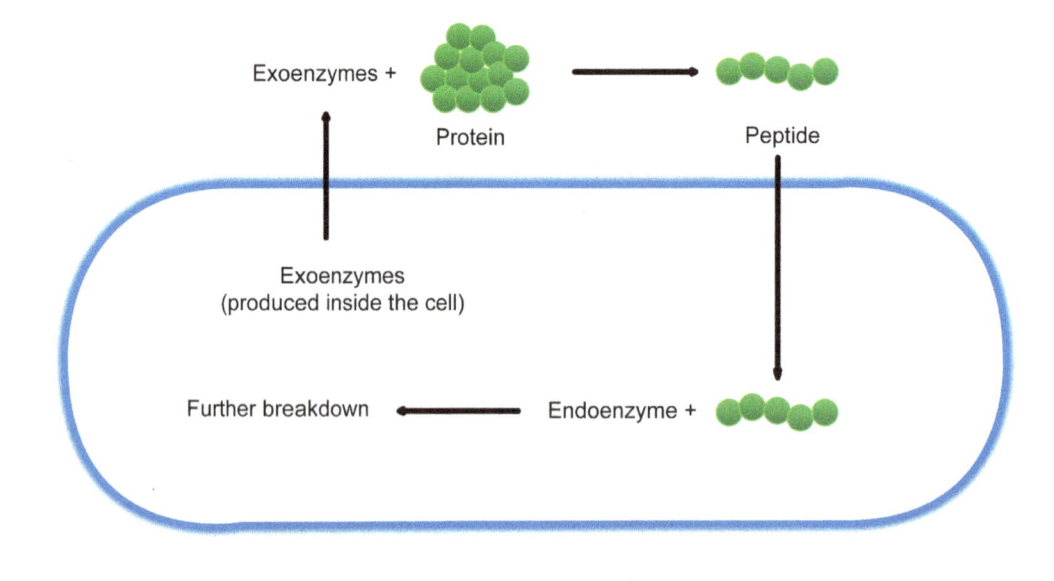

FIGURE 4.9 Endo- and exoenzymes

extracellular protein gelatin. We will examine the bacterial cells for the presence of gelatinase by applying gelatin-coated strips "to bacterial suspensions (Box 3)" instead of to the growth media (Box 3).

Similarly, adding peptides and free amino acids to the growth media can be used to detect the presence of endoenzymes. An example of such a growth medium is tryptone broth, which detects the presence of the tryptophan-degrading endoenzyme tryptophanase. Kligler Iron Agar (KIA) is another example of a medium that can be used to detect the presence of a certain endoenzyme. Thus, aside from detecting carbohydrate usage, the KIA medium can detect the breakdown of sulfur-containing amino acids by the endoenzyme desulfhydrase.

INTERPRETATION OF AMINO ACID AND GELATIN BREAKDOWN

Tryptophanase activity:

Prior to testing bacteria for tryptophanase activity, the organisms must be grown in a tryptone broth medium. The medium contains high levels of the amino acid tryptophan in addition to other amino acids and required nutrients. In order to utilize tryptophan, a bacterium must produce the endoenzyme tryptophanase, which catalyzes the hydrolysis of tryptophan to pyruvate, ammonia, and indole. Tryptophanase activity can be verified after incubation by detecting the presence of indole in the medium.

$$\text{L-tryptophan} + H_2O \xrightleftharpoons{\text{Tryptophanase}} \text{indole} + \text{pyruvate} + NH_3$$

Kovac's reagent is used to test for the presence of indole in the medium. The reagent contains a chemical (4-dimethylaminobenzaldehyde) that reacts with indole to form a red layer or ring that appears at the top of the broth. Thus, the addition of this reagent to an indole-positive (tryptophanase-producing) culture results in the development of a red layer or ring layer. If the layer appears green or yellow after the addition of Kovac's reagent, there is no indole present, and the organism is considered to be indole negative and thus does not produce tryptophanase.

Figure legend The appearance of a red layer indicates that the organism is indole-positive (tryptophanase +). The formation of a green or yellow layer indicates that no indole has been produced, and that organism is indole-negative (tryptophanase negative).

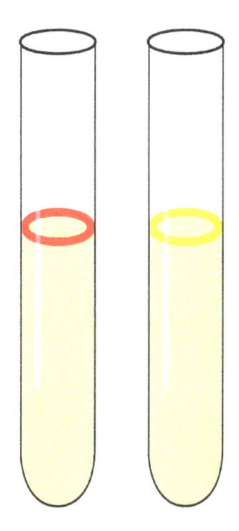

FIGURE 4.10 Kovac's reagent and reaction results

Desulfhydrase activity:

$$H_2S\uparrow + FeSO_4 = H_2SO_4 + FeS\downarrow$$

Desulfhydrase activity is detected by the formation of a black precipitate (FeS) of the KIA slant (see **Box 3** for further details).

Gelatinase activity:
Gelatin is a large protein that first was used by Robert Koch (see Module 1) in his attempts to provide a solid surface for the pure culture streak technique of microbial organisms. However, while working with gelatin, Dr. Koch found two noteworthy disadvantages associated with using gelatin as a solidifying agent:

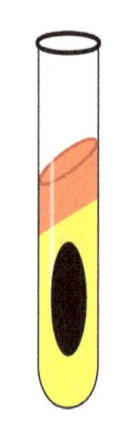

1) gelatin liquefies at 37°C; and
2) gelatin can be used by many microorganisms as an energy source, which causes the medium to liquefy at an even lower temperature.

Acid produced
No Gas produced
Glucose used
No Lactose used
Protein used
Desulfhydrase produced

KIA result showing desulfhydrase production

Agar soon replaced gelatin as the solidifying agent used in microbiological media; however, the discovery of gelatin's potential to be used as an energy source for certain bacterial species became a useful tool for identifying bacteria.

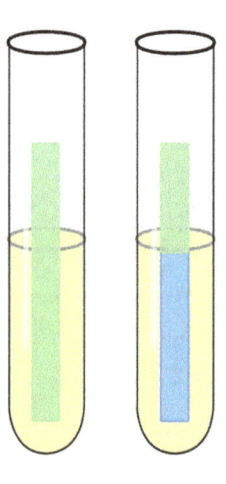

FIGURE 4.11 Gelatine degradation by gelatinase

In order to utilize a molecule as large as gelatin, microorganisms must produce the exoenzyme gelatinase to break down gelatin into polypeptides and, subsequently, amino acids. The amino acids are then readily available for uptake by the bacteria to be used for energy production by the cell.

Gelatin strips have an emulsion of gelatin attached to an acetate film strip. The gelatin strip is added to a liquid bacterial suspension, which is then incubated. Appearance of the blue color of the acetate film of the gelatin strip following incubation indicates that the organism utilized (degraded) the gelatin on the strip and that the organism is positive for gelatinase production.

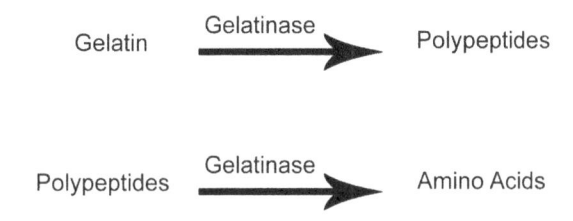

$$\text{Gelatin} \xrightarrow{\text{Gelatinase}} \text{Polypeptides}$$

$$\text{Polypeptides} \xrightarrow{\text{Gelatinase}} \text{Amino Acids}$$

Figure legend: If gelatin has been liquefied by the gelatinase, the blue color of the acetate base of the strip is visible. This (the blue color of the gelatin strip after incubation) is considered a positive test for gelatinase production by the organism. If the strip is still opaque and the blue acetate is not visible, no gelatinase activity is produced by the organism, and the result is negative.

Exercise 4-2

Protein Utilization

In this exercise, we will test for protein and amino-acid utilization as well as the activities of their respective endo- and exoenzymes. Specifically, bacteria will be tested for their ability to break down the protein gelatin and the amino acid tryptophan, as well as sulfur-containing amino acids.

Learning Objectives

To understand tests used to monitor protein and amino-acid utilization by bacteria as an energy source.
To use the results of the tests to draw conclusions about intracellular and extracellular peptidase activities.

Day 1

Materials

- TSB cultures of bacteria (4)
    - *E. coli*
    - *B. subtilis* 848
    - *E. hoshinae*
    - *B. subtilis* 494
- Tubes of:
    - Tryptone broth (2)
    - KIA
    - Sterile water (2)
- Gelatin strips (2)
- Inoculating loop
- Forceps
- Alcohol jar
- Dropper (2)
- Bunsen burner

Work in groups of four.

Procedure

Tryptophanase activity

1. Use label tape and a Sharpie to label each of the two tryptone broth tubes, including the name of each of the following bacterial strains:

   Escherichia coli

   Bacillus subtilis 848

2. Use a sterile inoculation loop to inoculate each of the two tubes.

Desulfhydrase activity

1. Use label tape and a Sharpie to label the KIA tube, including the name of the bacterial strain:

   Edwardsiella hoshinae

2. To inoculate the KIA medium use the inoculating needle to streak and stab the medium as shown in Figure 4.12.

Gelatinase activity

1. Use label tape and a Sharpie to label each of the two tubes of sterile water, including the name of each of the following bacteria strains:

   Escherichia coli

   Bacillus subtilis 494

2. Use a sterile dropper to add three drops of culture to the appropriate sterile water tubes. Use a fresh dropper for each bacterial strain.

   Note: Dispose of the dropper and any culture left inside in the red biohazard bins.

3. Use an alcohol jar to flame-sterilize a pair of forceps, and aseptically drop one gelatin strip into each labeled tube.
4. Incubate all culture tubes at 37°C for 24–48 hours.

   Caution: Alcohol is flammable! Use caution when handling jars of alcohol near open flames.

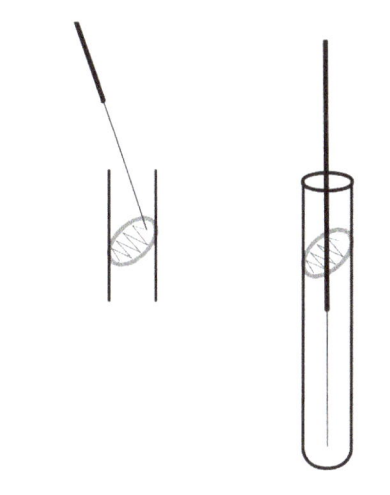

FIGURE 4.12 KIA inoculation

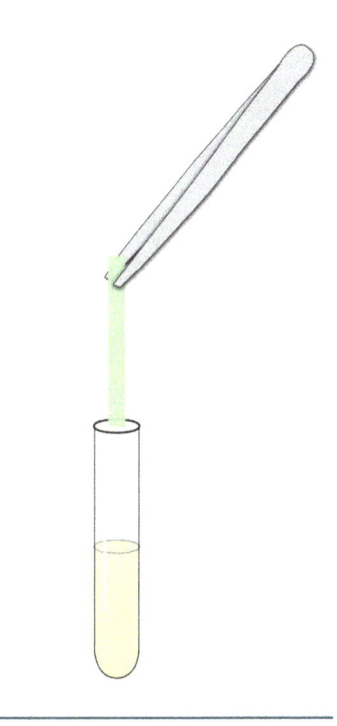

FIGURE 4.13 Gelatin test

Exercise 4-2

Day 2

Procedure

1. Examine the gelatin strips in the tubes.
2. Record your results in the *R & Q* section.
3. Before interpreting the results of the tryptone broth cultures, use the following procedure to add Kovac's reagent to each of the tubes.
   a. Vortex the tryptone broth tubes to resuspend the cells in the cultures.
   b. Add 6–8 drops of Kovac's reagent to each tryptone broth tube.

   Caution: Wear gloves when adding Kovac's reagent.

   c. Observe each tube for the appearance of a red layer or ring at the top of the broth.
4. Record your results in the *R & Q* section.

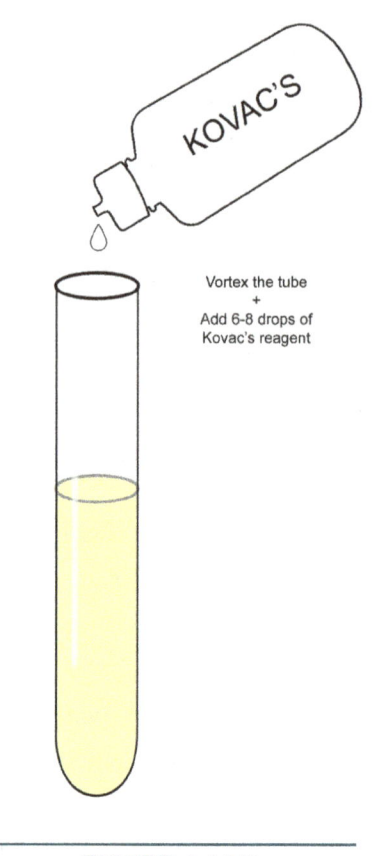

FIGURE 4.14 Tryptone test

Exercise 4-2   177

R & Q

Organism	Tryptone Broth	Kligler Iron Agar (KIA)	Gelatinase Activity
Bacillus subtilis 848			
Escherichia coli			
Edwardsiella hoshinae			
Bacillus subtilis 494			

Is gelatinase an endoexyme? Explain your answer.

___
___
___

Explain the role of gelatinase in bacterial protein usage.

___
___
___

Explain the reasons why Dr. Koch found gelatin unsuitable as a solidifying agent in agar plates.

___
___
___

Describe the enzymatic activity of tryptophanase.

___
___
___

Exercise 4-2

Which degradation product is monitored in the tryptophanase-activity test?

_____
_____
_____

Explain why the activity of desulfhydrase results in the development of a dark precipitate in the KIA medium.

_____
_____
_____

Mention two sulfur-containing amino acids.

_____
_____
_____

CATALASE AND OXIDASE ACTIVITIES

Microbes living in the presence of oxygen (e.g., obligate aerobes, facultative anaerobes, and micro-aerophiles) are organisms that produce cytochrome oxidase, catalase, or peroxidase. The activity of these enzymes can be used to investigate if an organism uses aerobic respiration to create energy. Cytochrome oxidase catalyzes oxidation-reduction reactions of the electron transport chain, and catalase and peroxidases remove the resulting toxic reactive oxygen species of the aerobic respiration process. The latter two enzymes play vital roles in determining the level of oxygen tolerance in a given organism. In this exercise, the presence or absence of cytochrome oxidase and catalase activities will be examined.

Interpretation of Cytochrome Oxidase and Catalase Assay

Catalase catalyzes the breakdown of hydrogen peroxide, producing water and oxygen:

$$2\ H_2O_2 \longrightarrow 2\ H_2O + O_2\uparrow$$

A culture can be tested for catalase activity by adding hydrogen peroxide to an aliquot of the culture. Typically, the test can be carried out on a microscope slide. If catalase is produced by the bacterial organism, the hydrogen peroxide is broken down to yield H_2O and O_2, and bubbles will develop on the slide. If no bubbles are produced, catalase is not produced by the bacterial organisms, and the test is considered negative.

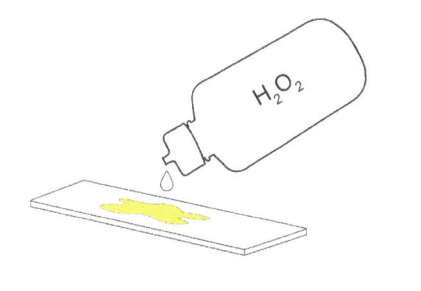

FIGURE 4.15 Catalase results

Whether a bacterial organism produces cytochrome oxidase activity can be determined by adding oxidase reagent to an aliquot of a bacterial culture. If the oxidase reagent (which is a solution of N,N,N',N'-tetramethyl-p-phenylenediamine dihydrochloride or p-aminodimethylaniline) has been oxidized via cytochrome oxidase, a dark purple color will develop. Thus, the appearance of a dark purple color within 30 seconds of the test indicates that the reagent has been oxidized and that the organism is oxidase-positive.

Note: Cytochrome oxidase does not directly oxidize the oxidase reagent. Rather, it oxidizes cytochrome c3, which subsequently oxidizes the oxidase reagent, producing the purple color. Therefore, a positive test is an indirect indication of the presence of cytochrome oxidase, since it monitors the presence of oxidized cytochrome c3. Oxidase-negative organisms do not possess either cytochrome c3 or cytochrome oxidase and will not produce the purple color.

Important: If a purple color develops after the 30-second period, it is considered a false-positive result.

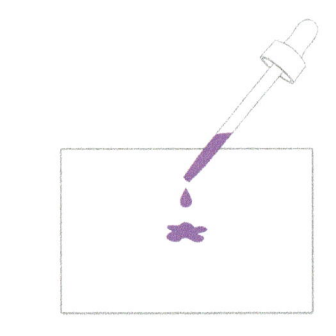

FIGURE 4.16 Cytochrome oxidase results

Exercise 4-3

Catalase and Oxidase Activities

Learning Objectives

To become acquainted with the roles of cytochrome oxidase and catalase in respiring organisms.
To evaluate and interpret cytochrome oxidase and catalase results.

Day 1

Materials

- TSB cultures of bacteria (3)
    - *S. epidermidis*
    - *P. fluorescens*
    - *S. salivarius*
- TSA plates (3)

Work in groups of four.

Procedure

1. Label the three TSA plates, including the name of the organisms.
    Staphylococcus epidermidis
    Pseudomonas fluorescens
    Streptococcus salivarius
2. Perform a three-phase streak of each of the organisms.
3. Incubate plates for 24 hours at 37°C, except the plate inoculated with *P. fluorescens*, which will be incubated at 30°C.

Day 2

Materials

- *S. epidermidis*, *P. fluorescens*, and *S. salivarius* three-phase streak plates from previous lab

Exercise 4-3

- Filter paper
- Sterile toothpicks
- 5% hydrogen peroxide (H_2O_2) solution
- Oxidase reagent

Work in groups of four.

Procedure

1. Test for cytochrome oxidase production.
   a. Label a piece of filter paper with the bacterial names.
   b. Using a **sterile toothpick**, remove a pea-sized amount of culture from the pure culture plates to make a smear on the filter paper.
   c. Repeat with fresh toothpicks for the other cultures.

   Note: It is important to use toothpicks and not a wire loop to smear the cultures; otherwise, the test may give a false-positive result.

   d. Add one drop of oxidase reagent to each smear.
   e. Examine the reaction area and record the result in the *R & Q* section.
   f. Discard the filter paper in the red biohazard bin.

2. Test for catalase production
   a. Use a sterile inoculation loop to transfer a small amount of the three cultures to one clean microscope slide each.
   b. Add one drop of H_2O_2 solution to the samples on the slide and watch for the production of bubbles in the suspension.
   c. Record your results in the *R & Q* section.

Use a sterile toothpick to remove a "pea sized" amount of culture from a colony on the plate

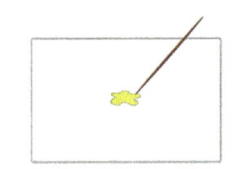

Use the toothpick to smear the culture on the filter paper

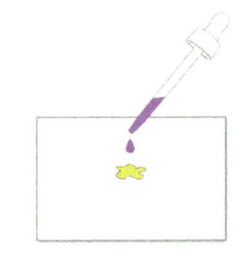

Add one drop of oxidase reagent to the smear on the filter paper

FIGURE 4.17 Cytochrome Oxidase Procedure

Use a sterile loop to transfer a small amount of culture to a clean microscope slide

Add one drop of H_2O_2 and watch for the production of bubbles in the suspension

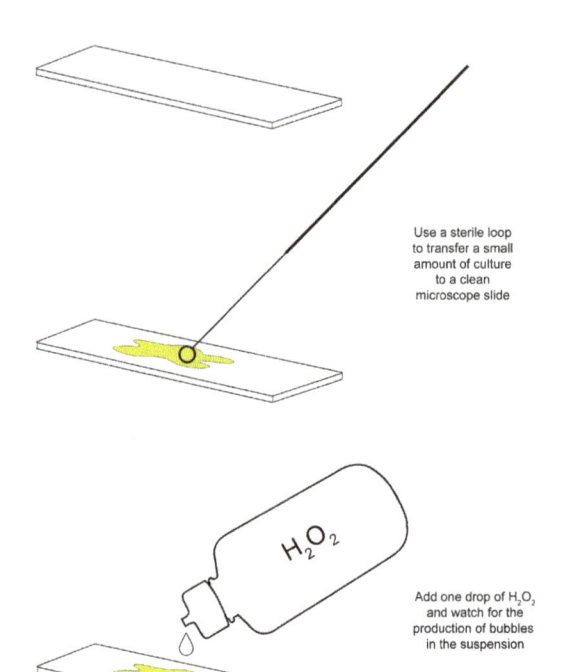

FIGURE 4.18 Catalase Procedure

Exercise 4-3

R & Q

Organism	Cytochrome Oxidase Activity	Catalase Activity
Staphylococcus epidermidis	−	+
Pseudomonas fluorescens	+	+
Streptococcus salivarius	−	−

Explain which cellular activity the cytochrome oxidase test identifies.

_____
_____
_____

Which organism(s) produce cytochrome oxidase?

_____
_____
_____

Explain the role of catalase.

_____
_____
_____

If an aerobic organism performing aerobic respiration does not produce catalase, can it still live if H_2O_2 is formed?

_____
_____
_____

AEROBIC AND ANAEROBIC GROWTH

In this exercise, you will produce plate cultures of aerobes as well as obligate (strict) anaerobes that can only live in environments depleted of oxygen (O_2) because oxygen is toxic to them. The anaerobic bacteria that you will be introduced to, however, are somewhat aerotolerant. This means that the microbes can survive brief exposure to gaseous oxygen, but they will not be able to grow and divided in its presence.

The generation of pure cultures requires growth of the bacterial organisms on solid agar plates so that isolated colonies can be produced and examined. Working with anaerobic organisms can be a major challenge, and it is important to provide the appropriate conditions for their growth.

Anaerobic Growth of Bacterial Organisms

Today, microbiologists have several reliable systems in place to produce suitable conditions for the growth of anaerobic organisms. However, some of the old ways of creating anaerobic conditions were truly imaginative; these included the use of a candle to burn off all the oxygen present in a large glass jar that served as a growth chamber (see Figure 4.19).

Today, a typical way to incubate smaller batches of agar plates anaerobically involves the use of chemicals that, combined with gaseous oxygen, remove oxygen from the environment by physical exclusion.

The system that will be used in this exercise is the GasPak Anaerobic System. This system consists of an incubation jar into which agar plates and a GasPak EZ Gas Generating Sachet (see Figure 4.21 "GasPak Jar") are placed. The sachet, which resembles a large tea bag, is gas-permeable. Inside the sachet are inorganic carbonate, activated carbon, ascorbic acid, and water.

FIGURE 4.19 Depleting oxygen with candle

Ernst Hempelmann, https://commons.wikimedia.org/wiki/File%3ATrager_%26_Jensen.jpg. Copyright in the Public Domain.

FIGURE 4.21 GasPak Anaerobic System

To activate the contents of the sachet, it is first removed from its original airtight wrapper and then placed in the jar together with the inoculated plates. An oxygen indicator (a methylene blue strip) is also added to the jar. Once the jar is sealed, the activated carbon and ascorbic acid in the packet remove the free oxygen in the container by absorption, and CO_2 is generated from carbonate. As the condition in the sealed jar becomes anaerobic, the indicator strip turns from blue to white, which validates that gaseous oxygen is no longer present.

Varying the contents of the sachet, the incubation jar can be used to cultivate a range of anaerobic, microaerophilic, or carbon dioxide-requiring bacteria.

The GasPak® Anaerobic System is one of the most widely used techniques for producing anaerobic conditions in the laboratory. However, when working with organisms that do not tolerate even brief exposure to oxygen, more sophisticated techniques and expensive equipment are used, such as an anaerobic chamber (see Figure 4.22 "Anaerobic Chamber").

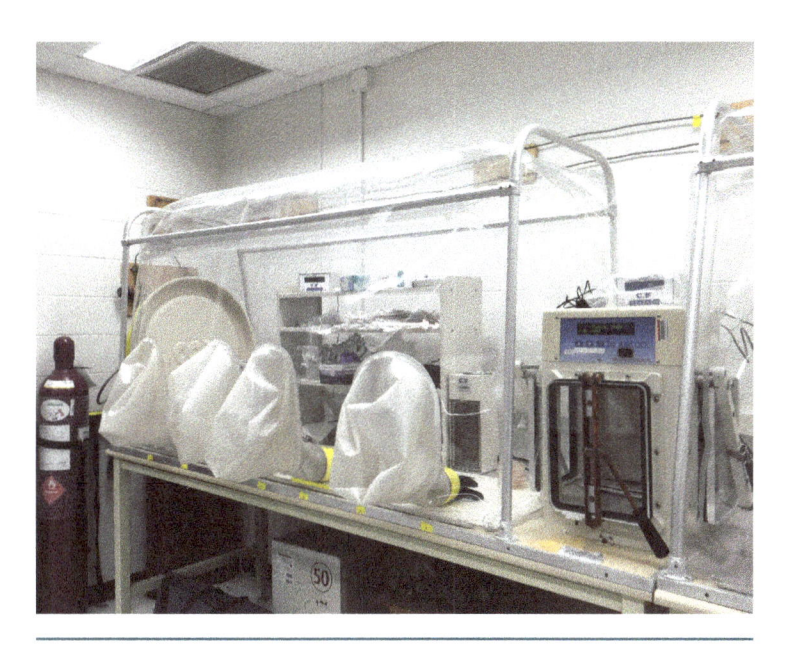

FIGURE 4.22 Anaerobic Chamber

Exercise 4-4

Aerobic and Anaerobic Growth

Learning Objectives

To compare bacterial growth under aerobic and anaerobic conditions.
To become familiar with methods used to grow anaerobic bacteria.
To determine if an organism is an obligate aerobe, obligate anaerobe, or facultative anaerobe.

Day 1

Materials

- Broth cultures (3)
    - *E. coli*
    - *M. luteus*
    - *C. sporogenes* (*Clostridium Sporogenes*)
- BHI agar plates (2)
- Sterile swabs (3)

Work in groups of four.

Procedure

1. Use a permanent marker to divide each of the two BHI plates into three equal sections.
2. Label the plates, including the names of the bacteria according to the sections. Add the aerobic/anaerobic conditions at which the plates will be incubated.
3. Vortex the cultures to properly resuspend the cells.
4. Use sterile swabs (one per organism) to zigzag streak each section of the plates with the indicated organism.

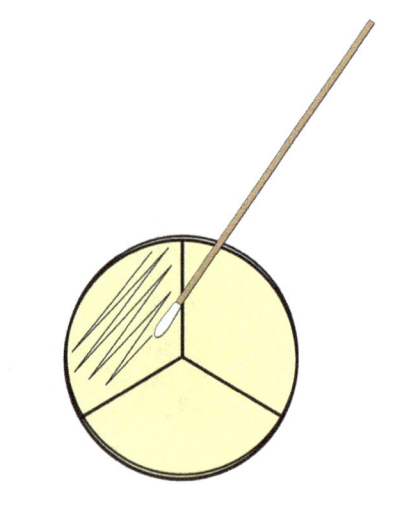

FIGURE 4.23 Zigzag streak with swab

Note: Before streaking the plates, gently twist the swab against the inside of the culture tube to remove excess cell suspension. This will reduce the chances of the culture dripping onto the bench top or contaminating the other sections of the plate.

Exercise 4-4

5. For anaerobic growth, place the plates into the provided GasPak jar. Your lab instructor will place the sachet and the oxygen indicator strip in the jar before closing it.
6. Incubate all plates under aerobic and anaerobic growth condition at 37°C for 24–48 hours.

Day 2

Material

- Aerobically and anaerobically grown cultures on agar plates

Note: Your lab instructor will open the GasPak jar in the fume hood due to strong odor.

Procedure

1. Observe the plates and describe the relative amount of growth of each organism under aerobic vs. anaerobic conditions in the *R & Q* section.

Organism	Aerobic Growth	Anaerobic Growth
E. coli	+	+
M. luteus	+	−
C. sporogenes	−	+

R & Q

Do some research and suggest three habitats for anaerobic cells.

lake bottoms
ocean floor
water treatment plants
intestines
groundwater

Do some research and suggest a few places where microaerophilic organisms may grow.

Exercise 4-4

Which of the above organisms can be classified as obligate anaerobe(s)?

_____
_____
_____

Which enzymes are absent in anaerobic bacteria that makes gaseous O_2 toxic to them? Explain your answer.

_____
_____
_____

Define obligate aerobe.

_____
_____
_____

Are there any facultative anaerobes among the three organisms you tested? Explain your answer.

_____
_____
_____

ANAEROBIC RESPIRATION AND NITRATE REDUCTION

Obligate aerobes can only use oxygen as the terminal electron acceptor in the respiratory process. However, specialized electron-transport systems exist in bacteria capable of anaerobic respiration that allow the use of other terminal electron acceptors than oxygen.

This section focuses on the ability of bacterial microbes to use nitrate as the terminal electron acceptor. The resulting nitrate-reducing reactions taking place within anaerobically respiring organism differ with respect to the enzymes produced by the respective bacterial organisms. The nitrate-reducing pathways utilized by the bacteria can be identified by examining the resulting end products.

Thus, usage of nitrate as a terminal electron acceptor can produce the following nitrate-reducing end products:

1. Nitrate reduction: commonly is used by enteric facultative anaerobes in the absence of oxygen.

    Nitrate (NO_3^-) is reduced to nitrite (NO_2^-) or ammonia (NH_3).

Pathways of Nitrate Reduction:

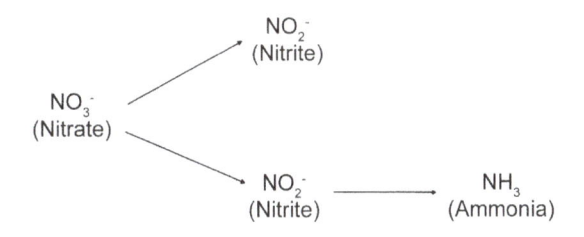

$$NO_3^- \text{ (Nitrate)} \longrightarrow NO_2^- \text{ (Nitrite)}$$
$$NO_3^- \text{ (Nitrate)} \longrightarrow NO_2^- \text{ (Nitrite)} \longrightarrow NH_3 \text{ (Ammonia)}$$

2. Denitrification: a complex series of reactions that many soil bacteria utilize.

General Pathway of Denitrification:

$$NO_3^- \text{ (Nitrate)} \xrightarrow{\text{Nitrate Reductase}} NO_2^- \text{ (Nitrite)} \xrightarrow{\text{Nitrite Reductase}} NO\uparrow \text{ (Nitric Oxide)} \xrightarrow{\text{Nitric Oxide Reductase}} N_2O\uparrow \text{ (Nitrous Oxide)} \xrightarrow{\text{Nitrous Oxide Reductase}} N_2\uparrow \text{ (Nitrogen Gas)}$$

Nitrate is ultimately reduced to nitrogen gas (N_2). However, other gaseous forms of nitrogen are also produced during this stepwise reduction of nitrate. These are nitric oxide (NO), and nitrous oxide (N_2O).

Denitrification and the Environment

Denitrifying bacteria and the denitrification process are important parts of the nitrogen cycle. The process serves to return nitrate produced by nitrifying and nitrogen-fixing bacteria back to the atmosphere.

Under certain conditions, denitrification can also have harmful environmental effects. This is because green plants usually use nitrogen in the form of nitrate. The denitrification process removes nitrates from the soil that are naturally present. Furthermore, the process causes loss of nitrogen from applied fertilizers. The consequence of reduced nitrate availability to plants can result in an unfavorable decrease in crop yield. This situation is seen often in waterlogged soils, since oxygen is unable to permeate the soil and the bacteria found there must respire anaerobically.

Other environmental problems can occur when denitrification results in the production of nitrous oxide (N_2O). Nitrous oxide, a greenhouse gas, causes warming of the earth's atmosphere. In addition, nitrous oxide (N_2O) is converted to nitric oxide (NO) in the atmosphere. Since nitric oxide (NO) reacts with and breaks down ozone (O_3) in the upper atmosphere, denitrification also contributes to the depletion of Earth's ozone layer, the essential barrier between life on earth and deadly ultraviolet radiation produced by the sun.

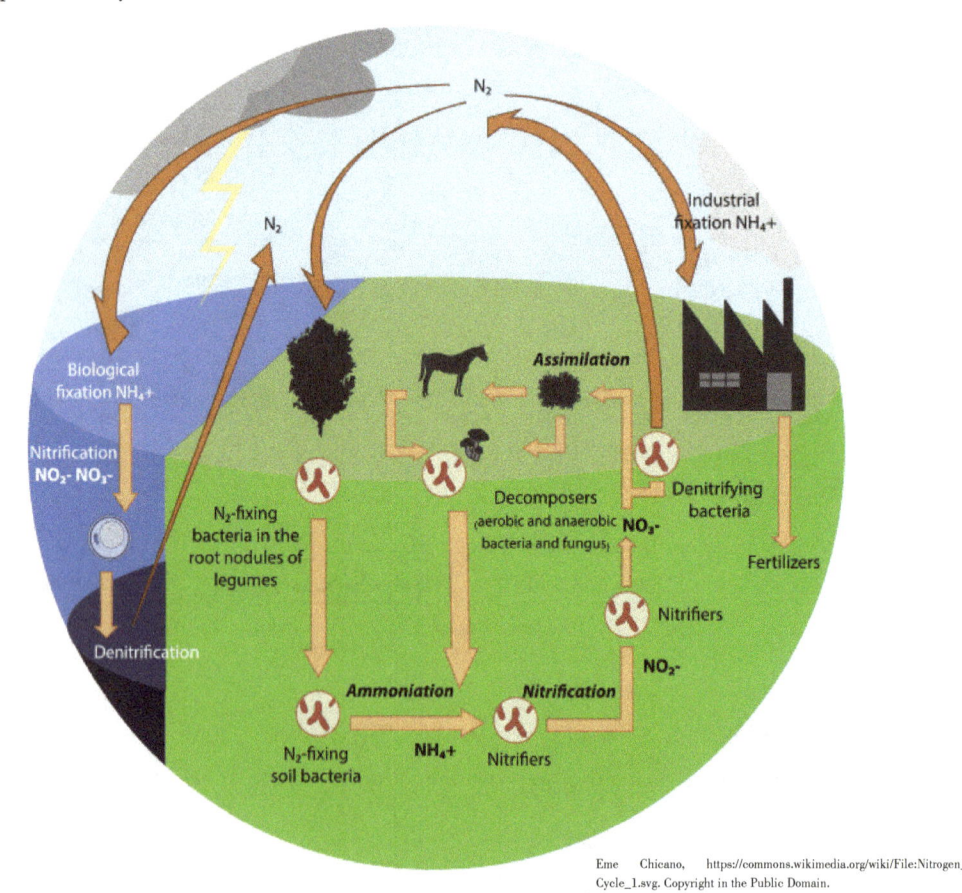

Eme Chicano, https://commons.wikimedia.org/wiki/File:Nitrogen_Cycle_1.svg. Copyright in the Public Domain.

Anaerobic Respiration and Nitrate Reduction

In this exercise, you will inoculate nitrate-containing growth medium (nitrate broth medium) with selected bacteria. Following incubation and examination of end products, you will be able to determine which pathway the respective bacterial species are using to reduce nitrate.

Learning Objectives

To get familiar with anaerobic respiration and nitrate reduction and how these can affect the environment. To determine the specific nitrate-reduction pathway used by the bacterial organisms by examining the nitrate-reducing end products.

Day 1

Materials

- TSB cultures of bacteria (3)
    - *E. hoshinae*
    - *B. subtilis*
    - *P. denitrificans*
- Nitrate broth medium with Durham Tube (3)

Work in groups of four.

Procedure

1. Label each of the three tubes of nitrate broth containing Durham tubes, including the name of the organism.

    Note: Nitrate both tubes contain Durham tubes—do not vortex!

2. Use a sterilized inoculating loop to inoculate each of the tubes with the indicated organism.
3. Incubate the tubes at 37°C for 24–48 hours without shaking.

Exercise 4-5

Day 2

Materials

- Nitrate broth cultures (3) inoculated in previous lab and incubated
- Sulfanilic acid
- Naphthylamine solution
- Zinc dust
- Fume hood

Work in groups of four.

Procedure

1. Carefully resuspend the cultures by rolling the tubes gently back and forth in your hands. Avoid introducing air bubbles into the Durham tubes (do not vortex).
2. Add 12–15 drops of sulfanilic acid solution to each nitrate tube and mix gently (see procedure outlined Figure 4.24 Nitrate Broth Procedure).
3. Determine if nitrate has been reduced to nitrite by adding 12–15 drops of naphthylamine solution, one drop at a time, to each of the nitrate broth tubes.
4. Record your observation in the R & Q section.
5. For cultures that did not turn red after the addition of the naphthylamine, use a spatula to add a very small amount of zinc dust to these culture tubes.

   Caution: Be careful handling zinc; wear gloves and keep the reagent in the fume hood.

Exercise 4-5 193

Nitrate Reduction Procedure and Interpretations

Add 12–15 drops **sulfanilic acid** solution to each tube

Add 12–15 drops **naphthylamine** solution to each tube

Red → The organism reduced $NO_3^- \rightarrow NO_2^-$ TESTING COMPLETE do NOT add zinc dust

No Color Change → Add a small amount of zinc dust (wear gloves)

Red → The organism did NOT use NO_3^-

No Color Change → Check the Durham tube

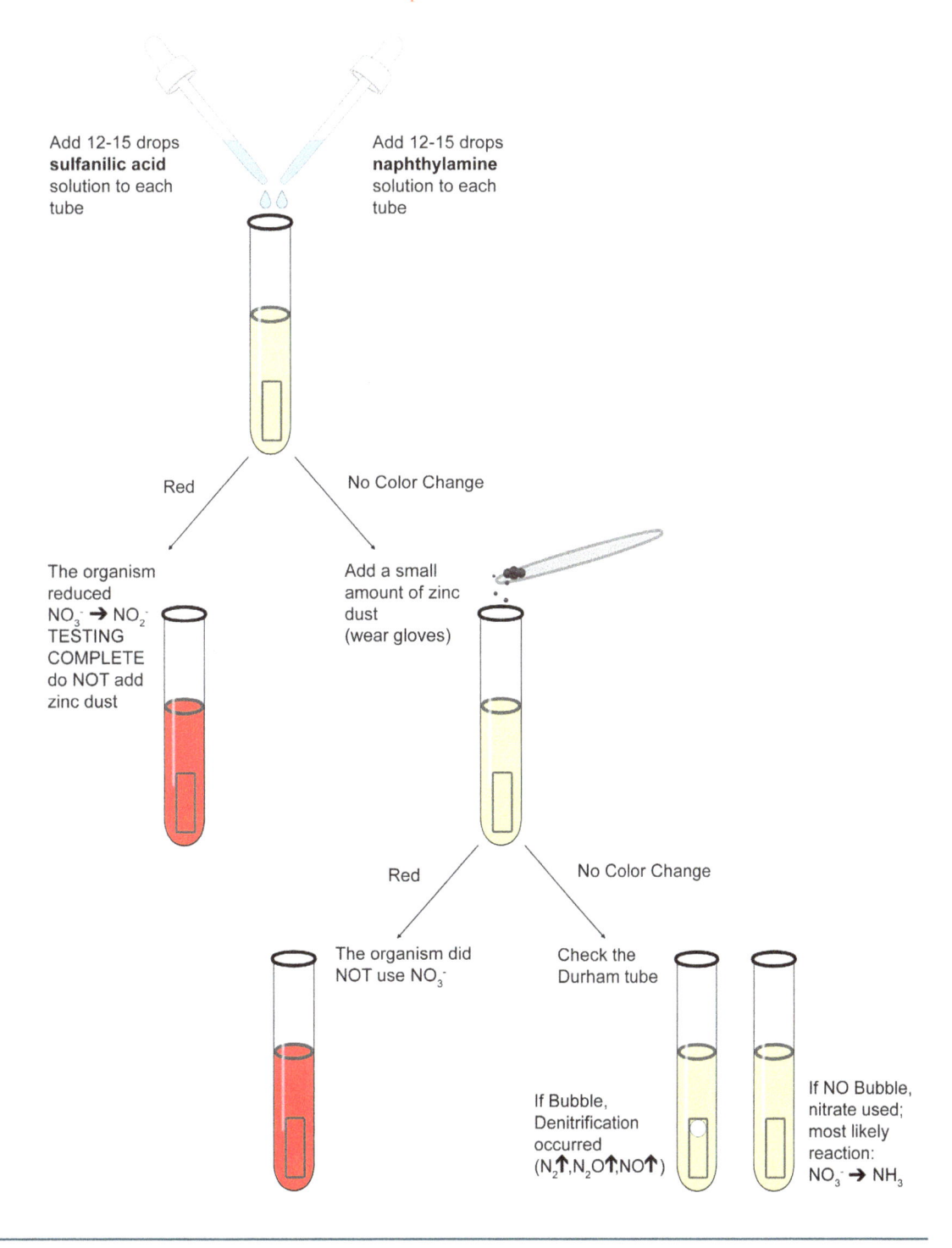

If Bubble, Denitrification occurred ($N_2\uparrow, N_2O\uparrow, NO\uparrow$)

If NO Bubble, nitrate used; most likely reaction: $NO_3^- \rightarrow NH_3$

FIGURE 4.24 Nitrate Broth Procedure

Exercise 4-5

Result summary:

NO₃⁻ → NO₂⁻

Red color develops after addition of sulfanilic acid and naphthylamine.

No NO₃⁻ utilized

Red color develops after addition of zinc dust.

NO₃⁻ → NH₃

No red color develops after addition of zinc dust, and no gas is present in Durham tube.

NO₃⁻ → N₂, N₂O, NO (Denitrification)

No red color develops after addition of zinc dust, and gas is present in Durham tube.

R&Q

Record your observation in the table below as follows.

Organism	Color Change after addition of sulfanilic acid and naphthylamine	Color change after addition of zinc dust	Bubble in Durham tube	Extent of Nitrate (NO₃⁻) Reduction
Edwardsiella hoshinae	yes	N/A	N/A	Nitrate Reduction
Bacillus subtilis	No	Yes	N/A	did not use NO₃⁻
Pseudomonas denitrificans	No	No	yes	denitrification

When studying nitrate reduction in anaerobic respiration, why is it important not to incubate the nitrate broth tubes on a shaker for aeration of the culture medium?

_____
_____
_____

Explain the goal of this exercise and include definitions of nitrate reduction and denitrification.

_____
_____
_____

SELECTIVE, DIFFERENTIAL, AND SELECTIVE-DIFFERENTIAL MEDIA

MacConkey agar plates, Starch agar plates, and Pseudomonas isolation Agar

As mentioned previously, the isolation and identification of a single bacterial species from its natural environment is often a challenge. However, it is possible to facilitate isolation of certain bacteria by taking advantage of known variations in microbial nutrition and metabolism. One way to do this is to use selective, differential, or selective-differential media.

We will be working with three agar media:
1. one used to select for members of the genus *Pseudomonas* (Pseudomonas Isolation Agar or PIA);
2. another differentiating between the ability of bacteria to use starch as a carbon source; and
3. a third selecting for Gram-negative enterics that also contains the differential property to distinguish between lactose-fermenting enterics (coliform enterics) and non-lactose-fermenting enterics (non-coliform enterics).

In the exercise, we will also revisit the fact that some enzymes, although produced inside the cell, are active only after being exported from the cells.

Selective media such as PIA (Pseudomonas Isolation Agar) are used to select for the growth of some organisms while inhibiting the growth of others. The inhibition of growth may be accomplished by omitting certain required nutrients or by adding compounds to the medium (such as dyes and antibiotics) which affect the growth of unwanted organisms.

Differential media such as Starch Agar may allow a variety of organisms to grow but enable the observer to visually distinguish among the different types of bacteria. The differentiation may be assisted by components added to the media and the metabolism of the bacteria. For example, starch can be included in the media; this will be utilized (degraded) only by bacteria that produce the exoenzyme α-amylase. After growth, examination can be done that reveals if starch is still present in the medium or has been degraded. Another way to distinguish among bacterial species growing on a certain medium is to add an appropriate pH indicator to the medium. Acid production by a given organism will result in a color change of the colonies and the surrounding medium. In contrast, no color change will occur for organisms growing on the medium that do not produce acid.

Selective-differential media (such as MacConkey agar plates) demonstrate both selective and differential properties. These media select for a limited number of organisms but also allow the observer to distinguish among those that do grow.

Selective, Differential, and Selective-differential Media—Interpretation of Results

Pseudomonas isolation agar

PIA is a selective medium that is used to isolate members of the genus *Pseudomonas*. PIA contains a broad-spectrum antimicrobial agent (Irgasan) that inhibits the growth of a wide variety of organisms but does not inhibit growth of *Pseudomonas* strains such as *Pseudomonas aeruginosa* and *Pseudomonas* spp.

Starch Agar

This medium is a differential medium used to determine if an organism has the ability to utilize starch (amylose) as a carbon and energy source. Utilization of starch depends on the organism's ability to break down this large complex carbohydrate (amylose) to glucose units. The breakdown of starch is catalyzed by the exoenzyme α-amylase (**Box 1**).

Growth of an organism on starch agar is not indicative of starch utilization. Therefore, after growth on the starch-containing medium, iodine must be added to the medium in order to determine if the tested organism could degrade starch. If starch has been utilized, a clear area around the streak indicates that the bacterium produces α-amylase and is able to hydrolyze starch.

Figure legend: After growth on the starch medium, the determination of whether the bacterium is able to degrade starch includes flooding the agar plate with an iodine solution. If starch is still present, iodine will turn starch in the medium deep blue to black in color. Thus, if the organism

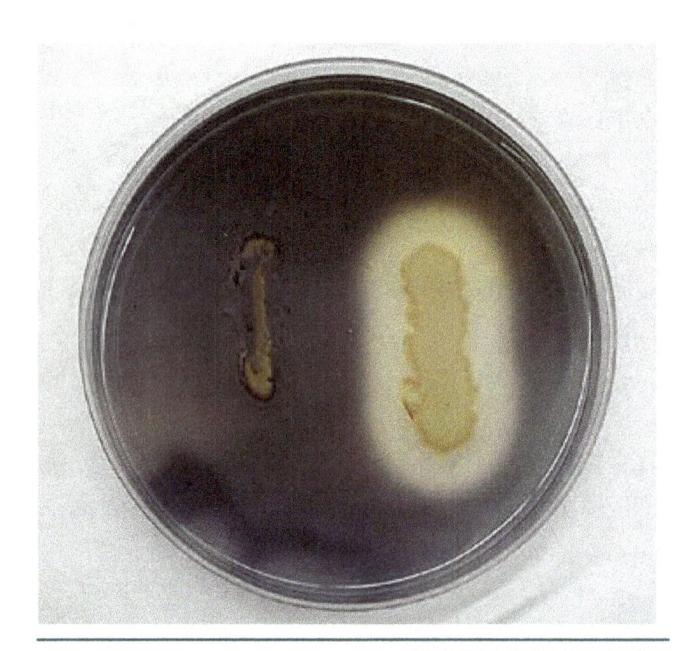

FIGURE 4.25 Starch plate

does not produce α-amylase, the starch remains in the medium, and the area immediately surrounding the organism will appear the same color as the rest of the medium after the iodine has been added. However, if an organism produces α-amylase, it will be able to degrade the starch in the medium, and a clear area will appear around the streak of growth after the addition of iodine. This means that the organism can utilize starch as a carbon and energy source.

MacConkey agar

This medium selects for the growth of Gram-negative enteric organisms.

Enterics are selected for growth on MacConkey agar due to the presence of bile salts and crystal violet in the medium; this inhibits the growth gram-positive organisms. MacConkey agar can also be used to differentiate between lactose-fermenting enterics (coliforms) and non-lactose-fermenting enterics (noncoliforms), which are able to grow on the medium. Organisms that ferment lactose and produce acid will develop bright pink or fuchsia colonies due to presence of the neutral red pH indicator in the medium.

Thus, organisms that can grow on MacConkey are usually Gram-negative enterics, and they may or may not be able to ferment lactose:

- Colonies appearing hot pink after incubation on the media reflects that the organism can ferment lactose and therefore is a coliform.

- Colonies appearing light yellowish to colorless after incubation on the media reflects that the organism cannot ferment lactose
and is therefore not a coliform.

MacConkey's agar showing both lactose and non-lactose fermenting colonies. Lactose fermenting colonies are pink whereas non-lactose fermenting colonies are colorless or light yellowish.

Medimicro, https://commons.wikimedia.org/wiki/File:MacConkey_agar_with_LF_and_LF_colonies.jpg. Copyright in the Public Domain.

MacConkey Agar Flowchart

Selective due to bile salts and crystal violet

- MacConkey Agar
  - Growth → Gram negative enterics
  - No Growth → Gram positives and all other Gram negatives

Differential due to neutral red pH indicator

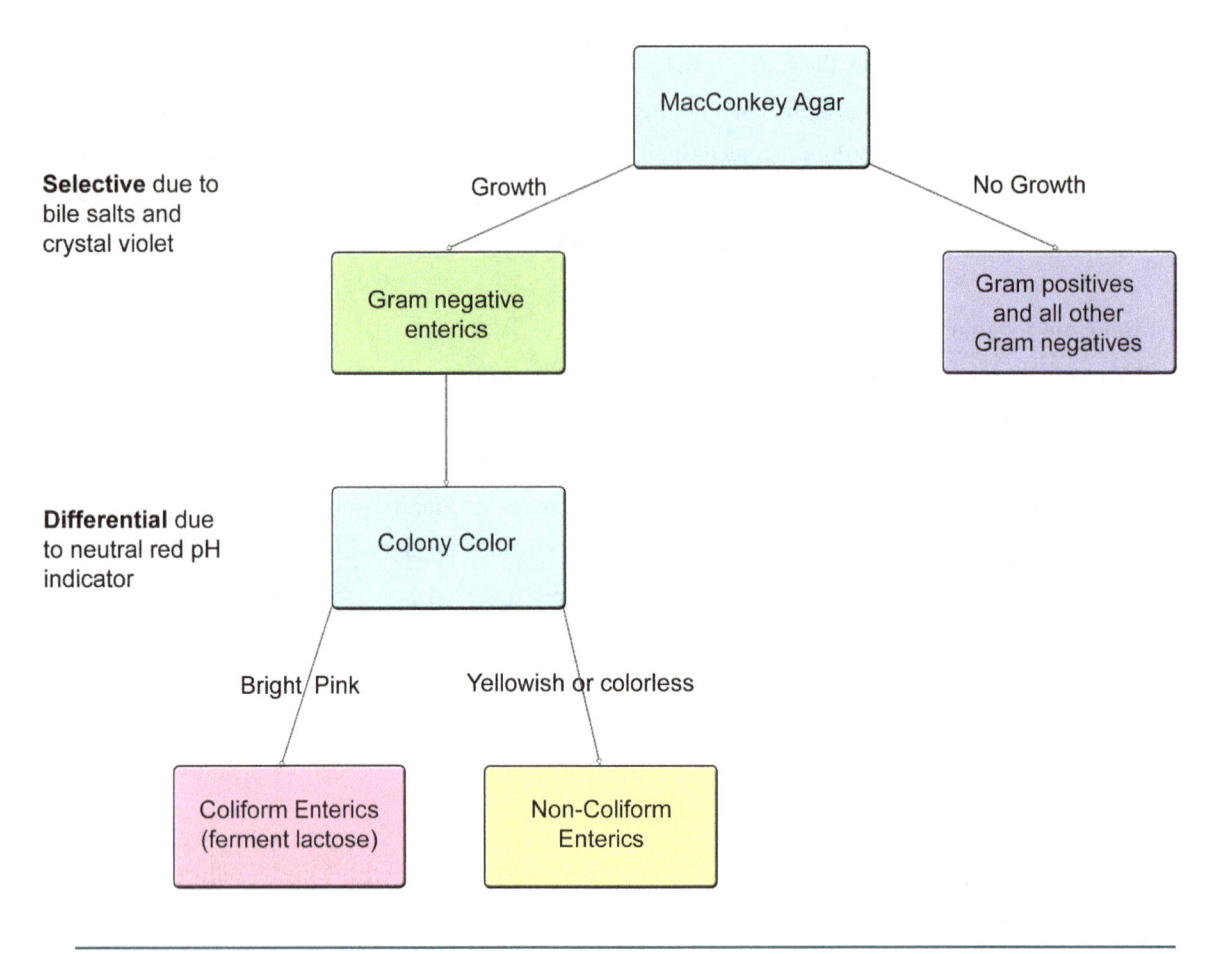

- Colony Color
  - Bright Pink → Coliform Enterics (ferment lactose)
  - Yellowish or colorless → Non-Coliform Enterics

FIGURE 4.26 MacConkey Agar Flowchart

Enterics

Gram-negative enterics commonly grow in the intestinal tracts of humans and other warm-blooded animals, although they can also be found naturally in other environments. The microbes are facultative anaerobes (can live with or without gaseous oxygen), gram-negative rods and are currently grouped together in the same family, the Enterobacteriaceae.

Only certain members of the Enterobacteriaceae family are found as normal microbiota (normal flora) of the gut; others may be present only in a disease state.

Examples of genera included in the Enterobacteriaceae family:

Escherichia—part of the normal microbiota of human intestines; typically used as an indicator of fecal contamination in water and food.

Salmonella—often associated with meat (especially poultry); the cause of common forms of food-borne illnesses.

Serratia—important in nosocomial (hospital-acquired) infections of the urinary and respiratory tracts.

Selective, Differential, and Selective-Differential Media

Learning Objectives

To become familiar with selective, differential, and selective-differential media and to interpret the observed the results.

Day 1

Materials

- TSB cultures of:
    - *B. subtilis*
    - *P. fluorescens*
    - *E. coli*
    - *E. hoshinae*
- PIA plate
- Starch agar plate
- MacConkey agar plate
- Inoculating loop
- Bunsen burner

Work in groups of four.

Procedure

1. Divide Pseudomonas Isolation Agar (PIA) plate into three equal sections for each of the bacterial strains below and label the plate accordingly.
    - *Escherichia coli*
    - *Bacillus subtilis*
    - *Pseudomonas fluorescens*

Exercise 4-6

2. Similarly, divide a MacConkey agar plate into three equal sections and label accordingly.
   - *Escherichia coli*
   - *Edwardsiella hoshinae*
   - *Bacillus subtilis*
3. Light the Bunsen burner.
4. Use the sterilized inoculating loop to zigzag streak each section of the PIA and MacConkey agar plates with the respective organisms (Figure 4.27 "Zigzag Streak").
5. Divide a starch agar plate into two equal sections (Figure 4.28 "Starch Streak"). Label the plate accordingly, including the name of the organisms.
   - *Escherichia coli*
   - *Bacillus subtilis*
6. Use a sterilized inoculation loop to make a small (about two inches long), straight single-line streak of the indicated organism on each section of the starch agar plate.
7. Incubate your inverted plates at 37°C for 24–48 hours, except the PIA plate, which will be incubated at 30°C.

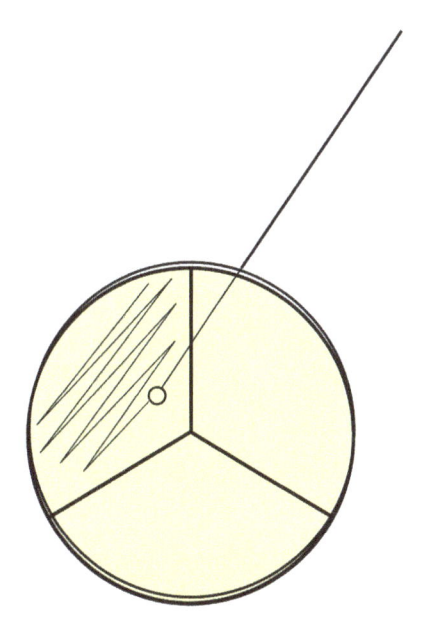

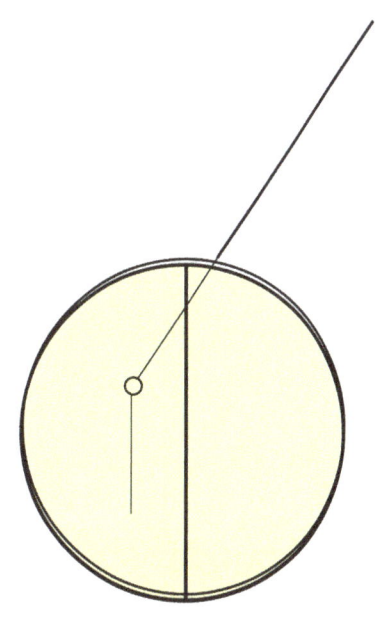

FIGURE 4.27 Zigzag streak

FIGURE 4.28 Starch streak

Exercise 4-6

Day 2

8. Examine the bacterial strains streaked on the PIA plate for growth. Record your observation in the *R & Q* section.
9. Examine the bacterial strains streaked on the MacConkey agar plate for growth and record your observation in the table in the *R & Q* section. If growth occurred, record the appearance of the colonies and the medium. Both the ability of the organism to grow on MacConkey agar and the color the colonies develop are important for the interpretation of the result.
10. Examine the bacterial strains streaked on the starch agar plate for growth and record your observation in the *R & Q* section.
11. Examine if the stains were able to use starch by adding iodine to the plate in the following way:
    a. Flood the starch agar plate with Gram's iodine.
    b. Allow the reagent to penetrate into the agar for about 3–4 minutes.
    c. Examine if the agar surrounding the bacterial streaks turned deep blue/black or if a clear zone developed.
12. Record your observation in the table in the *R & Q* section.

R&Q

Organism	Pseudomonas isolation agar	Starch agar	MacConkey agar
A — Escherichia coli	—	+ No clearing	+ Pink
B — Edwardsiella hoshinae	✗	✗	+ Colorless
C — Bacillus subtilis	—	+ clearing	—
Pseudomonas fluorescens	+	✗	✗

gram-enteric

— A: (coliform enteric) Ferment lactose, bright red
B: growth, non-coliform enterics
C: ∅

Exercise 4-6

Describe the function of α-amylase; include where the enzyme is produced and where it is catalytically active.

Explain why we add iodine to the starch plate after incubation.

What does a clear zone surrounding the bacterial strain on the starch plate indicate?

Explain the idea of using PIA to select *Pseudomonas* strains.

How effective does PIA appear to be as a selective medium?

Based on the results from the MacConkey agar, explain the metabolism of the three organisms tested.

Which other medium did you use in a previous exercise (or will you use in a future exercise) that is also a selective-differential medium?

Identification of Unknown Bacteria

In this module, you will use the experience you gained in all the previous modules, as well as your acquired hands-on skills, to work toward identifying two unknown bacterial species.

During the previous exercises, it became evident that bacteria can be categorized according to their morphology, cellular arrangements, staining characteristics, catabolic capabilities, and the pathways they employ. You will use these features to identify your unknown organisms.

Before we start this exercise, we will be briefly introduced to how identification of unknown infectious agents occurs in the clinical setting. We will see that clinical work also takes advantage of knowledge about species-specific bacterial traits. We will get a feeling for how important microbial research throughout the past many years has been, and still is, for the efficient identification of unknown infectious agents and the subsequent successful treatment of the diseased individuals.

IDENTIFICATION OF INFECTIOUS AGENTS IN THE CLINICAL SETTING

In the clinic, it is important to rapidly and efficiently identify an agent causing an infection in order to quickly determine an appropriate treatment for the infected individual. Therefore, efficient multiple-test systems have been developed. Among those are the EnteroPluri-Test system and the API 20E system. These two systems are commonly used once the infectious agent has been isolated and a pure culture has been achieved.

Typically, a nonselective, nondifferential medium is first used in an attempt to grow the microbe. Subsequently, the microbe will be analyzed microscopically, and data from the multi-test systems will be collected.

The two multi-test systems, the EnteroPluri-Test and the API 20E systems, consist of several individual metabolic tests that are being assayed all at once. Both systems are normally used to identify genera belonging to the family Enterobactericiae, which includes species that are responsible for approximately 50% of all nosocomial (hospital-acquired) infections.

Box 1 EnteroPluri-Test System

The EnteroPluri-Test system allows for the inoculation of several different types of media while using the very same inoculum (Figure 5.1 EnteroPluri-Test).

After incubation of the inoculated media included in the EnteroPluri-Test system, results will be obtained for glucose utilization/gas production, lysine utilization, ornithine utilization, indole/H2S production, adonitol, lactose, arabinose and sorbitol utilization, acetoin production as detected by the Voges-Proskauer(VP) test, dulcitol utilization, phenylalanine deaminase production, urease production, and citrate utilization, many of which we worked with in Module 4.

As we previously learned, the indole and VP tests require the addition of specific reagents after incubation before the results can be interpreted. This is also true for the EnteroPluri-Test system. Therefore, such agents will be added prior to interpretation.

As soon as all the test results are achieved and a five-number code has been obtained, it will be entered into the Computer Coding and Identification System, which is a computerized database that processes the results and provides an identification of the organism. Test results may also be interpreted by visually scanning a printed version of the database test codes.

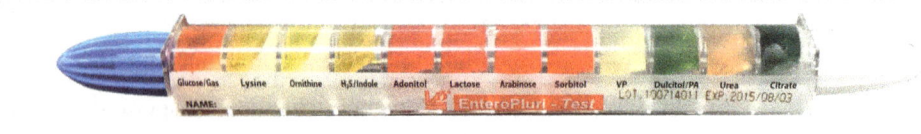

FIGURE 5.1 EnteroPluri-Test

> **Box 2 API 20E System**
>
> The API 20E system works along the same principles; however, a huge difference between the systems is that the media of the API20E system are provided in a dehydrated form.
>
> The system consists of twenty separate cupules contained in a plastic strip (Figure 5.2 "API 20E System"). Each cupule must be inoculated individually. It is necessary for the inoculum to rehydrate the medium contained in each cupule. Mineral oil is added to the cupules where an anaerobic growth environment is required.
>
> The twenty different media included in the kit provide results for biochemical tests such as glucose, lactose and mannitol fermentation, citrate utilization, H_2S production, indole production, acetoin production, and gelatin utilization.
>
> When inoculated, the API 20E system is incubated in the same manner as the EnteroPluri-Test system, and again, some of the tests require the addition of chemicals before they can be interpreted. Once all these data are obtained, a seven-digit code is generated and used for the identification of the bacterial organism. This is done by looking up the seven-digit code in an API catalog or by using a computer database (apiweb), which cites the corresponding organism(s).
>
> **FIGURE 5.2** API 20E System

These highly efficient screening methods are very useful, but they still have drawbacks. For example, they are very costly. Therefore, if conventional ways of identifying bacteria are less costly and speed is not an issue, those avenues could be taken.

Also, these test systems can be used to identify only a limited number of organisms. If an organism is isolated that is not included in the system (either because it is not present among the species in the database or because it cannot be identified using the media included in the test system), other tests may be required to identify that specific unknown organism.

When comparing the two types of systems, it is clear that the EnteroPluri-Test system is far easier to inoculate than the API 20E system. However, compared to the API 20E system, it is difficult to add the chemicals necessary for interpretation. Both systems have advantages and disadvantages that should be taken into consideration when choosing the appropriate method for the identification of an unknown organism.

Note: Although the EnteroPluri-Test and the API 20E systems provide a relative quick and sufficient way to identify unknown infectious organisms, other far more advanced systems exist in the clinic for rapid and accurate microbial identification and diagnosis of infectious diseases. Examples of such systems are; automated molecular diagnostic systems, which integrate automated sample preparation, extraction and purification of nucleic acids, and real time PCR (Polymerase Chain Reaction); and MALDI TOF Mass Spectrometry, which generates a mass spectrum unique to individual microbial species.

You can read more here about recent developments of systems to efficiently identify bacteria in the clinic: Robin Patel, New Developments in Clinical Bacteriology Laboratories, Mayo Clin Proc 2016 91(10):1448-1459.

Identification of Unknown Bacteria in the Clinic

Learning Objectives

To become familiar with the two biochemical test systems (EnteroPluri-Test and API 20E) used in the clinic for rapid identification of bacterial species.
To be aware of the advantages and disadvantages of the two systems.
To understand how EnteroPluri-Test ID Value Codes are used to identify bacteria species.

Materials

- Uninoculated EnteroPluri-Test
- Inoculated EnteroPluri-Test
- Inoculated API 20E

Work individually.

Procedure

The following protocol was used to prepare the EnteroPluri-Test demos.

1. The EnteroPluri-Test system was inoculated by dipping the tip of the sterile wire (which runs through the tube) into the cells of an isolated pure colony of *Escherichia coli*. To ensure that all media were inoculated, the wire was pulled through the system twice using a rotating motion.
2. A notch on the wire was thereafter aligned with the opening of the tube, and the wire was bent until broken off at the notch. This procedure ensures the required anaerobic conditions in the appropriate compartments.
3. To allow for aerobic conditions, holes were punched in the foil covering the appropriate compartments after inoculation.
4. Steps 1–3 were repeated for *Proteus vulgaris*.
5. The systems were incubated at 37°C for 18–24 hours.
6. After incubation, chemical reagents were added to the appropriate cupules to retrieve the results.

The following protocol was used to prepare the API 20E demo.

1. The inoculum was prepared by suspending an isolated colony of *E. coli* in 5 ml of sterile saline. A sterile Pasteur pipette was used to fill each section of the API 20E strip with the inoculum.
2. The appropriate cupules were topped off with mineral oil to create an anaerobic environment
3. The steps were repeated using *P. vulgaris*.
4. The systems were thereafter incubated at 37°C for 18–24 hours.
5. After incubation, chemical reagents were added to the appropriate compartments to retrieve the results.

Observation of the API 20E photograph and demo

To determine the identity of the bacterium, a seven-digit code must be generated. This is done by identifying the positive results for the tests. The seven-digit code is introduced into a computer database, which identifies the organism. Alternatively, the code is interpreted based on written information available in the API Index. You will not attempt to interpret the results shown in the figure or demo provided in the lab.

Observation of the EnteroPluri-Test photographs and demos

Compare the inoculated tubes to the uninoculated control tube. Use the table and the handout to interpret the result of each test.

For each organism tested, record "+" for positive and "-" for negative for all tests, and answer the questions in the *R and Q* section.

Exercise 5-1

EnteroPluri-Test legend:

In order to identify the organism, a five-digit Identification (ID) Value code must be generated from the test results. Depending on the test, a positive result has an assigned score of 4, 2, or 1. All negative results are given a score of zero (0). The tests are grouped into five sets of three tests. Each individual test score within a given set is added to produce a total score for each set of tests.

Example: the first set of tests.

For the first set of tests, if the result for the glucose fermentation was positive (yellow color) the score would be 4. If there was no gas detected, the gas score would be 0. If the test for lysine was positive (purple color) the score would be 1. The total score would then be 5 (4 + 0 + 1), and is the first number in the five-digit code used to identify the organism tested.

After all of the tests are evaluated and scores are assigned to each of the five sets of tests, the five-digit ID Value code can be determined.

	Glucose	Gas	Lysine	Ornithine	H_2S	Indole*	Adonitol	Lactose	Arabinose	Sorbitol	VP*	Dulcitol	P.A.	Urea	Citrate
Control	red-orange	no cracks	yellow	yellow	yellow	yellow	red-orange	red-orange	red-orange	red-orange	color-less	yellow-green	yellow-green	yellow	green
Positive Reaction	yellow	cracks	purple	purple	black	red	yellow	yellow	yellow	yellow	red	yellow	grey-brown ppt	bright pink	blue
Score for Positive	4	2	1	4	2	1	4	2	1	4	2	1	4	2	1
E. coli Result	+	+	+			+					−				
E. coli Score	4	2	1			1					0				
I.D. Code Value	7														

* The results of this test are not visible from this angle. Results and scores would be as indicated.

Exercise 5-1

Control

P. vulgaris

	Glucose	Gas	Lysine	Ornithine	H₂S	Indole*	Adonitol	Lactose	Arabinose	Sorbitol	VP*	Dulcitol*	P.A.	Urea	Citrate
Control	red-orange	no cracks	yellow	yellow	yellow	yellow	red-orange	red-orange	red-orange	red-orange	color-less	yellow-green	yellow-green	yellow	green
Positive Reaction	yellow	cracks	purple	purple	black	red	yellow	yellow	yellow	yellow	red	yellow	grey-brown ppt	bright pink	blue
Score for Positive	4	2	1	4	2	1	4	2	1	4	2	1	4	2	1
P. vulgaris Result	+	-	-			+					-	-			
P. vulgaris Score	4	0	0			1					0	0			
I.D. Code Value		4													

* The results of this test are not visible from this angle. Results and scores would be as indicated.

R & Q

Record the five-digit code for each of the organisms tested:

  E. coli _____   *P. vulgaris* _____

Use the provided printed version of the Computer Coding and Identification System Database to confirm the identities of these two organisms.

Describe the advantages of using these systems.

_____
_____
_____

Describe the disadvantages of using these systems.

_____
_____
_____

Discuss two major differences between the EnteroPluri-Test and the API 20E systems.

_____
_____
_____

IDENTIFICATION OF UNKNOWN BACTERIA IN THE LABORATORY

To conclude Modules 1–4, you will now use the knowledge gained to identify two unknown bacterial organisms. You will create and maintain a pure culture of each of the unknown organisms, microscopically examine them, and pick and perform biochemical tests that will help you identify them. This exercise will include an extensive report that you will submit to your lab instructor for grading.

During this exercise, you will also familiarize yourself with how the different biochemical tests can be used to distinguish one microbe from another. You will also know how to pick the right test in order to determine the usage of a specific carbohydrate or protein and to confirm the activity of specific biochemical reactions within the cells.

In Module 4, you learned that each type of bacterium is capable of utilizing specific energy and carbon sources while employing a characteristic set of pathways. These patterns of carbon and energy usage, in combination with knowing which pathways are applied utilizing these sources, together can identify a bacterium.

In order to determine the metabolic pathways used by a particular bacterium (as well as any other of its traits), it is necessary first to generate a pure culture. By doing that, we ensure that no contaminants are present, which otherwise would give rise to misleading results.

To identify an organism, Gram staining is commonly among the first tests to be performed. Obtaining the Gram status of an unknown bacterium greatly helps an investigator to determine which laboratory tests will be most useful to perform next.

Exercise 5-2

Identification of Unknown Bacteria in the Laboratory

The task for this exercise is simple: you will identify two types of bacteria from a list of a few possible species. With respect to the results you will obtain, you proceed through the identification of the two bacteria using a simple process of elimination. However, the identification process can take up to six laboratory periods. During those lab periods, you will also perform exercises from other modules in the lab manual.

After you have identified the two unknown species, you will submit a written summary of your work. In addition to a statement of the purpose of the exercise, the summary should include the identity of each of your two unknown bacteria, the approach taken to identify the organisms, and an analysis of results you obtained. You are also asked to write a paragraph describing any other known facts about the identified organisms. Remember to cite any reference you may have used to used to complete this work.

Forms and tables to be used for the summary, as well as further information and helpful details, can be found on the following pages.

Learning Objective

To use microscopy and metabolic tests for bacterial identification.

Day 1

Materials

- Saline suspension with two unknown bacteria
- TSA plate

Work individually.

Procedure

1. Each student will receive one saline suspension containing a Gram-positive (G+), and Gram-negative (G–) organism.
2. Record the number of your saline suspension in the *R & Q* section.
3. Vortex the saline suspension.
4. Perform a three-phase streak to separate the two bacterial organisms present in the saline suspension.

Exercise 5-2

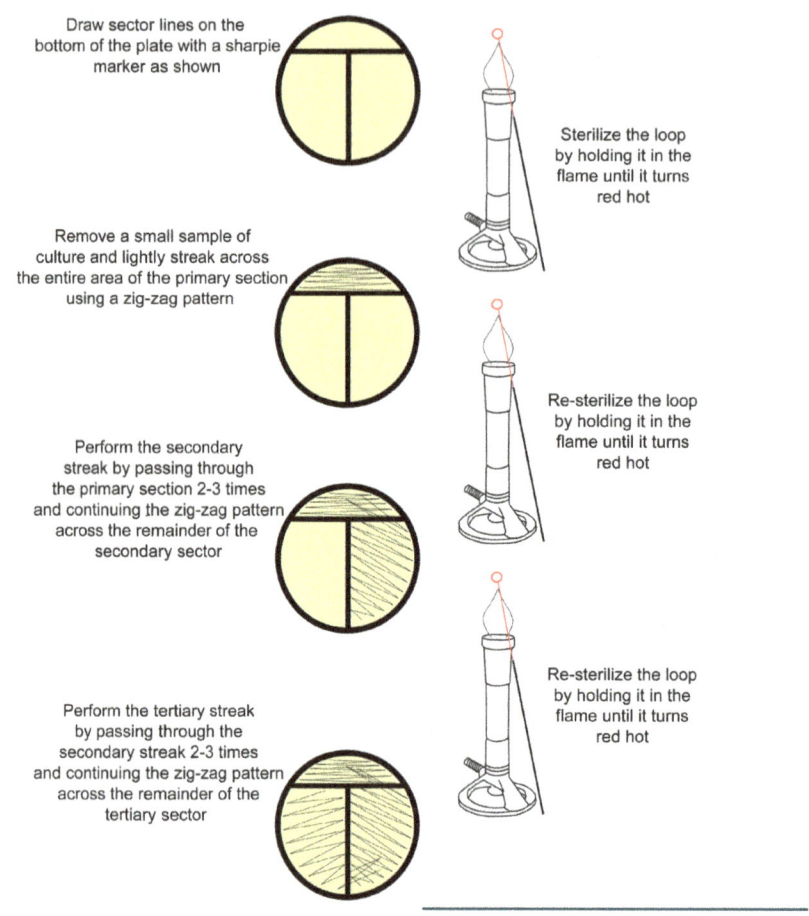

Draw sector lines on the bottom of the plate with a sharpie marker as shown

Sterilize the loop by holding it in the flame until it turns red hot

Remove a small sample of culture and lightly streak across the entire area of the primary section using a zig-zag pattern

Re-sterilize the loop by holding it in the flame until it turns red hot

Perform the secondary streak by passing through the primary section 2-3 times and continuing the zig-zag pattern across the remainder of the secondary sector

Re-sterilize the loop by holding it in the flame until it turns red hot

Perform the tertiary streak by passing through the secondary streak 2-3 times and continuing the zig-zag pattern across the remainder of the tertiary sector

FIGURE 5.3 3 phase streak technique

Note: It is crucial to use good aseptic technique!

5. Incubate the TSA plate at 37°C for 24 hours.
6. Store the saline suspension at 4°C.

Note: It is important to keep your suspension in case you are unable to generate isolated colonies on the first try.

7. Fill out the two flowcharts in the *R & Q* section. As you fill out the flowcharts, refer to Table "Characteristics of Bacteria" when selecting which media/tests to perform.

Note: Filling out the flowcharts will provide you with a helpful identification plan to identify your unknown bacteria.

8. Turn in your completed flowcharts at the end of the period.

Exercise 5-2

Edwardsiella tasn?nc |A+G| — |A+G| — | — | — | K|A|H₂S| — | + |

Characteristics of Unknown Bacteria

Organism	Cellular Characteristics	Gram Rxn	Glucose	Lactose	Mannitol	V-P	Cytochrome Oxidase	Citrate	KIA** slant/butt	Tryptone	Catalase
Staphylococcus aureus	cocci, clusters	+	A	A	A	–	–			–	+
Staphylococcus epidermidis	cocci, clusters	+	A	A	–	–	–			–	+
Streptococcus salivarius	cocci, chains	+	A	A	–		–			–	–
Bacillus subtilis	large bacilli, endospores	+*	A	–	A*	+	+	–		–	+
Bacillus megaterium	large bacilli, endospores	+*	A*	–	A*	–	+	–		–	+
Citrobacter freundii	small bacilli, single	–	A+G	A+G	A+G	–	–	+	A/A, H₂S, G	–	+
Escherichia coli	small bacilli single	–	A+G	A+G	A+G	+	–	–	A/A, G	+	+
Enterobacter aerogenes	small bacilli single	–	A+G	A+G	A+G	+	–	+	K/A, G	–	+
Proteus vulgaris	small bacilli single	–	A+G	–	A*	–	–	+	K/A, H₂S	+	+
Proteus mirabilis	small bacilli single	–	A+G	–	A*	–*	–	+	K/A, H₂S	–	+
Alcaligenes faecalis	small bacilli single	–	–	–	–	–	+	+	K/K K/no change	–	+
Hafnia alvei	small bacilli single	–	A+G*	–	A+G	+	–	–	K/A, G*	–	+

*Results are variable **KIA results not reliable for G+ organisms A = acid K = alkaline G = gas

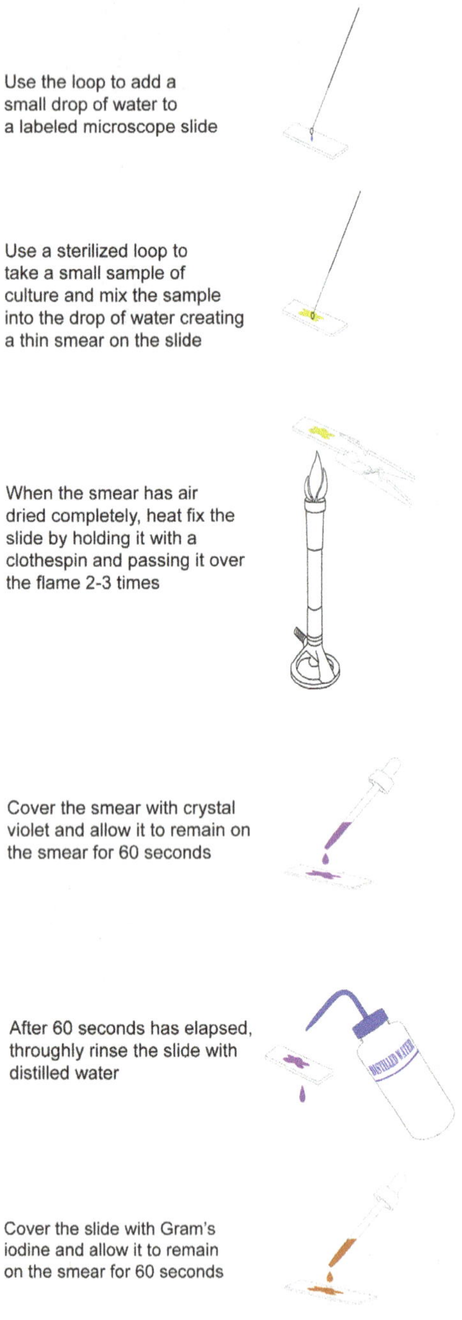

Exercise 5-2

Figure 5.4 steps (left column):

- Use the loop to add a small drop of water to a labeled microscope slide
- Use a sterilized loop to take a small sample of culture and mix the sample into the drop of water creating a thin smear on the slide
- When the smear has air dried completely, heat fix the slide by holding it with a clothespin and passing it over the flame 2-3 times
- Cover the smear with crystal violet and allow it to remain on the smear for 60 seconds
- After 60 seconds has elapsed, throughly rinse the slide with distilled water
- Cover the slide with Gram's iodine and allow it to remain on the smear for 60 seconds

FIGURE 5.4 Gram stain procedure

Day 2

Materials

- Incubated TSA plate of streaked saline cultures (1)
- TSA plates (2)
- Approved flowcharts

Work individually.

Procedure

1. Your TA will return the flowcharts from Day 1. The flowcharts may be approved or may contain comments about changes that you need to make before you begin testing your unknown cultures.

2. If your flowcharts are approved, and if you have well-isolated colonies of both types of bacteria on your plate, you are ready to perform a Gram stain and generate pure cultures of each type of organism.

   Note: If your colonies are not well isolated, or if you cannot differentiate the colonies of the two bacteria, it is important to consult your TA.

3. Circle a well-isolated colony of each type of organism on your plate.

4. Use a small sample of cells from each of two circled colonies to perform a Gram stain. Label each slide so you know which colony each sample originated from.

5. When Gram status has been obtained for each of your unknown bacteria, use a small amount of cells from the same colonies to produce three-phase streak plates. This step is done in order to generate pure cultures of each of the organisms. Include Gram status when labeling the plates.

6. Incubate the plates at 37°C for 24 hous.

   Note: After Gram staining and streaking, store mixed plates at 4°C in case you are unable to generate pure cultures on the first try.

Day 3

Materials

- TSA plates with pure cultures of the two unknown bacterial orgainsms
- Selected biochemical tests
- Gram stain reagents
- TSA plates

Work individually.

Procedure

1. Examine your two pure-culture plates. Verify with your TA that you have obtained two pure cultures.
2. Redo the Gram stain to verify the Gram status of the two organisms.
3. Examine your approved flowcharts to determine how to proceed with the identification of your unknown organisms.

   Note: You will lose points if you carry out an unnecessary test or inoculate a medium that is not needed to identify your unknown organisms.

4. Perform the appropriate tests that will help you to identify your two pure organisms. Use the Biochemical Media Quick Reference Guide for a quick reference on how to perform the tests.
5. Record all observations of test results in the *R & Q* section.
6. Make sure you have the result of any test performed before you carry out the next test. Many tests will need freshly grown cells for best test results. Therefore, it may be necessary to perform yet another three-phase streak on a fresh TSA plate before inoculating the next test medium.

After 60 seconds has elapsed, throughly rinse the slide with distilled water

Briefly rinse the slide with acetone-alcohol for 2-3 seconds

Immediately rinse the slide with distilled water

Completely cover the smear with safranin and allow it to remain on the smear for 90 seconds

After 90 seconds has elapsed, throughly rinse the slide with distilled water

Blot the slide dry using Bibulous Paper

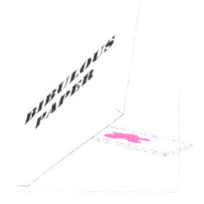

FIGURE 5.4 Gram stain procedure, cont.

Note: Each mix contains one Gram-positive species and one Gram-negative species. All possible bacteria and relevant cellular and metabolic characteristics are listed in the table "Characteristics of Bacteria". It is helpful to know that all unknown organisms are mesophiles and neutrophils; none of the unknown organisms are halophiles, and none are obligate anaerobes.

After recording your observation of the tests already performed, you should dispose of the tubes by placing them in the designated racks on the disposal cart after removing the tape.

When both of your unknown bacteria are correctly identified, dispose of all of your stored plates.

Days 4–6

Materials

- Pure cultures of unknown organisms, as needed
- Selected biochemical tests
- TSA plates

Work individually.

Procedure

1. Record all observations in the *R & Q* section.
2. Examine your approved flowcharts to determine if further testing is necessary. If you have any concerns about the results of your tests, consult your TA.
3. If more tests are needed, continue to run the appropriate tests of your two pure organisms that will help you to identify them. Use the Biochemical Media Quick Reference Guide and other material provided in this module to identify the two unknown organisms.
4. Make sure you have the result of any test performed before you carry out the next test. Many tests will need freshly grown cells for best test results. Therefore, it may be necessary to perform yet another three-phase streak on a fresh TSA plate before inoculating the next test medium.

After recording your observation of the tests already performed, you should dispose of the tubes by removing the tape and placing them in the designated racks on the disposal cart.

When both of your unknown bacteria are correctly identified, dispose of all of your stored plates.

Biochemical Media Quick Reference Guide

Cytochrome Oxidase

Period 1: Use a sterile **toothpick** to transfer a pea-sized amount of culture to make a smear on filter paper. Add one drop of oxidase reagent and observe the smear to see if it changes to a dark purple color within 30 seconds (dark purple = positive result). Positive result indicates the production of cytochrome oxidase which catalyzes oxidation-reduction reactions of the ETC during aerobic respiration

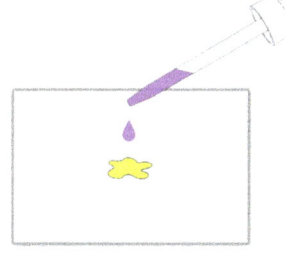

Catalase

Period 1: Use a sterile loop to transfer a visible sample of culture onto a clean microscope slide. Add 1-2 drops of H_2O_2 and look for the production of bubbles (bubbles = positive result). Positive result indicates the production of the enzyme Catalase which breaks down toxic H_2O_2 produced in aerobic respiration into the non-harmful byproducts H_2O and O_2

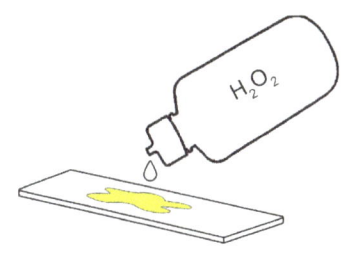

Glucose, Lactose and Mannitol Broth

Period 1: Inoculate medium by dipping an inoculated loop down into the medium (avoiding the Durham tube) Incubate at 37°C

Period 2: Observe for color change to yellow indicating acid production (carbohydrate fermented) and a bubble in the Durham tube indicating gas production

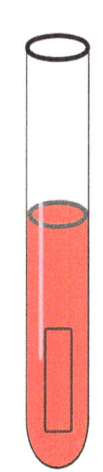

KIA

Period 1: Inoculate medium by using an inoculated **needle** to zig-zag streak the surface of the slant, then stab the medium almost all the way down to the bottom of the tube. Incubate at 37°C

Period 2: Observe for: Color change (red = protein use, yellow = acid production and carbohydrate fermentation of glucose and/or lactose), Cracks or breaks in the agar = Gas production (CO_2) and Black Precipitate = H_2S production (Desulfhydrase produced)

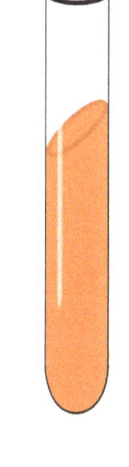

FIGURE 5.5 Biochemical Media Quick Reference Guide

Exercise 5-2

Biochemical Media Quick Reference Guide

Citrate

Period 1: Inoculate medium by using an inoculated loop to zig-zag streak the surface of the slant. Incubate at 37°C

Period 2: Observe for color change (color change to blue = positive result) Presence of a blue color indicates a pH change in the medium and the ability of the organism to use Citrate (citric acid) as a carbon source

Tryptone

Period 1: Inoculate medium by dipping inoculated loop down into the medium. Incubate at 37°C

Period 2: Vortex. Wear gloves. Add 6-8 drops of Kovac's solution and observe for color change (red ring = positive result, yellow ring = negative result) Positive result indicates tryptophanase is produced and the organism is able to break down tryptophan into pyruvate, ammonia and indole

MRVP

Period 1: Inoculate medium by dipping inoculated loop down into the medium. Incubate at 37°C

Period 2: Vortex. Transfer 0.5ml of culture in MRVP medium to a small test tube. **Wear gloves**. Add 15 drops of α-naphthol and 5 drops of KOH. Vortex and leave undisturbed for 15 min. Observe for color change (red ring = positive result) Positive result means acetoin is produced and glucose is fermented using the butanediol pathway

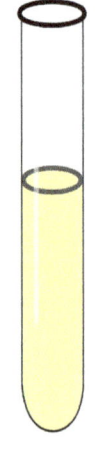

Exercise 5-2

R & Q

Record the number of your saline suspension

Unknown # _____

Explain why it is important to create pure cultures before examining the metabolic properties and other traits of an unknown bacterium.

_____
_____
_____
_____
_____
_____

Exercise 5-2

Report on Identification of Unknown Bacteria

Name: _____   Section: _____

Unknown #: _____   Date: _____

STATEMENT OF PURPOSE:

_____
_____
_____

Identification of Gram-positive unknown:

_____
_____
_____

Identification of Gram-negative unknown:

_____
_____
_____

Gram Reaction	Cellular Morphology	Cellular Arrangement	Colony Morphology
+			
−			

Exercise 5-2 225

Flow Chart PLAN for Identification of G+ Unknown

Name:_____   TA approval:_____

*Note: Use Catalase and Cytochrome Oxidase tests first since they yield immediate results

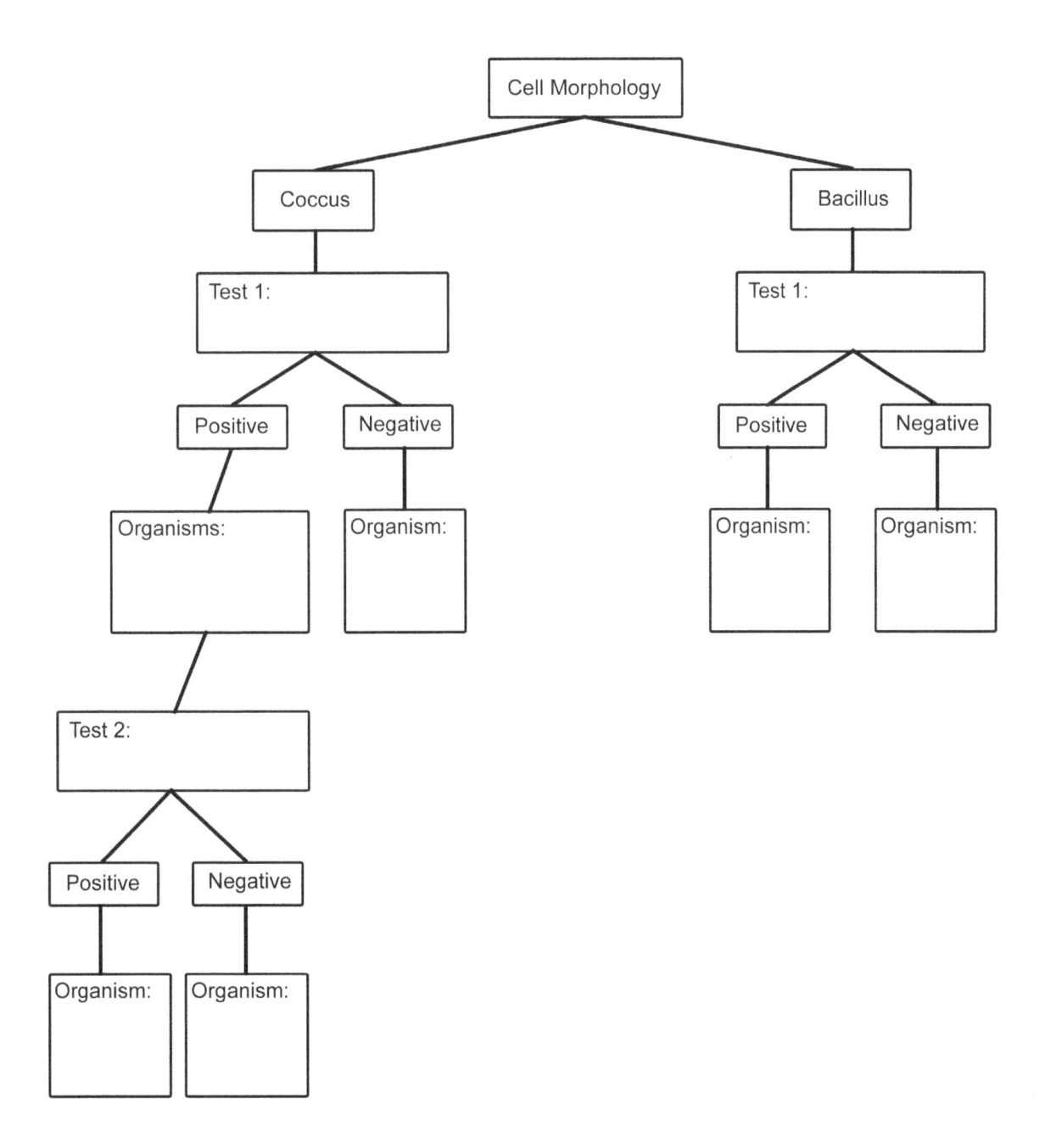

```
                        Cell Morphology
                        /             \
                    Coccus           Bacillus
                      |                 |
                   Test 1:           Test 1:
                   /     \           /      \
              Positive  Negative  Positive  Negative
                 |         |         |         |
             Organisms: Organism: Organism: Organism:
                 |
              Test 2:
              /     \
         Positive  Negative
            |         |
        Organism: Organism:
```

Exercise 5-2

Flow Chart PLAN for Identification of G- Unknown

Name:_____   TA approval:_____

```
                          ┌──────────────┐
                          │     KIA      │
                          │  pH of Tube  │
                          └──────────────┘
                 ┌────────────────┼────────────────┐
         ┌───────────────┐ ┌───────────────┐ ┌───────────────┐
         │  Result A:    │ │  Result B:    │ │  Result C:    │
         │     A/A       │ │ K/K, K/no chg │ │     K/A       │
         └───────────────┘ └───────────────┘ └───────────────┘
                 │                 │                 │
           Organisms:         Organism:         Organisms:
                 │                                   │
         ┌───────────────┐                 ┌───────────────┐
         │ KIA- H₂S prod │                 │ KIA- H₂S prod │
         └───────────────┘                 └───────────────┘
           Positive / Negative               Positive / Negative
           Organisms     Organisms           Organisms     Organisms
                             │                    │            │
                          Test 2:              Test 2:      Test 2:
                         Pos / Neg           Pos / Neg    Pos / Neg
                         Organism            Organism     Organism
```

- KIA — pH of Tube
  - Result A: A/A — Organisms:
    - KIA- H₂S production
      - Positive — Organisms:
      - Negative — Organisms:
        - Test 2:
          - Positive — Organism:
          - Negative — Organism:
  - Result B: K/K, K/no change — Organism:
  - Result C: K/A — Organisms:
    - KIA- H₂S production
      - Positive — Organisms:
        - Test 2:
          - Positive — Organism:
          - Negative — Organism:
      - Negative — Organisms:
        - Test 2:
          - Positive — Organism:
          - Negative — Organism:

DICHOTOMOUS KEY/Flowchart:

Include only your two unknown organisms in the flowchart

Exercise 5-2

Results of Metabolic Tests Used for the Identification of the Gram-Positive Unknown

Test	Results
1	
2	

Gram +

Gram −

Test	Results
1	
2	

Get to know your identified organisms. Do some research and describe your two organisms. Use approximately 200 – 250 words for each organism.

Describe, in your own words, anything you find interesting about your identified organisms. This could include information such as preferred habitats or whether your organism has been in the news regarding topics related to medicine, the environment, humans, or animals. Don't forget to cite your sources.

Organism 1

_____
_____
_____
_____
_____
_____
_____
_____
_____
_____

Organism 2

Exercise 5-2

Scientific references:

Control of Bacterial Growth

PHYSICAL FACTORS CONTROLLING BACTERIAL GROWTH

The examination of bacterial growth and the creation of growth curves provide essential information about how well microbes grow under certain circumstances. In the research laboratory, growth curves are often performed to examine the growth of microbial organisms such as bacteria and yeast.

Growth curves provide information about the growth of a microbial population over a given period of time. When bacteria grow in an environment with unlimited nutrients, they divide exponentially (at a constant rate), and their generation time can be determined. Factors such as the type of medium, pH, temperature, and the bacterial species themselves impact the length of the given organism's generation time. Most bacteria do not have access to unlimited nutrients, and their growth cannot remain exponential continuously; consequently, most bacterial growth curves consist of specific phases (i.e., lag phase, log phase, stationary phase, and death phase) (**Box 1**).

> **Box 1 Growth Phases**
>
> When bacteria are transferred to a new medium or they encounter an alteration of environment, they initially experience a change in growth during which the cells either do not divide or they divide very slowly. During this phase (the **lag phase**), cells adapt to their new surroundings and synthesize any materials needed to sustain growth under the new conditions. Once the cells have adapted, they begin to grow exponentially and enter the **log phase**. Eventually, when essential nutrients are depleted and waste products build up, the growth rate of the cells slows down, causing the cells to enter the **stationary phase**. During the stationary phase, the number of new cells equals the number of dead cells. If the growth conditions do not improve and essential nutrients do not become available, the cells enter the **death phase**.
>
> Measuring growth and establishing a growth curve for a particular microorganism under a certain defined condition is important in many industrial applications. For example, growth curves are useful in food microbiology when preparing fermented food products that require the concentration of microorganisms to be accurately controlled. Growth curves are also useful in the production of antibiotics, since it is often necessary to maintain the antibiotic-producing microbial culture at a specific growth phase to maximize the yield of the antibiotic being produced.
>
> **FIGURE 6.1** Growth curve

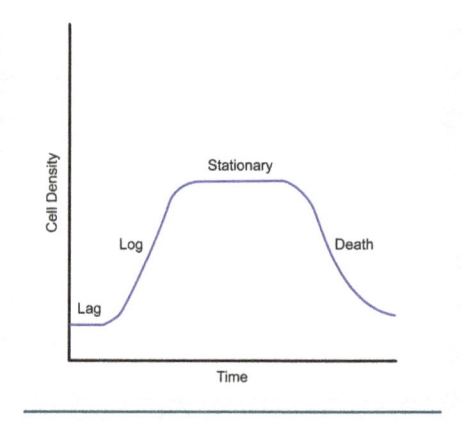

We have briefly seen that bacteria have a specific temperature range for optimal growth (Module 2) and that the microbes can be categorized according to their temperature optimums. Thus, temperature and media composition are components that affect bacterial growth. In this module, we will learn that other physical factors present in our environment can also control bacterial growth and even their survival. Such factors include pH, exposure to high salt concentrations, high temperatures, and UV rays.

Environmental pH plays a significant role in microbial growth. Every microbe has a specific pH range within which it can grow. The pH minimum of a given organism is defined as the lowest, and therefore the most acidic, pH level at which the organism can grow. The pH maximum is the highest and most alkaline pH at which the organism can grow. Between the maximum and minimum is the pH optimum. The microbe grows best at its pH optimum. As we will see in the following exercise, changes in environmental pH can result in reduced microbial growth rates or even elimination of growth altogether.

> **Box 2 Microbial Growth and pH**
>
> **pH** is a measure of the acidity or alkalinity of a solution, and it represents the relative number of hydrogen ions (H$^+$) versus hydroxide ions (OH$^-$) in a given solution. If the pH of a solution is 7, it is defined as neutral (i.e., the concentration of hydrogen ions equals that of the hydroxide ions). Below pH 7, the solution is acidic, and above pH 7, it is alkaline or basic.
>
> Some bacteria thrive best at low pH, and such organisms are called acidophiles. Other bacteria show optimal growth in alkaline environments, and these are the alkaliphiles. The majority of bacteria have a pH optimum of around pH 6.5 to pH 7.5, and these organisms are called neutrophiles.
>
> In general, carbohydrate-fermenting bacteria that produce acid by-products are tolerant of acidic pH. Proteolytic organisms, which produce alkaline by-products in the process of protein utilization, tolerate alkaline pH conditions well.

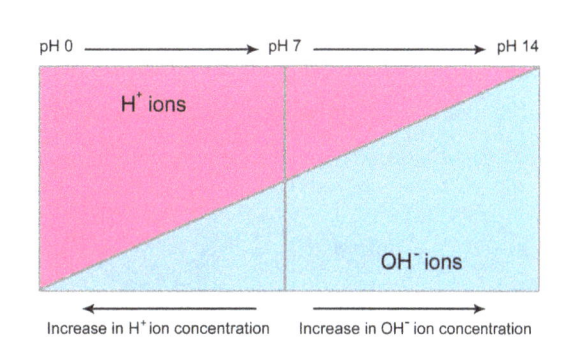

Just as bacteria have different pH and temperature tolerances, bacteria also exhibit dissimilar levels of salt tolerance. Indeed, some bacteria not only thrive in hypertonic solutions such as high salt solutions, but they also require higher salt concentrations to grow. Such organisms are called halophiles, and they typically grow in solutions containing from 5% up to 20% salt. Halotolerant organisms, on the other hand, can tolerate high salt concentrations but does not require salt to grow. A salt concentration around 0–2% is mostly used to grow nonhalophiles. In the exercise below, you will experience the effect that salt concentration has on controlling bacterial growth.

Fungi, bacteria, and viruses are killed by temperatures approaching the boiling point of water (100 °C), mostly due to the fact that enzymes and other cellular proteins are denatured at these high temperatures. Thus, high temperatures are often used as an efficient way to control the growth of microbes. Moist heat is more efficient in destroying microbial organisms. This is because the energy of moist heat is more readily transferred that the energy of dry heat. However, if endospore-forming bacteria such as *Bacillus* and *Clostridium* species have already undergone sporulation, their spores can survive even lengthy exposure to moist heat.

This resistance of endospores to high temperatures is caused by the presence of hydrophobic proteins in the endospore coat that help maintain the low internal concentration of water. Furthermore, heat-stable proteins located in the coat and inside the endospore itself function to maintain the stability of the endospore when exposed to high temperatures.

To ensure that endospores are killed by moist heat, it is best to apply heat under pressure. The best example of a device that can produce such conditions is the autoclave (Figure 2.1).

The increase in pressure inside an autoclave raises the boiling point of water and gives rise to steam temperatures around 121 °C, a condition that kills microbes; endospore-forming and non-endospore forming bacteria, viruses, and even endospores are destroyed within 15–20 minutes. Thus, the autoclave represents the fastest and most efficient means to eliminate the endospores. Most media and other laboratory materials are sterilized in an autoclave.

Ultraviolet (UV) radiation is another effective way to control the growth of microbes. Most effective at a wavelength around 260 nm, UV radiation is absorbed by nucleic acids, resulting in the formation of thymine dimers throughout the bacterial DNA. As these dimers are created, the likelihood of introducing an alteration in the genetic code of the microbial cells increases (Figure 6.2 "DNA and

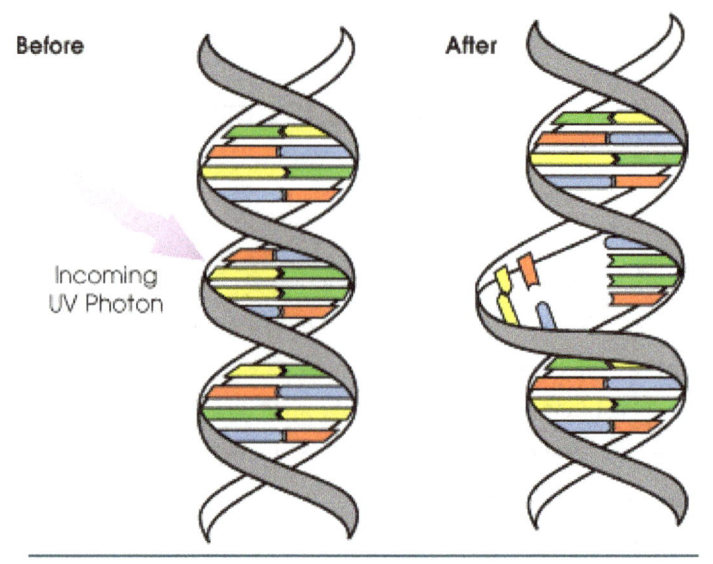

FIGURE 6.2 DNA and UV Radiation

UV Radiation"). This is because the presence of thymine dimers affects both DNA replication and transcription of DNA in the cells, and can therefore easily result in elimination of the microbial cell.

Although UV radiation can be used to control bacterial growth, there are several drawbacks associated with its use. The primary limiting factor is the poor ability of UV light to penetrate material such as glass, paper, cardboard, pus, or feces. These factors easily prevent the UV rays from coming into direct contact with the microbial cell.

Other limitations include the short distance that must be maintained between the source of radiation and the cells to be irradiated (about 15 cm) and the length of time needed to expose the bacteria to UV radiation (several minutes). In addition, UV radiation is not equally effective against all types of bacteria and, as above, endospores will survive longer UV light exposure than vegetative cells will.

Source: David Herring/NASA, https://commons.wikimedia.org/wiki/File%3ADNA_UV_mutation.png. Copyright in the Public Domain.

Osmosis is the diffusion of a solvent through a semipermeable membrane. In biology, the solvent is most often water; regarding bacteria, the membrane is the cell membrane.

Water moves freely across cell membranes, constantly flowing into and out of the cell. Osmosis occurs when there is an imbalance in the concentration of water molecules across the cell membrane. A net movement of water molecules takes place from the side of the cell membrane with the high water concentration to the side with the low water concentration. **Equilibrium** is reached when no *net* movement of water occurs: the rate of movement of water molecules into the cell is the same as the rate of movement of water molecules out of the cell.

The terms isotonic, hypertonic, and hypotonic describe the relative amount of solutes on either side of a semipermeable membrane.

> **Isotonic condition:** the concentration of solutes and water on either side of the membrane are the same. No net movement of water across that membrane takes place.
>
> **Hypertonic condition:** the concentration of solutes is higher (lower concentration of water) outside the cell compared to inside the cell (i.e., the cytoplasm). More water diffuses out of the cell than enters the cells until an equilibrium has been reached: the concentration of water is equalized on both sides of the membrane. If equilibrium cannot be reached, the cell's membrane may collapse due to the loss of water from the cytoplasm; this is called plasmolysis.
>
> **Hypotonic condition:** a lower concentration of solutes (and therefore a higher concentration of water) is present outside the cell compared to inside the cell (cytoplasm). More water will flow into the cell than out of the cell. If equilibrium is not obtained, the cell can swell as the cytoplasm gains water. This results in the buildup of osmotic pressure and increases the possibility that the cell will burst or lyse. In bacteria, lysis of cells generally does not happen because the bacterial cell membrane will be pressed against the rigid cell wall. However, a cell without a cell wall (such as a red blood cell) would burst when the osmotic pressure became excessive.

Osmotic pressure is the amount of pressure needed to stop the net flow of water across a semipermeable membrane. An imbalance in the concentration of solutes on either side of a membrane can result in the buildup of osmotic pressure if an equilibrium cannot be reached. If an equilibrium can be reached, the osmotic pressure determined by the solutions on each side will ensure that water is being pushed out of the cell at the same rate at which it enters the cell.

High osmotic pressures limit the growth of a variety of organisms that can cause food spoilage. High osmotica (e.g., solute concentrations like sugar or salt) are often used to preserve food. One example of a food with a high osmoticum is soy sauce.

Name two other foods that are preserved in a similar manner and indicate the type of solute employed in each case.

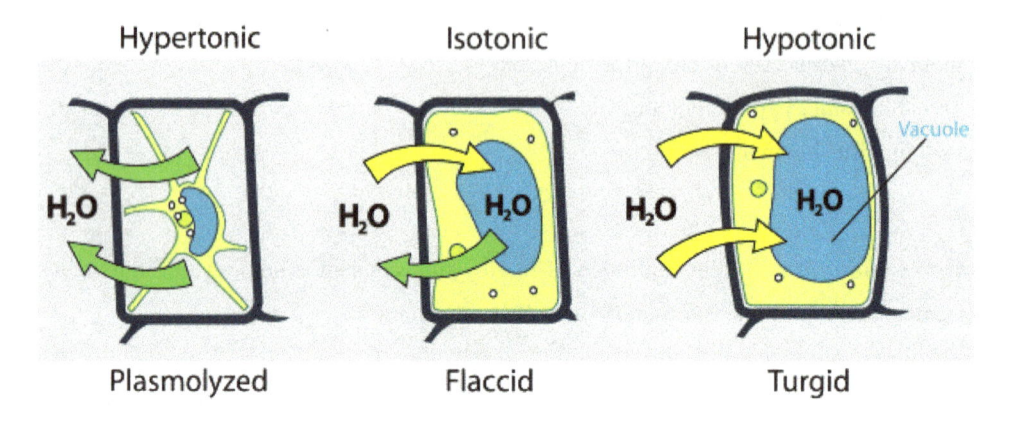

In biology, turgor pressure or turgidity, is the pressure of the cell contents against the cell wall. In plant cells, turgidity is determined by the water content of the vacuole, resulting from osmotic pressure.

Potato slices in hypo- and hypertonic solutions

This is a simple demonstration that can be done in the lab or simply at home. It is an excellent example that demonstrates the macroscopic effects of cells' gaining or losing water.

Materials

- Two bottom-half Petri dishes, one containing distilled water and the other containing a 20% salt solution
- Two thick slices of potato

Before each slice of potato is placed in the respective solutions, both slices have the same amount of turgor (rigidity). After immersing the slices for 20 minutes or longer in the hypotonic (distilled water) or hypertonic (20% salt) solutions, the changes in the amount of turgor of the potato slices can be examined. This is done by picking up each slice of potato and gently flexing it.

Source: LadyofHats, https://commons.wikimedia.org/wiki/File:Turgor_pressure_on_plant_cells_diagram.svg. Copyright in the Public Domain.

FIGURE 6.3 Potato in 20 % and 0 % water.

Relate the amount of water contained within each potato cell to the amount of turgor.

In the exercises to follow, you will challenge bacterial growth by incubating them in media with different pH levels and salt concentrations. You will also investigate survival of bacteria after exposure to high temperatures and UV radiation. However, first you will compare the effect of nutritional availability on the growth rate of a bacterial organism.

Exercise 6-1

Growth Curve

Objectives

To learn about bacterial growth and the respective growth phases.
To understand the basic principles of the growth curve.
To become familiar with the spectrophotometer and how it is used.

In this exercise, you will generate growth curves of a bacterial organism grown in minimal and in rich medium. In order to do so, you will use a spectrophotometer to collect OD (optical density) measurements. You will determine generation times (doubling times) and illustrate the various stages of the growth curve by plotting data onto graph paper.

To determine cell numbers and illustrate the growth phases of bacterial cultures, it is necessary to measure the **optical density** (**OD**) using a **spectrophotometer**. A spectrophotometer measures the amount of light of a specified wavelength that passes through a sample of bacterial cells. Wavelengths of light are measured in nanometers (nm) (e.g., 600nm). The principle behind these turbidity measurements is that the light that is scattered by the bacterial cells is proportional to the concentration of bacterial cells in the culture. In order to relate the absorbance reading to the cell density (cells/ml), a standard curve has been constructed and saved in the spectrophotometer memory. An OD =1 corresponds approximately to 10^9 cells /ml.

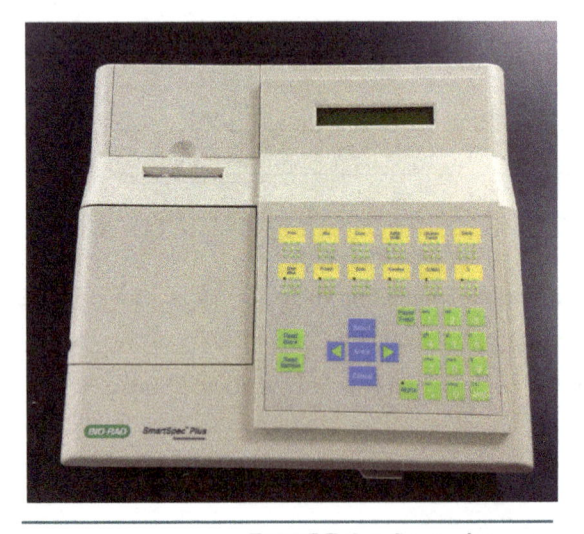

When measuring the concentration of a sample, uninoculated growth medium is first placed in a cuvette and then inserted into the spectrophotometer. This first reading serves as a reference (a blank). Next, a sample of the bacterial culture grown in the same type of medium is inserted into the machine and the OD is recorded. These steps are repeated to obtain measurements at consistent time intervals. The results are then graphed to illustrate the growth curve for the organism.

FIGURE 6.4 Spectrophotometer

Materials

- *E. coli* culture grown in minimal medium (MM1 broth) (1)
- *E. coli* culture grown in rich medium (BHI broth) (1)
- P1000 and P200 micropipettes or 1 ml serological pipettes
- Tips

Work in groups of four and with the entire class.

Procedure

As a class, you will collect OD_{600} measurements at various time points of *Escherichia coli* cultures grown in a shaker at 37°C. You will be collecting samples starting at zero minutes and ending after 5–8 hours. You may need your lab instructor's help to collect the late time points.

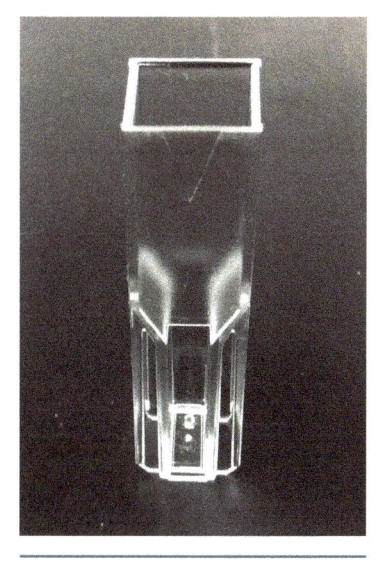

FIGURE 6.5 Cuvette

1. At your assigned time point, use the micropipettes or a 1 ml serological pipette to remove 1000 µl (1 ml) from the 250 ml *E. coli* culture growing in BHI. Dispense the 1000 µl of culture into a clean cuvette.

   Note: It is important to only touch the top portion of the cuvettes when handling them. This must be done in order to prevent leaving fingerprints on the bottom half of the cuvette, which will interfere with the OD reading.

2. Insert a BHI blank (cuvette containing uninoculated medium) into the spectrophotometer. Make sure to follow the provided instructions for how to insert the cuvettes into the spectrophotometer correctly.
3. Follow the instructions for how to read the blank, and set it to zero.
    Remove the blank.
4. Insert the cuvette containing the 1000 µl of E. coli culture grown in BHI into the spectrometer. Read the sample as the instructions indicate. Record the reading and remove the cuvette.
5. Repeat the procedure for the *E. coli* culture growing in MM1.

Exercise 6-1

Note: If your OD_{600} reading is higher than 0.8, you will need to dilute your sample 10X for an accurate reading. To do this, transfer 200 µl culture to a tube containing 1800 µl of uninoculated medium. Vortex the tube and transfer 1000 µl of the diluted cells into a fresh cuvette. Multiply your reading by ten before recording the reading.

Note: If your OD_{600} reading is higher than 10, you will need to dilute your sample 20X for an accurate reading. To do this, transfer 200 µl of culture to a tube containing 1800 µl of un-inoculated medium. Vortex the tube and transfer 1000 µl into a tube containing 1000 µl of uninoculated medium. Vortex the tube and transfer 1000 µl of the 20X diluted culture into a fresh cuvette. Multiply the reading by twenty before recording reading.

6. As a class, continue to record readings every 15 minutes until all necessary OD measurements have been the obtained. Make sure you have all OD measurements from the individual groups of the entire class.
7. Use the data to graph the growth curve on the graph paper in the *R & Q* section. Label lag phase, exponential phase, stationary phase, and dead phase, if present.

Exercise 6-1

R & Q

Time (minutes)	BHI OD$_{600}$	Number of cells per ml of culture	MM1 OD$_{600}$	Number of cells per ml of culture
0 Provided				

For bacterial cells: OD$_{600}$ = 1, corresponds to approximately 10^9 cell/ml culture. Use this information to calculate the number of cells per ml of culture.

Graph Time (minutes) vs. OD$_{600}$ for both BHI and MM1 on the graphs provided on the following pages.

Exercise 6-1

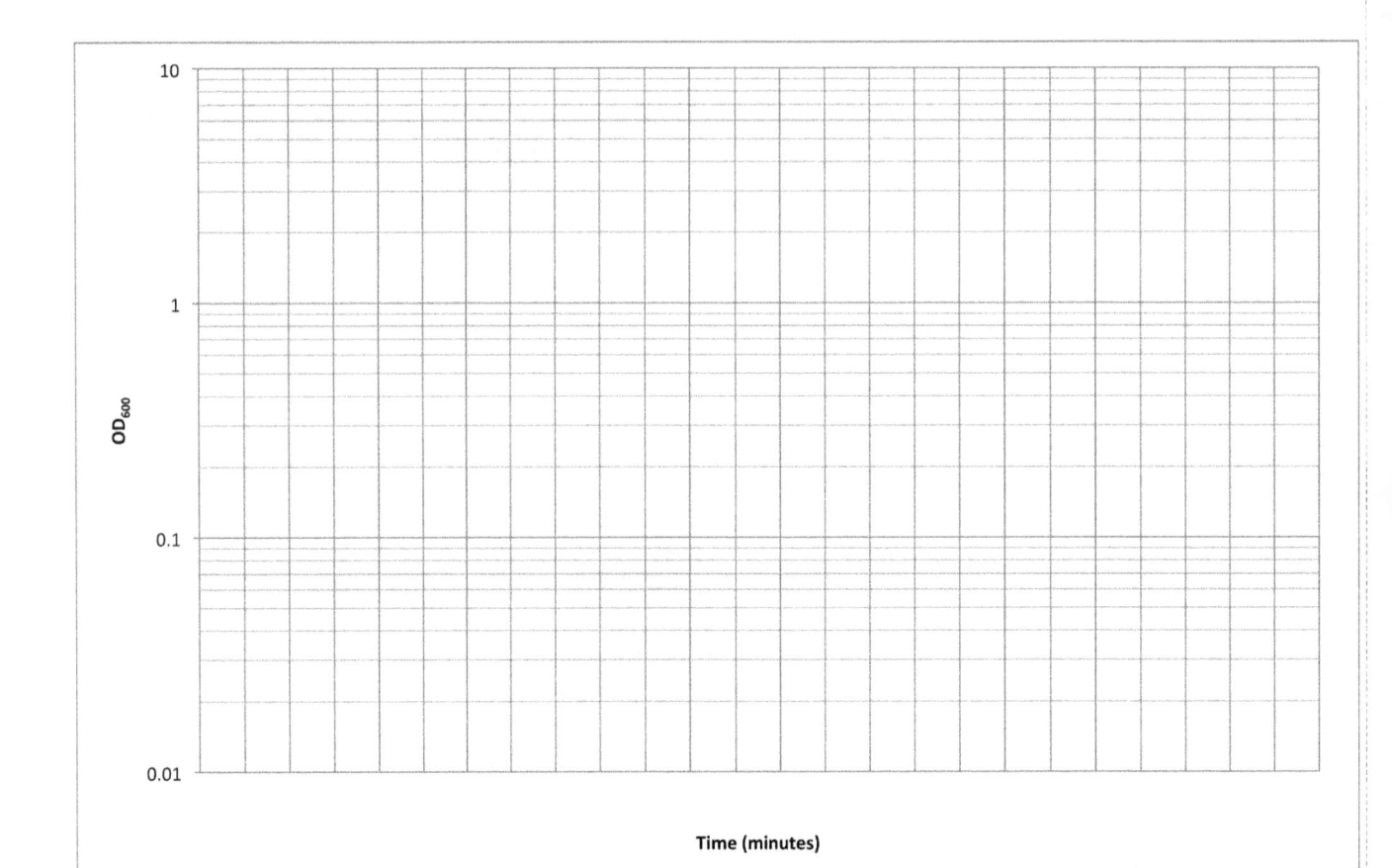

OD$_{600}$

10

1

0.1

0.01

Time (minutes)

Exercise 6-1 243

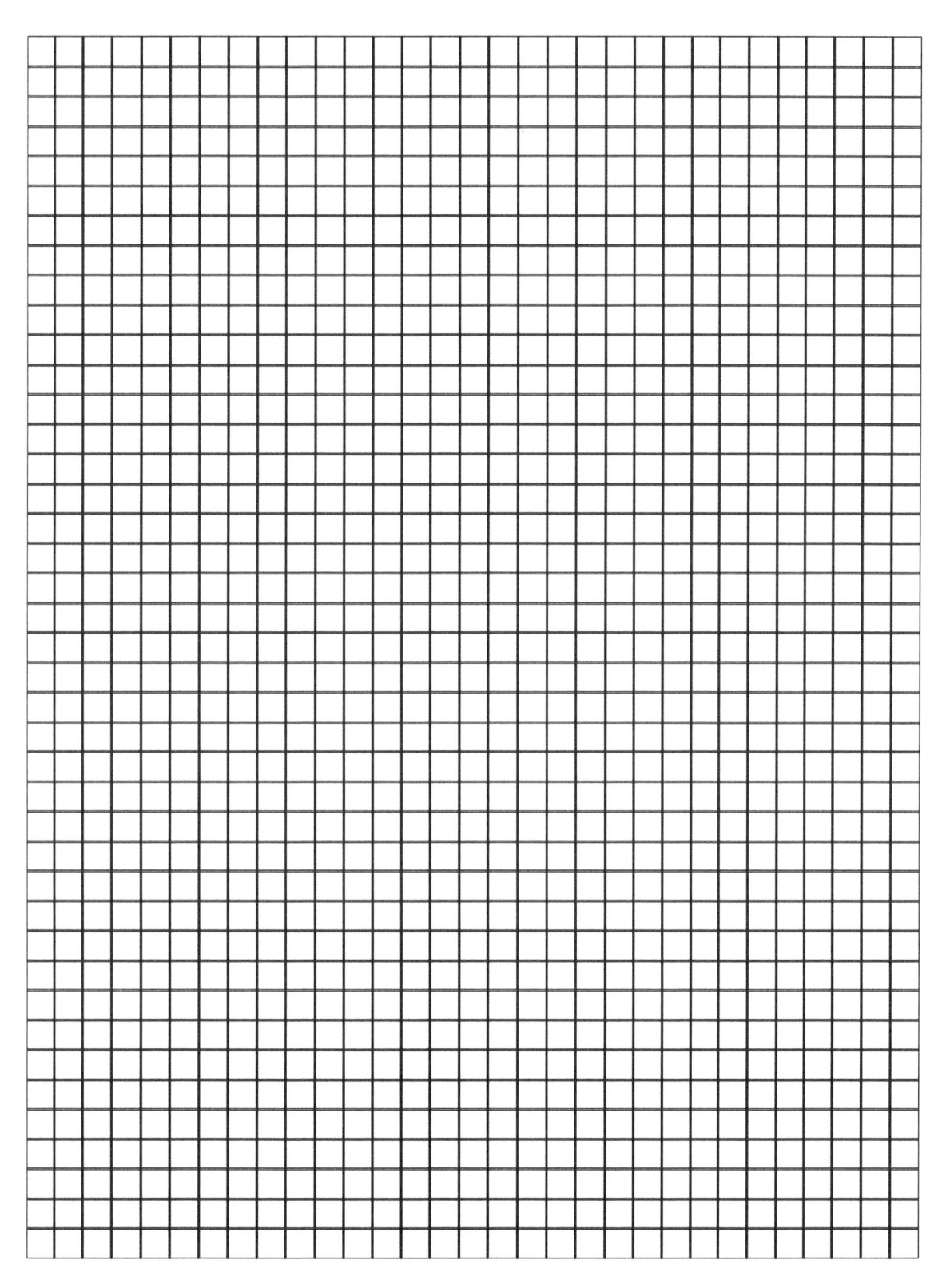

OD$_{600}$

Time (minutes)

Exercise 6-1

Calculate the number of cells per ml of culture. Record your values in the table on the previous page.

> Note: to obtain cells/ml culture, multiply the OD_{600} reading by 10^9. If you have diluted the samples, remember to include the dilution factor in the calculation. $OD_{600}=1$ corresponds to about 10^9 *E. coli* cells per ml.

Explain what you notice when comparing the growth curves and cells/ml of the *E. coli* cultures grown in MM1 and BHI.

_____
_____
_____

Define generation time.

_____
_____
_____

Using the graphs you created, extrapolate the generation time of *E. coli*.

_____
_____
_____

Describe the advantage of plotting the data using semilogarithmic graph paper.

_____
_____
_____

If the growth curve was conducted at 25°C instead of 37°C temperature, would this change the growth rate of the organisms?

_____
_____
_____

Effect of pH on Bacterial Growth

Learning Objectives

To observe the effects of environmental pH on the growth of microbes.

To get familiar with the terms pH maximum, pH minimum, pH optimum, acidophile, alkaliphile, and neutrophile.

In this exercise, you will examine the effects of pH on microbial growth by inoculating growth media that have been adjusted to acidic, neutral, or alkaline pH, respectively.

Day 1

Materials

- Broth Cultures (3)
    - *E. coli*
    - *S. griseus*
    - *S. cerevisiae*
- Nutrient Agar plate pH 4
- Nutrient Agar plate pH 7
- Nutrient Agar plate pH 10

Work in groups of four.

1. Label each plate according to the pH of the media.
2. Label each sector of the plate with one of the following:
    Escherichia coli
    Streptomyces griseus
    Saccharomyces cerevisiae
3. Use a sterile inoculating loop, inoculate the plates with each of the bacterial strains by performing a zig-zag streak.
4. Incubate the plates at 30°C 24 hours.

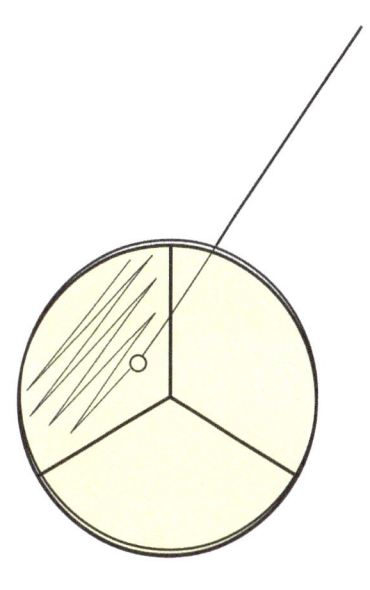

Exercise 6-2

Day 2

Material

- pH-adjusted Nutrient Agar plates inoculated in previous lab period.

1. Record your observations regarding the growth in the various pH- adjusted Nutrient Agar plates in the table in the *R & Q* section.

R & Q

Organism	pH 4	pH 7	pH 10
Escherichia coli			
Streptomyces griseus			
Saccharomyces cerevisiae			

Which of the organism(s) appears to be the least tolerant to low pH?
___
___
___

Are any of the organisms above acidophiles? Explain your answer.
___
___
___

Which organism(s) appears to show the broadest range of pH tolerance?
___
___
___

Which organism(s) appears to show the narrowest range of pH tolerance?

If you wanted to culture a bacterium that has an optimum pH at 8.0, will media adjusted to pH 6.5 be a good choice? Explain your answer.

Exercise 6-3

Effects of Osmotic Pressure on Bacterial Growth

Learning Objectives

To understand how relative solute concentrations can affect the movement of solvent particles across a semi-permeable membrane (osmosis).

To define the terms hypotonic, hypertonic, and isotonic and how such conditions affect bacterial growth.

In this exercise, you will expose bacteria to broth media containing various salt concentrations and examine their abilities to tolerate hypertonic conditions.

Day 1

Materials

- Droppers (3)
- Bacterial Broth Cultures (3)
    - *E. coli*
    - *S. epidermidis*
    - *H. volcanii*
- Haloferax volcanii medium (HVM):
    - 0% NaCl (3)
    - 5% NaCl (3)
    - 10% NaCl (3)
    - 20% NaCl (3)

Work in groups of four.

1. Label tubes, including the type of medium, the concentration of NaCl, and the respective bacterial strains.
    Escherichia coli
    Staphylococcus epidermidis
    Haloferax volcanii

2. Using a sterile dropper, inoculate each set of four HVM tubes with two drops of the indicated culture.
3. Set aside the four tubes that were inoculated with Haloferax volcanii. This organism needs incubation in a shaker at 37°C, since it requires aeration in order to grow properly.
4. Incubate all other tubes at 37°C without shaking.
5. Incubate all cultures for 48 hours.

Day 2

Material

- HVM cultures inoculated in previous lab period.

Work in groups of four.

Procedure

1. In the table in the *R & Q* section, record your observations of the growth of each organism at the various salt concentrations.

   Note: Remember to resuspend each culture by vortexing before you examine each tube for growth. Why?

R & Q

Organism	0% NaCl	5% NaCl	10% NaCl	20% NaCl
Escherichia coli				
Staphylococcus epidermidis				
Haloferax volcanii				

Exercise 6-3

Are any of the organisms tested salt tolerant? If so, which one(s)?

_____
_____
_____

Halophiles can not only thrive in media with high salt concentrations; they require salt to grow. This means that relatively high concentrations of salt must be present in a medium/environment before the organism is able to grow. Are there any salt-requiring organisms among the three that you tested? Explain your answer.

_____
_____
_____

Effect of High Temperature on Viability of Bacteria

Learning Objective

To get familiar with the heat resistance of bacterial endospores in comparison to vegetative endospore-forming and non-endospore-forming bacterial organisms.

In this exercise, you will expose different bacterial species to high temperature (80°C) for various lengths of time. The bacterial organisms are resuspended in saline and include *Staphylococcus epidermidis* (which does not form endospores), *Bacilus subtilis* vegetative cells, and *Bacillus subtilis* endospores. Following incubation, you will observe which bacterial suspension(s) was the most resistant to high temperatures.

Day 1

Materials

- Saline suspension of bacteria
- TSB tubes (6)

Work in groups of four.

Procedure

1. Label the saline suspension and the set of six TSB tubes, including the name of your assigned bacterial organism:

    Staphylococcus epidermidis
    or
    Bacillus subtilis endospore
    or
    Bacillus subtilis vegetative

2. Label each TSB tube with the following time points:

    Control (0 min.)
    2 min.

Exercise 6-4

       5 min.
       10 min.
       20 min.
       30 min.

3. Using aseptic technique, inoculate the 0-min. TSB control tube with a loopful of your assigned organism.
4. Place the tube containing the saline cell suspension into a test tube rack in the 80°C water bath.
5. After incubating the saline culture for 2 minutes in the 80°C water bath, aseptically remove a loopful of the cells from the saline suspension.
6. Use this loopful of saline cell suspension to inoculate the 2-min.-labeled TSB tube.
7. Return the original tube of saline cell suspension to the water bath immediately.
8. Leave the saline suspension in the water bath for an additional 3 minutes and inoculate the 5-minutes TSB tube as above.

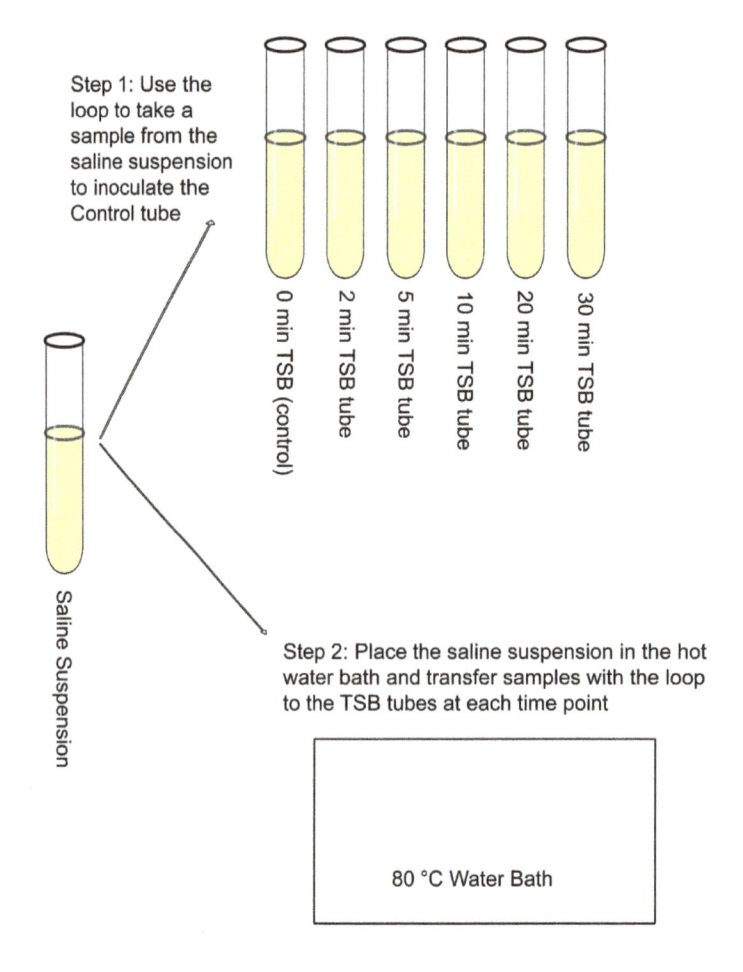

Step 1: Use the loop to take a sample from the saline suspension to inoculate the Control tube

0 min TSB (control)
2 min TSB tube
5 min TSB tube
10 min TSB tube
20 min TSB tube
30 min TSB tube

Saline Suspension

Step 2: Place the saline suspension in the hot water bath and transfer samples with the loop to the TSB tubes at each time point

80 °C Water Bath

Exercise 6-4

9. Repeat for all time points.
10. Incubate all the inoculated TSB tubes at 37 °C for 24 hours.

Day 2

Materials

- TSB tubes inoculated previous lab period

Work in groups of four.

Procedure

1. Record your observations of the growth of each of the bacterial organisms after exposure to high temperature for the indicated times.

   Note: Remember to vortex each tube before examining for growth.

R & Q

Organism	Control	2 min	5 min	10 min	20 min	30 min
Staphylococcus epidermidis						
Bacillus subtilis vegetative cells						
Bacillus subtilis endospores						

Which of the cell types tested was most resistant to exposure to high temperature?

_____
_____
_____

Was this result expected? Explain your answer.

_____
_____
_____

Effect of UV Radiation on Bacterial Viability

Learning Objectives

To understand the effects of UV radiation as well as its limiting factors associated with the control of microbial growth.

To compare the effects of UV radiation on the viability of bacterial endospores, vegetative endospore-forming bacterial organisms, and non-endospore-forming bacterial organisms.

Day 1

Materials

- Saline suspension (3)
    - *S. epidermidis*
    - *B. subtilis* vegetative
    - *B. subtilis* endospores
- TSA plates (18)
- Sterile swabs (3)
- UV crosslinker

Work as an entire class.

In this exercise, both vegetative cells and endospores of *Bacillus subtilis*, as well as vegetative cells of the non-endospore former *Staphylococcus epidermidis*, will be exposed to ultraviolet radiation, and their viability will be assessed. The bacteria will be exposed to UV rays at a wavelength of 254 nm using an ultraviolet crosslinker. We will examine the limits of UV penetration and the length of time required to achieve sterilization.

Procedure

1. Label a set of six TSA plates. Include the name of one of the bacterial strains and the length of time of UV exposure

    Staphylococcus epidermidis
    Control 0 min.

0.2 min.
0.5 min.
1 min.
5 min.
5 min. with lid

2. Similarly, label the set of six plates for each of the two remaining types of bacteria:
   Bacillus subtilis vegetative cells
   Bacillus subtilis endospores
3. Using a sterile swab, aseptically streak the six *S. epidermidis* plates with culture to form a lawn of growth. Carefully reinoculate the swab between each plate.
4. Use a second and third sterile swab to similarly inoculate the remaining two sets of six plates with either *B. subtilis* vegetative cells or *B. subtilis* endospores.
5. Set aside the control plates, as they will not be exposed to UV radiation. These plates will serve as **positive controls** to confirm viability of the bacteria prior to UV exposure.
6. Use the provided instructions to set the timer on the UV crosslinker for 0.2 minutes.
7. Remove the lids from all three of the 0.2-min. plates and place them into the exposure chamber of the UV crosslinker. Irradiate the plates for 0.2 minutes, replace the lids back on the plates, and remove the plates from the chamber.
8. Repeat the steps for the remaining plates (except the plates labeled "5 min. with lid"), exposing each for the time intervals indicated on the plate (0.5 min., 1 min. and 5 min.).

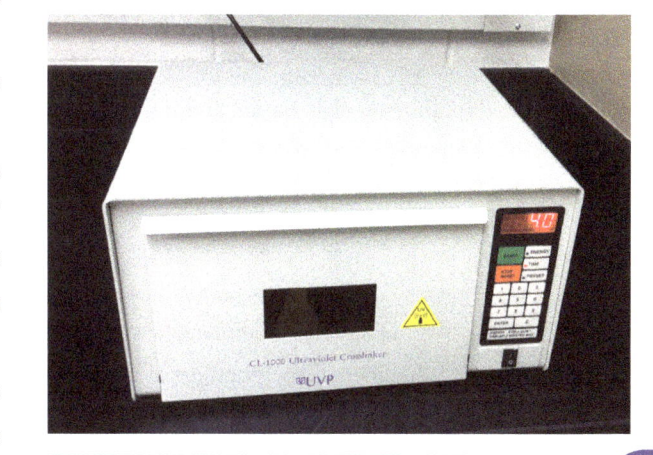

FIGURE 6.6 UV Crosslinker

9. Place the plates labeled "5 min. with lid" into the chamber without removing the lids. Expose the covered plates to UV radiation for 5 minutes.
10. Invert the plates and incubate at 37°C for 24 hours.

Exercise 6-5

Day 2

Material

- Plates exposed to UV radiation in previous lab period.

Work as an entire class.

Procedure

Examine and record the growth of each organism after the various time periods of exposure to UV radiation.

Organism	Control	0.2 min	0.5 min	1 min	5 min	5 min with lid
Staphylococcus epidermidis						
Bacillus subtilis vegetative cells						
Bacillus subtilis endospores						

Explain your observation and if the results are as you expected.

_____
_____
_____

In some laboratories, laminar flow hoods are used to help reduce contamination problems. These open-front chambers direct the flow of air through the hood to filters that collect airborne contaminants. They are also equipped with UV lights. Describe which limitations may prevent the UV light from controlling contamination in this hood.

_____
_____
_____

CHEMICAL FACTORS CONTROLLING BACTERIAL GROWTH

Human skin provides a distinct habitat for microorganisms, just as hot sulfur springs and salt marshes do. Our sweat and oil glands secrete a variety of components like urea, amino acids, lactic acid, lipids, fatty acids, and salts, many of which affect the pH of the skin and create a suitable habitat for certain microbes. Combined with periods of drying, these conditions and components assist in determining which microbes will comprise the **normal microbiota** of the skin. Together, these factors also produce an environment that generally is uninviting for **transient microbiota (Box 3)**.

Box 3 Transient Microbiota

Transient microbiota are the bacteria, mold spores, etc. that are temporarily found on our skin as a result of touching objects in our environment.

Normal microbiota are the bacteria that usually inhabit our body (either on the skin or internally), and they cause us no harm under normal circumstances. The normal microbiota of the skin include *Staphylococcus aureus, Staphylococcus epidermidis, Corynebacterium, Acinetobacter* species, and certain yeasts such as the *Pityrosporum* species. Most normal skin microbiota is situated in the natural open spaces on the skin provided by oil glands or sebaceous glands that are associated with hair follicles.

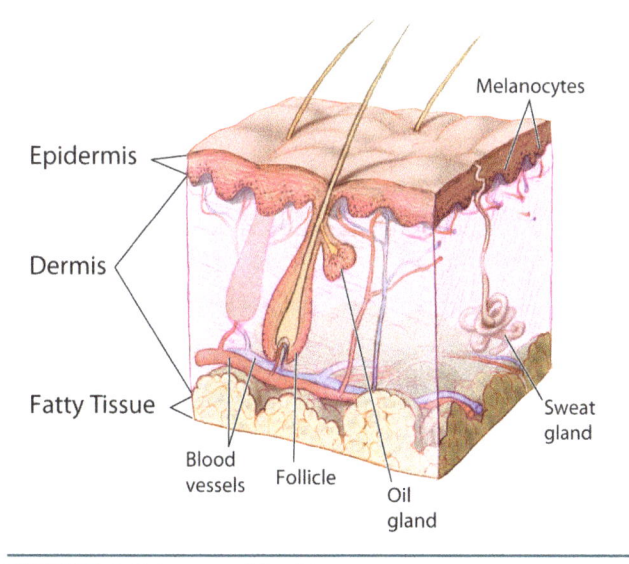

FIGURE 6.7 Anatomy of the skin

Don Bliss, https://commons.wikimedia.org/wiki/File%3AAnatomy_The_Skin_-_NCI_Visuals_Online.jpg. Copyright in the Public Domain.

> **Box 4 Antiseptics**
>
> **Antiseptics** are agents used for topical (surface) application to living tissues.
>
> **Disinfectants** are applied topically to only inanimate (nonliving) materials. These agents may cause damage to living tissue.
>
> Depending on the circumstances, some of these chemical agents may be used as either antiseptics or disinfectants. One example is hydrogen peroxide (H_2O_2), which can damage living tissue but is also used for cleaning deep wounds like puncture wounds. When hydrogen peroxide comes in contact with catalase that has been released from the damaged cells, the enzymatic action on H_2O_2 results in the release of oxygen (recall the catalase exercise). The release of oxygen reduces the probability of becoming infected by obligate anaerobes such as *Clostridium tetani*, the causative agent of tetanus. Iodine is another example of this type of dual-purpose agent. Other agents that are strictly used as disinfectants are bleach and Lysol.

The extensive eradication of bacteria from the human body may seem appealing to people who are unaware of the positive aspects of our associations with normal microbiota. However, total elimination of normal microbiota can be quite harmful. For example, normal microbes found in the oral cavity help prevent the colonization of harmful organisms such as the yeast *Candida albicans*, the causative agent of candidiasis.

Although the total elimination of normal microbiota is undesirable, it is still important to control microbial growth, both on living and nonliving surfaces, in order to prevent disease. Two groups of chemical agents typically used for controlling microbial growth are **antiseptics** and **disinfectants** **(Box 4)**.

Antibiotics are among the most widely used (and abused!) antimicrobial agents. Antibiotics are chemicals that are naturally produced by some soil bacteria and fungi and either inhibit or kill other microbial organisms. The best-known antibiotic, penicillin, is made by fungi that belong to the genus *Penicillium*. The largest number of bacterial antibiotic-producing species belongs to the genus *Streptomyces*.

Generally, the mode of actions of antibiotics on bacterial species include:

> Inhibition of cell wall synthesis (e.g., penicillin);
> Inhibition of protein synthesis (e.g., erythromycin);
> Inhibition of nucleic-acid synthesis (e.g., rifampin);
> Negative alteration of the plasma membrane (e.g., polymyxin B).

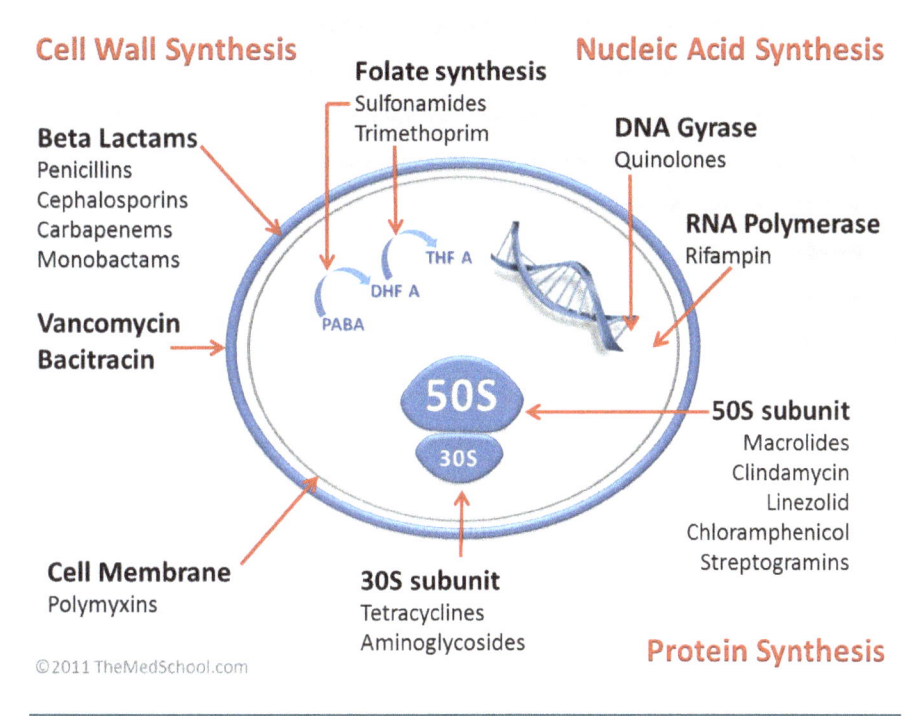

FIGURE 6.8 Action of antibiotics

Copyright © Kendrick Johnson (CC BY-SA 3.0) at https://commons.wikimedia.org/wiki/File%3AAntibiotics_Mechanisms_of_action.png.

Most microorganisms are either killed or inhibited by antibiotics; viruses are rarely affected by these antimicrobials (rifamycins, such as rifampin, are one exception; they inhibit poxvirus replication).

Do some research. Describe how penicillin was discovered and specify its mode of action.

_____
_____
_____

If a bacterium is killed, the antibiotic is referred to as bactericidal towards that specific organism. Antibiotics that—instead of killing the organism—inhibit the growth of the organism are said to be bacteriostatic. However, some antibiotics might be bacteriostatic under a given set of conditions and bactericidal under a different set of conditions. For example, changing the concentration of the antibiotic, or using it against the bacteria in certain growth phases, can change the effectiveness of the antibiotic.

Antibiotics can be categorized based on the range of microorganisms they kill or inhibit. **Broad-spectrum antibiotics** affect a wide range of bacteria, while **narrow-spectrum antibiotics** are effective against a limited range of bacteria. If possible, it is preferable to use a narrow-spectrum antibiotic for the treatment of disease. As we already know, this is because normal microbiota (in intestines, mouth and nasal passages, etc.) must be maintained. A broad-spectrum antibiotic will affect not only disease-causing organisms but also normal microbiota.

In the following exercises, you will determine the effect of different chemical antibacterial compounds. You will become familiar with, and take advantage of, the different methods available to evaluate the effectiveness of the compounds. Such methods include the minimal inhibitory concentration (MIC), the Kirby-Bauer method, and the determination of the zone of inhibition, including the Etest strip method.

The minimum inhibitory concentration

The minimum inhibitory concentration (or MIC) of an antibiotic is the lowest concentration of an antibiotic needed to inhibit the growth of a particular organism under laboratory conditions. The MIC test is performed by serial diluting a bacterial culture. Known concentrations of the antibiotic to be tested are added to each of the dilutions. The lowest concentration of antibiotics that results in inhibition of the bacterial growth is the MIC. The measurements are made in µg/ml, and the information is used to determine the concentration of an antibiotic to be administered to treat the given bacterial infection.

Disadvantages of using this method include the fact that MIC is assessed in vitro, (outside of the body) and the concentrations determined may not actually be suitable to treat the infection inside the body. For example, MIC may be so high that the concentration of the antibiotic is toxic to the patient, or it may be low and quickly metabolized by the body, making it difficult to mimic MIC in the human body.

For most of the common bacterial infections, MICs do not need to be calculated, since methods like the Kirby-Bauer disk-diffusion method will provide sufficient data for determining which antibiotic to use to clear the infection. However, when more precise information concerning possibly antibiotic-resistant bacterial strains is needed, a rapid way of determine MIC is through the use of the Etest.

The Kirby-Bauer method

The Kirby-Bauer method, named after two researchers who developed the test in the mid-1960s, examines microbial sensitivity to antibiotics by taking advantage of special filter disks containing standard test concentrations of antibiotics. The organisms to be tested are spread onto a agar plate to form a lawn of growth, the antibiotic-containing filter disks are dispensed onto the plate, and the plate is incubated. If the organism is susceptible to an antibiotic, a zone of inhibition will appear surrounding the disk (Figure 6.9 "Kirby-Bauer").

To determine whether the effect of the antibiotic on the bacterial species is bactericidal (kills the bacterium) or bacteriostatic (inhibits growth of, but does not kill, the bacteria), a subculture can be made as follows: an inoculum from the zone of inhibition is transferred into/onto a fresh medium and incubated. Growth in/on this media indicates that the antibiotic is bacteriostatic; the absence of growth means that the antibiotic is bactericidal.

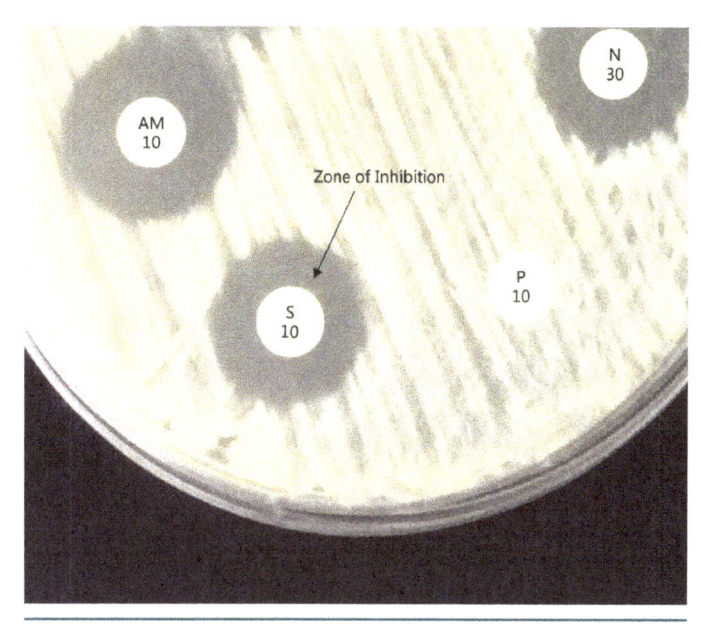

FIGURE 6.9 Kirby-Bauer method pointing out zone of inhibition

The Etest

The Etest uses plastic strips with a concentration gradient of a given antibiotic impregnated on one side. The strip can readily be positioned on the surface of a spread plate inoculated with cells of the bacterium in question. After incubation, the MIC can be directly read by observing where the growth intersects with the strip.

You will also transform bacterial cells using plasmid DNA that carries genes that, when expressed, will alter the susceptibility for certain antibiotics. Plasmids are circular pieces of DNA that replicate (copy themselves) independently of the chromosome of the bacterial cell. During the transformation procedure, cells take up the plasmid molecules and subsequently express the genes carried by the plasmid DNA. You will experience that the bacterial cells transform from antibiotic-sensitive to antibiotic-resistant cells when harboring such a plasmid.

Several bacterial genera are able to differentiate, or change, in response to certain environmental signals. You are already aware of the fact that members of the genus *Bacillus* produce endospores when exposed to nutritional stress.

Fungi and bacteria belonging to the genus *Streptomyces* also produce spores under conditions of stress; however, these spores are quite different from endospores. Fungal spores and spores of *Streptomyces* serve a reproductive function rather than a protective function. Compared to endospores, these spores are not as resistant to harsh stress and environmental conditions such as heat and drying.

Despite the differences of endospores and spores regarding structure and function, both are associated with the production of antibiotics. A number of *Bacillus, Streptomyces*, and fungal species produce antibiotics as their cells begin to sporulate. These antibiotics function to inhibit the growth of organisms located nearby. This decreases the competition for nutrients in the immediate vicinity and provides a distinct advantage for the antibiotic producers, at times with limited nutrients. In microbiological terms, this phenomenon is called antibiosis ("against life"); in ecological terms, it is known as allelopathy ("making your neighbor suffer").

The effects of antibiosis can be observed on agar surfaces, where a **zone of inhibition** develops, clearing the area on the agar plate between an antibiotic producer and its susceptible competitors.

The specific antibiotic produced by the antibiotic-producing bacteria differs. For instance, chloramphenicol and tetracycline are produced by two different species of streptomycetes. Many of the antibiotics produced by microbes have been shown to be commercially valuable for the treatment of infectious diseases caused by pathogenic bacteria and fungi.

It is noteworthy that a few nonsporulating bacteria also produce antibiotics. One example of a nonsporulating antibiotic producer is *Pseudomonas aeruginosa*. This organism produces a bluish-green pigment called pyocyanin, which causes lysis of susceptible organisms. Certain strains of *Pseudomonas aeruginosa* produce the pigment fluorescein. This yellowish-green pigment also demonstrates antimicrobial activity. Even though this organism does not produce spores, it is still able to minimize the competition for nutrients in its environment.

Exercise 6-6

The Effectiveness of Handwashing

Learning Objectives

To examine the diversity of skin surface microbiota.
To understand the differences between transient and normal skin microbiota.
To examine the effectiveness of various handwashing procedures for removing transient microbiota from the hand surface.

Washing your hands with warm water and mild soap emulsifies oils, removes transient microbiota, and brings greater numbers of normal microbiota to the surface of the skin.

In this exercise, you will have the opportunity to compare the types of changes in skin microbiota that can be produced by using different hand-cleaning procedures. These procedures will include the use of various soaps and a commercial hand sanitizer, rubbing your hands under running water without the use of soap, and rubbing your hands for different lengths of time.

Changes in both the number and diversity of organisms present on skin surfaces will be determined by observing the colonies that develop on TSA plates before and after the skin surfaces are cleansed.

Day 1

Materials

- TSA agar plate
- Various hand-cleansing agents

Work in pairs.

Procedure

1. Before you wash your hands, divide a TSA plate into four equal sections. Label the top two sections "before" and the bottom two sections "after." Label the left two sections "student 1" and the right two sections "student 2."

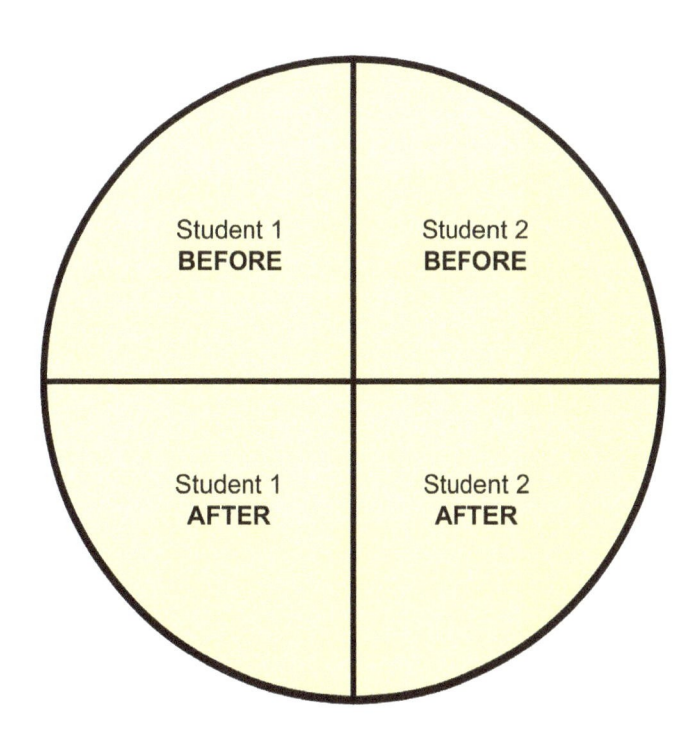

2. Carefully open the TSA plate. Inoculate the plate with your thumb by *gently* touching the thumb to the surface of the agar.
3. Close the plate and pass it on to your lab partner.
4. Refer to Table "Handwashing Procedures and Results" to determine which of the hand-cleaning agents and procedures you and your lab partner are assigned, and follow the instructions.
5. After inoculating the plate by gently touching it with the thumb after handwashing, incubate the plate at 37°C for 24 hours.

Less hardy microbes such as members of the enteric family (Enterobacteriaceae) may appear on the TSA plates. The chance increases if the bacteria were deposited on the skin surface shortly before the samples were inoculated. Enterics include *E. coli*, which are intestinal microbiota, as well as common environmental species such as *Serratia* and *Enterobacter*, some of which are pathogenic.

Day 2

	Colony Morphology
Staphylococcus aureus (normal microbiota)	small (1-2 mm); entire, smooth; pale to golden yellow; opaque
Staphylococcus epidermidis (normal microbiota)	small (1-2 mm); entire, smooth; white; opaque
Acinetobacter (normal microbiota)	medium (2-3 mm); usually smooth; often mucoid (mucus-like), sometimes spreading; off-white; translucent
Corynebacterium (normal microbiota)	highly variable; tan to translucent; entire
Bacillus sp. (transient)	large (3 mm or more); irregular, spreading; flat to raised; rough to smooth; dull to shiny; often white to off-white, opaque to translucent
Enterics (transient)	medium (2-4 mm); entire to undulating; flat, smooth, shiny; white to off-white to pigmented; translucent
Yeast (normal or transient)	large (3 mm or more); entire, smooth; raised, tan to white; opaque

Materials

- Plates from the entire class inoculated in previous lab period.

Procedure

1. In order to compare the effectiveness of the various hand-cleaning methods, your lab instructor will place all incubated plates at the common area space in the lab.
2. Record your observations in the table and answer the questions that follow in the *R & Q* section

R & Q

Handwashing Procedures and Results

Procedure	Soap or Agent Used	Appearance Before Washing (trancient/normal microbiota?)	Appearance After Washing (trancient/normal microbiota?)
Rub your hands with soap for 30 sec. Allow hands to air dry.	Water only		
	Non-antibacterial soap		
	Antibacterial soap		
Rub your hands with soap for 1 min. Allow hands to air dry.	Water only		
	Non-antibacterial soap		
	Antibacterial soap		
Rub your hands with soap for 2 min. Allow hands to air dry.	Water only		
	Non-antibacterial soap		
	Antibacterial soap		
Hand Sanitizer	Hand sanitizer		

No washing 30 sec, 1 min 2 min, water only, 1 non-antibactrial soap, 1 antibacterial, alchohol-based hand sanitizer.

Exercise 6-6

Based on your observation and the information provided in Table "Colony Morphology," which sector(s) on the TSA plates, if any, appear to include mostly transient microbes? Does that make sense?

_____
_____
_____

Which sectors appear to include mostly normal microbiota? Did you expect this result?

_____
_____
_____

Based on the results obtained today, does washing your hands for only fifteen seconds appear to be an effective way to eliminate transient microbes from your skin?

_____
_____
_____

Based on the results obtained today, if no soap was available, does it appear to be worthwhile to wash your hands with water alone?

_____
_____
_____

Based on the results obtained today, does the use of a hand sanitizer appear to be an effective way to eliminate transient microbes from your skin?

_____
_____
_____

Would you expect all transient microbiota to grown on the TSA plate? Explain your answer.

_____
_____
_____

Exercise 6-7

Effects of Mouthwashes and Rinses on Bacterial Growth

Learning Objectives

To understand the effects of mouthwashes/rinses on normal microbiota of the mouth.
To learn how to use the filter disk method to determine microbial susceptibility to antimicrobial agents.
To understand and recognize the appearance of a zone of inhibition.

Good oral hygiene—including brushing, flossing, and rinsing the mouth—is the best defense against dental caries. These processes reduce the number of microorganisms in the mouth without completely eliminating them.

In this exercise, the effects of various mouthwashes and rinses on oral microbiota will be assessed by applying the **filter disk method**. This technique employs sterile filter disks that are saturated with a given antimicrobial agent. The disks will be placed on a freshly made spread plate of a given culture.

After incubation, the plate is inspected for the appearance of clear areas surrounding the individual filter disks. This type of clearing is called a **zone of inhibition**.

The appearance of a zone of inhibition indicates that the applied agent has either inhibited or killed the organism that was spread on the plate and that the organism is susceptible to the given agent.

FIGURE 6.10 Mouthwash

Day 1

Materials

- Broth bacterial cultures (2)
    - *S. salivarius*
    - *S. epidermidis*
- TSA agar plates (4)
- Sterile swabs (2)

Exercise 6-7

- Alcohol jar
- Forceps
- Sterile filter disks
- Five mouthwashes/rinses:
    - Scope, Act, Listerine, Crest, and Cêpacol

Work in groups of four.

Procedure

1. Using a permanent marker, divide the bottom of two TSA plates into three equal sections.
2. Divide the bottom of the remaining two TSA plates into two equal sections.
3. Label one "three-section plate" and one "two-section plate," and include the bacterial name *Streptococcus salivarius*.
4. Label one "three-section plate" and one "two section plate," and include the bacterial name *Staphylococcus epidermidis*.
5. Label the "three-section plate" of *S. salivarius* with the antimicrobial agents Scope, Act, and Listerine.
6. Label the "two-section plate" of *S. salivarius* with the antimicrobial agent Crest and Cêpacol.
7. Repeat for the two plates labeled with *S. epidermidis*.
8. Resuspend the *S. salivarius* cells by vortexing the culture. Use a sterile swab to make a spread plate with the organism. Carefully reinoculate the swab between each plate.

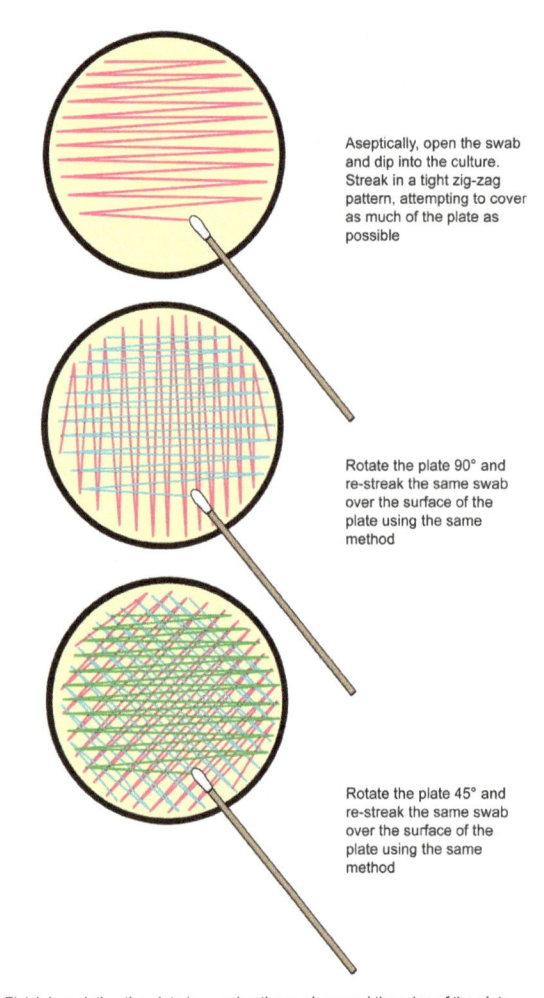

FIGURE 6.11 Spread plate procedure

Aseptically, open the swab and dip into the culture. Streak in a tight zig-zag pattern, attempting to cover as much of the plate as possible

Rotate the plate 90° and re-streak the same swab over the surface of the plate using the same method

Rotate the plate 45° and re-streak the same swab over the surface of the plate using the same method

Finish inoculating the plate by running the swab around the edge of the plate

9. Repeat step 8 for *S. epidermidis*.
10. To apply each antimicrobial agent to the plates, use sterile forceps to aseptically remove a sterile filter disk from its container. Hold the disk with the forceps while you use a dropper bottle to apply one drop of the agent to the disk. Place the saturated disk in the center of the appropriately labeled section of the plate and gently tap the disk onto the agar surface (do not press it into the agar).
11. Sterilize the forceps and repeat step 10 until all sectors of the four inoculated plates have received a disk soaked with the appropriate agent.

Alcohol is flammable. Use caution when working with alcohol near an open flame!

12. Incubate the inverted plates at 37°C for 48 hours.

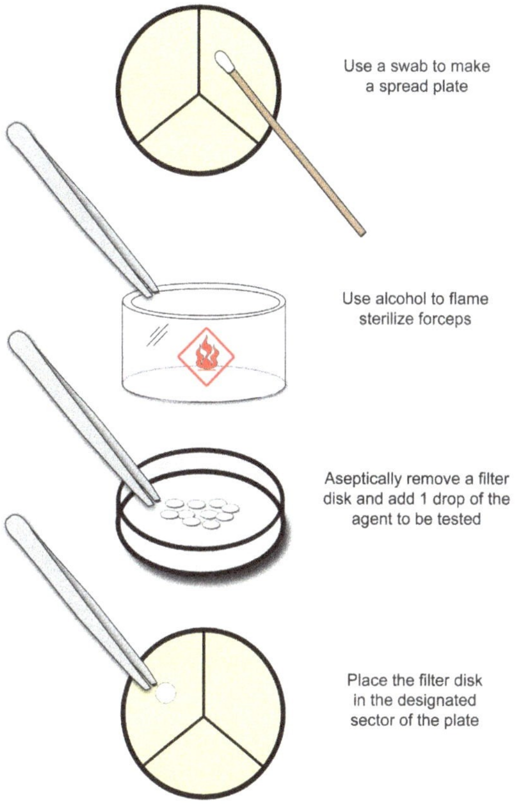

Day 2

Materials

- Plates inoculated in previous lab period

Work in groups of four.

Procedure

1. Examine the area immediately surrounding each disk to determine whether **zones of inhibition** have been produced. Use the provided ruler to measure (in mm) the diameter of each zone you detect.
2. In the table in the *R & Q* section, record the type of mouthwash/rinse used and the diameter of each zone of inhibition. If no zone is detected, record (R) to indicate that the organisms are resistant to the mouthwash/rinse.

FIGURE 6.12 Plate disk procedure

Exercise 6-7

R & Q

Organism(s)	Mouthwash/Rinse Used / Zone of inhibition (mm)				
	Scope	Act	Crest	Listerine	Cepacol
Streptococcus salivarius					
Staphylococcus epidermidis					

Explain your thoughts about using *S. salivarius* and *S. epidermidis* in this experiment.

_____

_____

_____

Which of the products tested seems to be the least effective at eliminating normal microbiota?

_____

_____

_____

Which of the agents tested seems to be the most effective at eliminating normal microbiota? Explain your thoughts about the result you obtained.

_____

_____

_____

Exercise 6-8

Effects of Antiseptics and Disinfectants on Bacterial Growth

Objectives

To understand the differences between antiseptics and disinfectants in regards to their use.
To observe the effects of selected antiseptics and disinfectants on gram-positive and gram-negative bacteria.

Day 1

Materials

- TSB cultures of bacteria (2)
    - *S. epidermidis*
    - *P. fluorescens*
- TSA agar plates (4)
- Sterile swabs (2)
- Alcohol jar
- Sterile filter disks
- Forceps
- Antiseptics and Disinfectants:
    - Bleach, Lysol, iodine, ethanol, hydrogen peroxide, and isopropyl alcohol

Work in groups of four.

In this exercise, you use the filter disk method to test the effects of various disinfectants and antiseptics on the Gram-positive bacterium *Staphylococcus epidermidis* and the Gram-negative bacterium *Pseudomonas fluorescens*. Following incubation, you will examine the plates for the appearance of zones of inhibition and determine which organism is more resistant to the agents tested.

Procedure

1. Use a permanent marker to divide the bottom of each of the four TSA plates into three equal sections.
2. Label two of the TSA plates with *Staphylococcus epidermidis*.

3. Label the other two TSA plates with *Pseudomonas fluorescens*.
4. Label each section of one *S. epidermidis* plate with each of the following chemical agents: bleach, Lysol, and iodine.
5. Label each section of the second *S. epidermidis* plate with each of the following chemical agents: ethanol, hydrogen peroxide, and isopropyl alcohol.
6. Repeat steps 4 and 5 for two *P. fluorescens* plates.
7. Resuspend the *S. epidermidis* culture, and use a sterile swab to make a spread plate. Carefully reinoculate the swab between each plate.
8. Similarly, use a fresh swab to inoculate the other two TSA plates with resuspended *P. fluorescens* cells.
9. To apply each agent to the plates, use sterile forceps to aseptically remove a sterile filter disk from its container. Hold the disk with the forceps while you use a dropper bottle to apply one drop of the agent to the disk. Place the saturated disk in the center of the appropriately labeled section of the plate and gently tap the disk onto the agar surface (do not press it into the agar).
10. Sterilize the forceps and repeat step 10 until all sectors of the four inoculated plates have received a disk soaked with the appropriate agent.

Caution: Alcohol is flammable. Use caution when working with alcohol near an open flame!

11. Incubate the inverted plates at 37°C for 24–48 hours, except the two plates inoculated with *P. fluorescens*, which will be incubated at 30°C.

Day 2

Materials

- Antimicrobial plates inoculated previous lab period

Procedure

1. Examine the area immediately surrounding each disk to determine whether **zones of inhibition** have been produced. Use the provided ruler to measure (in mm) the diameter of each zone you detect.

Exercise 6-8

2. In the table in the *R & Q* section, record the type of antiseptics and disinfectants used and the diameter of each zone of inhibition. If no zone is detected, record (R) to indicate that the organisms are resistant to the agent.

R & Q

Organism	Bleach	Lysol®	Iodine	70% Ethanol	3% H_2O_2	Isopropyl Alcohol
Staphylococcus epidermidis						
Pseudomonas fluorescens						

Pseudomonas aeruginosa is a common cause of infections in burn victims. Lysol is a disinfectant that is used in hospitals. Explain how you would apply Lysol in the hospital setting to help the victim fight the *P. aeruginosa* infection.

___
___
___

Are Gram-positive or Gram-negative bacteria more susceptible to the antiseptics/disinfectants tested? Include your observations in the explanation.

___
___
___

Antibiotics

Learning Objectives

To observe the effects of selected antibiotics on bacterial growth.

To learn how to determine MIC using the Etest.

To understand the meaning of the terms bactericidal and bacteriostatic and learn how antibiotics affect a given bacterium.

To understand the meaning of genetic transformation of bacteria.

To transform E. coli cells with plasmid DNA, which expresses a gene that gives rise to antibiotic resistance of the bacterial cells.

Day 1

Materials

- Antibiotic disk dispensers
- TSB cultures of bacteria (2)
    - *E. coli*
    - *S. epidermidis*
- TSA plates (3)
- LB +AMP plate
- LB+ KAN plate
- Etest strip
- Microfuge tube of competent cells
- Eppendorf tubes (2)
- Plasmid A and B
- Ice bucket
- P200 micropipette
- Tips

Work in groups of four.

Exercise 6-9

In this exercise, you will apply several antibiotic disks to one culture plate that has been inoculated with a Gram-positive organism, *Staphylococcus epidermidis*, and to another plate inoculated with a Gram-negative species, *Escherichia coli*. Following incubation, you will observe the plates for zones of inhibition. The exercise continues by examining the bactericidal or bacteriostatic properties of the antibiotics.

You will make a second spread plate of either *S. epidermidis* or *E. coli* and use the Etest strip to determine the minimal concentration of one of the antibiotics needed to inhibit growth of this specific organism. Finally, you will use plasmids, which carry genes that code for antibiotic resistance, to transform *E. coli*. You will be able to follow how the transformed cells will change from antibiotic-sensitive cells to antibiotic-resistant cells (**Box 5**).

Box 5 Plasmid A and Plasmid B

Plasmid A carries the gene *bla*, which, when expressed, codes for the enzyme beta-lactamase. This enzyme is responsible for the resistance of the bacterial cells to ampicillin, which normally would inhibit the growth of the bacterial cells by inhibiting cell-wall synthesis. Thus, if the bacterial cells express the *bla* gene from plasmid A (and thus produce beta-lactamase), the cells will be resistant to ampicillin and will grow on media containing this antibiotic. Plasmid A also contains the genetic material to synthesize a protein called GFPuv, a variant of the green fluorescent protein GFP, which is involved in bioluminescence. Bioluminescence can be found in organisms such as jellyfish, and GFP was initially isolated from the jellyfish *Aequorea victoria*. This jellyfish fluoresces green when irradiated with ultraviolet light, due to the production of the GFP. The bacteria transformed in the lab with Plasmid A will demonstrate the same luminescent properties as the jellyfish when irradiated with ultraviolet light.

Plasmid B carries a *KanR* gene, which, when expressed in the bacterial cell, is responsible for the resistance toward the antibiotic kanamycin. Kanamycin interacts with ribosomal proteins and thereby inhibits protein synthesis.

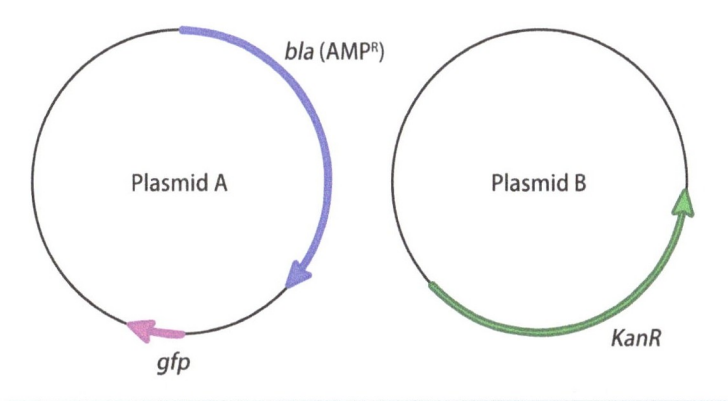

FIGURE 6.13 The two plasmids used to transform *E.coli*

Exercise 6-9

Procedure

Kirby-Bauer

1. In order to perform the Kirby-Bauer method, label two TSA plates, including the name of each of the strains, respectively.

   Staphylococcus epidermidis
   Escherichia coli

2. Resuspend the *S. epidermidis* cells by vortexing the culture, and use a sterile swab to make a spread plate of the culture.
3. Repeat step 2 for the *E. coli* culture.
4. Take the TSA plates inoculated with *S. epidermidis* and *E. coli* to the common area bench. Remove the lid from the *S. epidermidis*-inoculated plate. Center the dispenser over the inoculated agar. Gently push down on the knob located in the center of the dispenser and slowly release it. The dispenser will deposit six sterile antibiotic disks onto the surface of this plate.
5. Repeat for the TSA plate inoculated with *E. coli*.
6. If any of the disks do not lie flat on the agar, use a pair of sterilized forceps to gently tap the disks down onto the agar surface. Be careful not to tap it into the agar.
7. Incubate the **inverted** plates at 37°C for 24 hours.

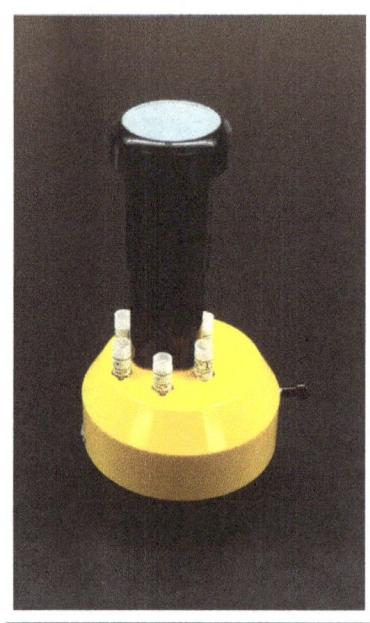

CAUTION: Alcohol is flammable. Use caution when working with alcohol near an open flame!

FIGURE 6.14 Antibiotic disk dispenser

Etest

1. To perform the Etest, label your third TSA plate with the organism assigned to you by your lab instructor (*E. coli* or *S. epidermidis*).
2. Resuspend the culture and use a sterile swab to produce a spread plate.
3. Collect your assigned Etest strip. Be careful to only touch the strip at the end with the large "E." Do not touch any other part of the strip.
4. While using good aseptic technique, carefully lay the strip, numbered side up, onto the surface of the plate. Once the strip has touched the surface of the plate, do not move it.
5. Incubate the inverted plates at 37°C for 24 hours.

Exercise 6-9

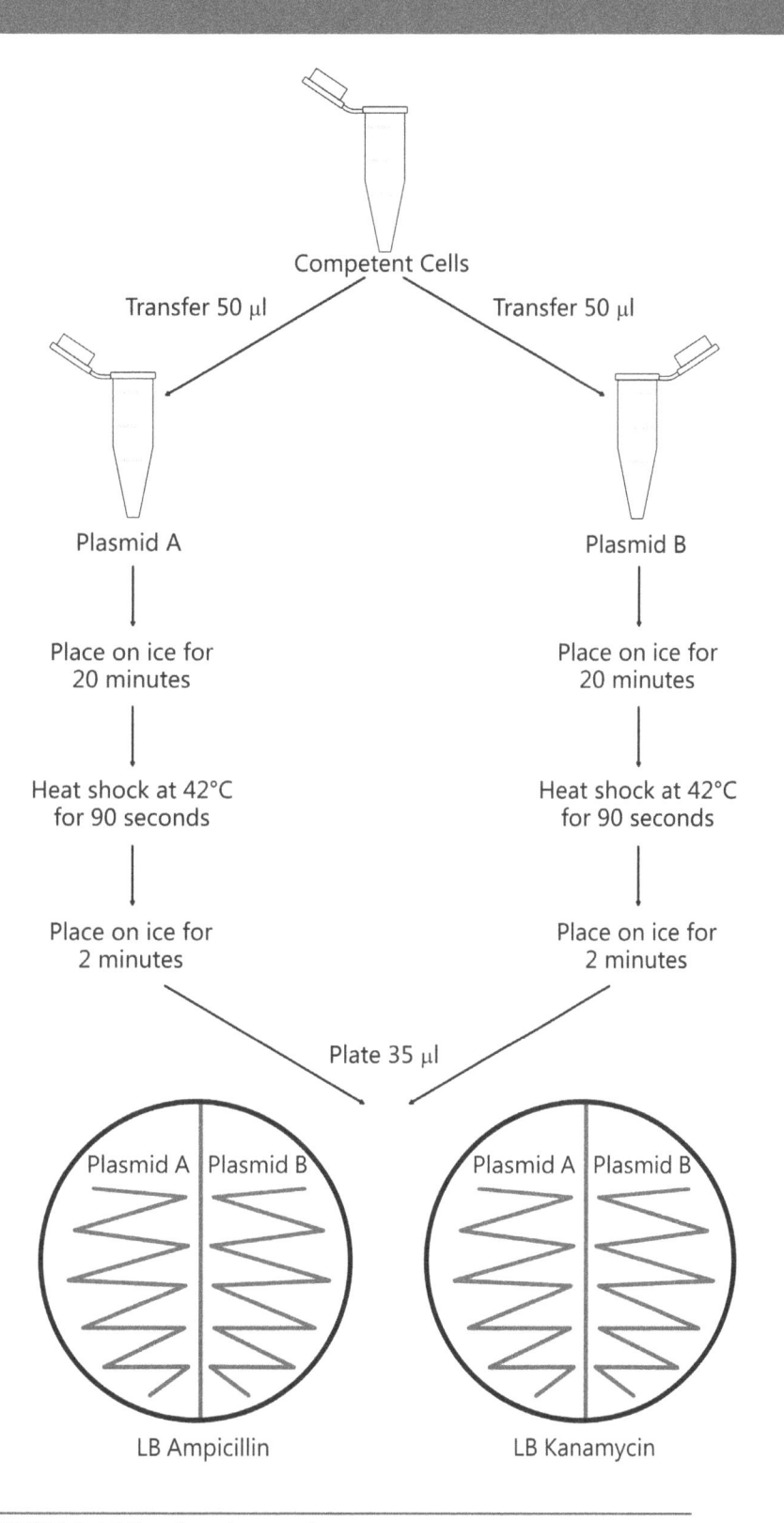

FIGURE 6.15 Transformation procedure

Transformation

1. In order to transform *E. coli* with plasmid DNA, label one microfuge tube of 100µl of competent cells with the number 1. Keep the tube on ice.

   Note: The *E. coli* cells have been made competent for transformation by treating the cells with high concentrations of calcium ions (Ca^{+2}). This increases the permeability of the cell and allows uptake of plasmid DNA by the bacterial cells. It is essential to keep the competent cells on ice all the time until the heat-shock step. Otherwise, they will lose their transformation efficiency.

2. Label an empty sterile microfuge tube "2." Put the tube on ice.
3. Use the micropipette to transfer 50µl of competent cells from tube "1" to tube "2." Return both tubes to ice.
4. Add 20µl of Plasmid A to tube "1." Flick the tube gently to mix the cells and DNA. Return the tube to ice.
5. Add 20µl of Plasmid B to tube "2." Flick the tube gently to mix the cells and DNA. Return the tube to ice.
6. Keep the competent cell/DNA mixtures on ice for 20 minutes.
7. Carry your ice bucket with your samples to the 42°C water bath. Heat-shock both of your samples for 90 seconds by placing the tubes in a floating rack in the water bath.
8. Remove the tubes from the water bath and keep them on ice for 2 minutes.
9. Collect two agar plates, LB + AMP and LB + KAN, respectively. Divide each plate in half and label the plates, including "A" or "B" for Plasmid A and B.
10. Using the P200 micropipette, place 35µl of cells from each tube near the edge of the appropriately labeled sector on each of the plates.
11. Use the inoculating loop to carefully streak cells from each spot in a zigzag pattern.
12. Incubate your inverted plates at 37°C for 24 hours.

   Note: LB + Amp contains the antibiotic ampicillin, and LB + Kan contains the antibiotic Kananmycin.

Exercise 6-9

Day 2

Materials

- Various plates inoculated in previous lab period
- TSA plate

Work in groups of four.

Procedure

1. For the plates concerning the **Kirby-Bauer method**, examine the area immediately surrounding each disk to determine if zones of inhibition have been produced.
2. Use the rulers provided to measure (in mm) the diameter of each zone detected.
3. Record your results in the table provided in the *R & Q* section. If no zone is detected, record (R) to indicate that the organisms are resistant to the antibiotic.
4. Make subcultures to determine the mode of action of selected antibiotics on the plates by first dividing the bottom of the fresh TSA plate into four equally sized sections with a permanent marker.

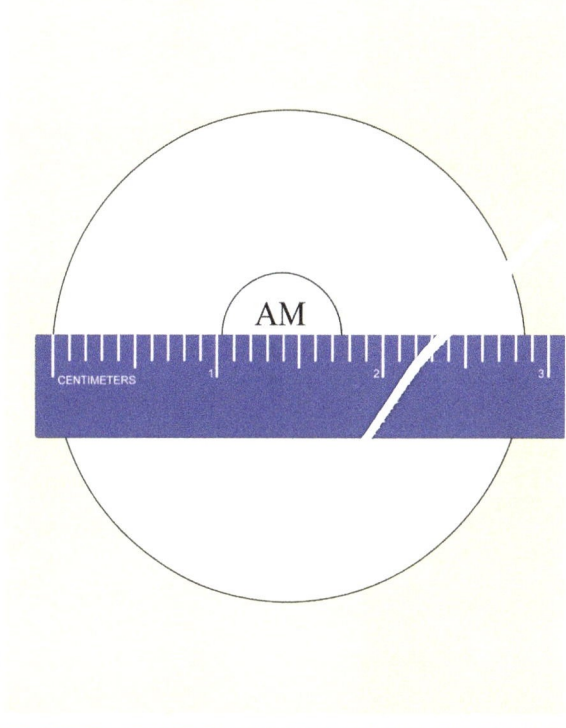

FIGURE 6.16 How to measure a zone of inhibition

5. Select two antibiotics that produced zones of inhibition on the plates with *S. epidermidis* and two that produced zones of inhibition on the plate with *E. coli*. These antibiotics will be tested to determine if their effects are bacteriostatic or bactericidal.
6. Label one section of the fresh TSA plate for each of your selected antibiotics, indicating which were used with *S. epidermidis* and *E. coli*.
7. Use a sterile loop to carefully remove a sample from the zone of inhibition surrounding your first selected antibiotic disk.

    Note: Avoid sampling any colonies that may appear within the zone; such colonies represent spontaneous mutants that show resistance to the antibiotic.

8. Streak the sample by making a single, short line (about 1.5 cm) on the appropriately labeled section of your fresh TSA plate.

9. Repeat steps 7 and 8 with your other three selected samples.
10. Incubate the TSA plate at 37°C for 24 hours.
11. All plates from the entire class concerning the **Etest strips** will be placed in the common lab area for all students to view.
12. Refer to Figure "Etest" for the explanation of how to read the Etest. Record the MICs obtained in the table in the *R & Q* section.
13. Examine the *E. coli* **transformation plates**, and record your observations in the *R & Q* section.

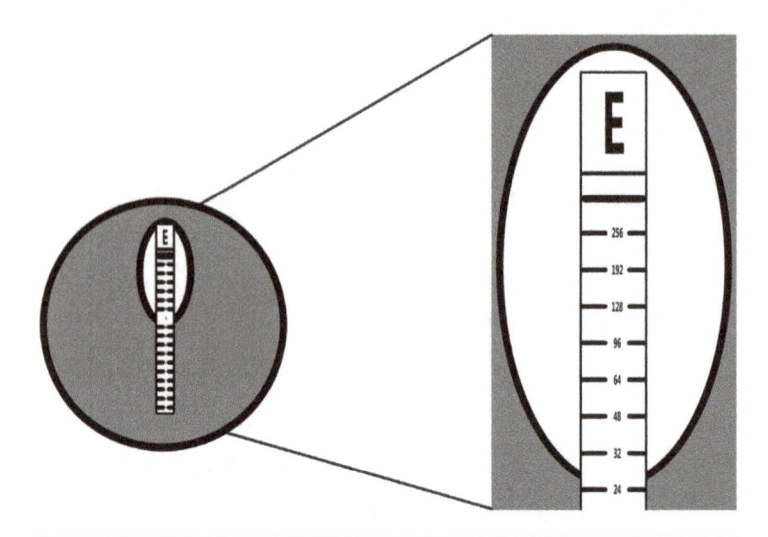

FIGURE 6.17 This diagram shows an Etest strip on a spread plate and the elliptical pattern of growth inhibition. You can see that the intersection of growth is between 24 and 32 µg/ml. When this occurs, the higher value should be recorded. The MIC in this example would be 32µg/ml.

Day 3

Materials

- TSA subculture plates performed in previous lab

Work in groups of four.

Procedure

1. Examine the plates to determine if growth has occurred.
2. Record your observations for each organism and antibiotic tested in the *R & Q* section. Include whether the mode of action of the antibiotics were bactericidal or bacteriostatic.

Kirby-Bauer continued

In a clinical setting, the size of the zones of inhibition around the antibiotic disks can be used to determine if the organism is susceptible, intermediate, or resistant to antibiotics tested.

Susceptible (S) indicates that the infectious organism is susceptible to the tested antibiotic, and the antibiotic may be the appropriate choice to treat this particular infection.

Intermediate (I) indicates that the antibiotic may be useful under certain circumstances; for example, it may be of use if the infection is located at a site of the body where the antibiotic is known to concentrate. It could also indicate that the antibiotic may be effective if high concentrations of the antibiotic are given.

Resistant (R) indicates that the infectious organism is resistant to the antibiotic and therefore not the appropriate antibiotic to administer in order to treat this particular infection.

The three categories are typically developed by extensive testing, including several MIC calculations, studies of actual achievable levels of the antibiotic in patients, how successful the antibiotic has been found to be therapeutically, etc.

For clinical use, the size of the zone of inhibition (adapted from BD) reflecting each of the three categories has been established by plotting zone diameters from tests of hundreds of clinical isolates of a particular species versus MIC values obtained from broth or agar dilutions.

Antibiotic	Organism	Zone diameter (mm) and Interpretive Standards		
		Resistant	Intermediate	Susceptible
Ampicillin	S. epidermidis	≤28	-	≥29
	E. coli	≤13	14-16	≥17
Erythromycin	S. epidermidis	≤13	14-22	≥23
	E. coli	NA	NA	NA
Kanamycin	S. epidermidis	≤13	14-17	≥18
	E. coli	≤13	14-17	≥18
Neomycin	None listed	≤12	13-16	≥17
Penicillin	S. epidermidis	≤28	-	≥29
	E. coli	NA	NA	NA
Polymyxin B	None listed	≤8	9-11	≥12
Streptomycin	S. epidermidis	NA	NA	NA
	E. coli	≤11	12-14	≥15

R & Q

Day 2

Organism	Antibiotic Used						
	Mm / S,I,R	mm / S,I,R	mm / S,I,R	mm / S,I,R	mm / S,I,R	mm / S,I,R
S. epidermidis						
E. coli						

Key to the antibiotics that may be used in this exercise:

E	Erythromycin		**N**	Neomycin
P	Penicillin G		**S**	Streptomycin
PB	Polymyxin B		**AM**	Ampicillin
K	Kanamycin			

Bacterial sensitivity to antibiotics varies. Generally, Gram-positive bacteria tend to be more susceptible to antibiotics, and Gram-negative bacteria tend to be more resistant. Explain how that compares to the results you obtained.

_____
_____
_____

Etest Plate

Organism	MIC (µg/ml)		
	Ampicillin	Erythromycin	Vancomycin
Staphylococcus epidermidis			
Escherichia coli			

Using the MIC information determined above to treat an infection, describe three other things you would need to consider before using the antibiotics to treat patients.

Transformation

Record your observations	LB +AMP	LB +Kan
E. coli + Plasmid A		
E. coli + Plasmid B		

Expose the LB + AMP and LB + Kan transformation plates to UV light to check for luminescence. Describe what you see and explain your observations.

Explain why *E. coli* cells transformed with Plasmid A are able to grow on the LB + AMP plate.

Explain the advantage for *E. coli* cells that carry a plasmid providing antibiotic resistance?

Is LB + AMP medium selective, differential, or selective-differential? Explain your answer.

Exercise 6-9

Day 3

Organism	Antibiotic Tested	Observed Result
Staphylococcus epidermidis		
Escherichia coli		

Do the bacteriostatic antibiotics appear to have a common mode of action? Do their effects appear to be influenced by the type of the cell wall? Explain your answer.

_____
_____
_____

If there is no growth in any one of the subcultures that you made, does this guarantee that the antibiotic is bactericidal? Explain your answer.

_____
_____
_____

Exercise 6-10

The Action of Natural Antibiotics

Learning Objectives

To understand the competitive advantages that antibiotics provide the organisms that naturally produce them.

To determine whether Gram-positive or Gram-negative organisms are more susceptible to the antibiotic produced by Paenibacillus polymyxa.

In this exercise, you will use a Gram-positive and a Gram-negative bacterial species to examine susceptibilities for the antibiotic produced by the endospore-forming bacterium *Paenibacillus polymyxa*.

Day 1

Materials

- TSB cultures of bacteria (2)
    - S epidermidis
    - E. coli
- TSA agar plate with *P. polymyxa*

Work in groups of four.

Procedure

1. Starting from the edge of the plate and perpendicular to the center streak of *Paenibacillus polymyxa*, use an inoculation loop to make a single straight line streak of the Gram-positive organism *Staphylococcus epidermidis*. Bring this streak close to, but do not touch, the center streak. Label this streak appropriately.
2. Use a loopful of the Gram-negative organism *Escherichia coli* to make a second single perpendicular streak on the opposite side of the plate. Again, be careful to not touch the center streak. Label this streak accordingly.
3. Invert the plate and incubate at 37°C for 48 hours.

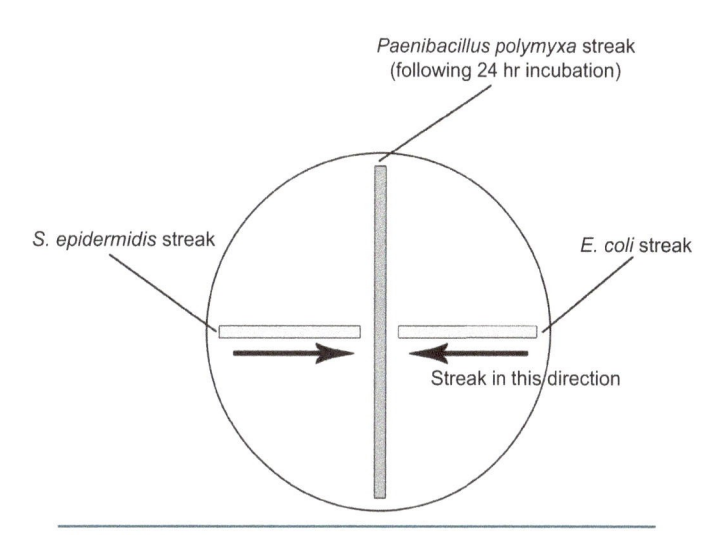

FIGURE 6.18 Polymyxa

Exercise 6-10

Day 2

Materials

- TSA plate inoculated in previous lab period

Work in groups of four.

Procedure

1. Examine the plate to determine the effects of the antibiotic produced by *P. polymyxa* on the Gram-positive *S. epidermidis* versus the Gram-negative *E. coli*.

   Note: The appearance of a clear area at the end of the test streak nearest the *P. polymyxa* streak indicates that inhibition of growth has occurred. This clear area is a zone of inhibition. The greater the effect of the antibiotic on the organism, the larger this zone will appear.

R & Q

Illustrate your results on the drawing provided below.

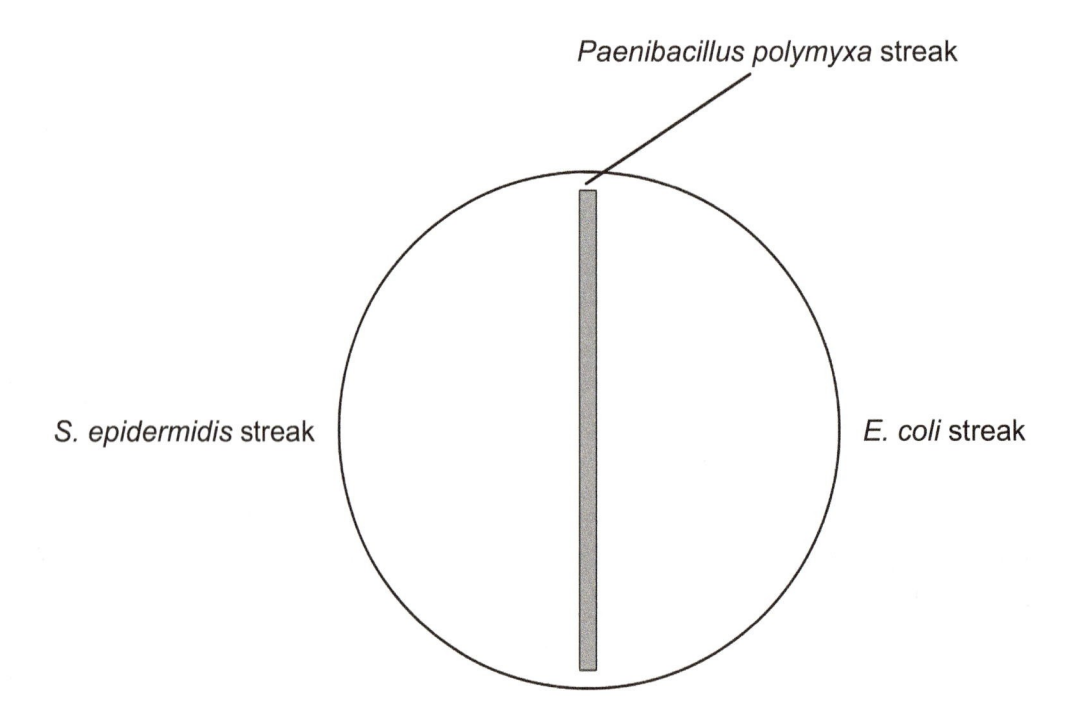

Paenibacillus polymyxa streak

S. epidermidis streak

E. coli streak

Which of the two organisms is more susceptible to the naturally produced antibiotic of *P. polymyxa*? Include the Gram status of the organisms in your answer, and describe your thoughts about the obtained result.

___
___
___

Name the antibiotic produced by *P. polymyxa*.

___
___
___

Symbiosis, Immunology, and Epidemiology

In this module, we will be touching on medical-related microbiology topics, including how bacteria may live in perfect harmony with humans or other animals and how they may evade hosts to cause disease. We will briefly discuss immunology-related topics such as the human host's defense mechanisms (e.g., phagocytosis, antibody and antigen interactions) and virulence factors that improve the chance of a pathogen evading a host to cause disease.

In the very end of the module, we will perform a simulated epidemic, during which we will "exchange fluids" with an already infected individual (the index case) and follow the spread of the disease around the lab. We will use ELISA (enzyme-linked immunosorbent assay, Figure 7.16 ELISA procedure) to verify which students have been infected and attempt to track down who was the first individual infected in our lab (the index case).

However, before we pursue the medical-related topics, the first part of this module will focus on symbiosis and symbiotic relationships. In this section of the module, you will gain an appreciation for the fact that bacteria entering or living in a host is not always undesirable.

SYMBIOSIS

Symbiosis (the way different organisms live close together and interact with each other) can be divided up into different groups of relationships, including commensalistic, mutualistic, and parasitic (Figure 7.1 Human symbiotic relationships).

The symbiotic relationship can be permanent (where the organisms are required to live closely together for survival) or transient (where the organisms are not required to live together for survival). In the latter relationship, the association could be short-term.

Bacteria can live in symbiotic relationships with a variety of other organisms, such as other bacteria, viruses, protists, fungi, plants, and animals. The specific symbiotic relationships are often defined by the particular conditions or environmental circumstances.

Box 1 Symbiotic Relationships

Examples of symbiotic relationships

Commensalistic relationship: only one of two different organisms benefits from the symbiotic relationship. The other organism does not benefit, nor is it harmed.

Mutualistic relationship: both organisms benefit from the symbiotic relationship.

Parasitic relationship: the symbiotic relationship is harmful to one organism while the other benefits.

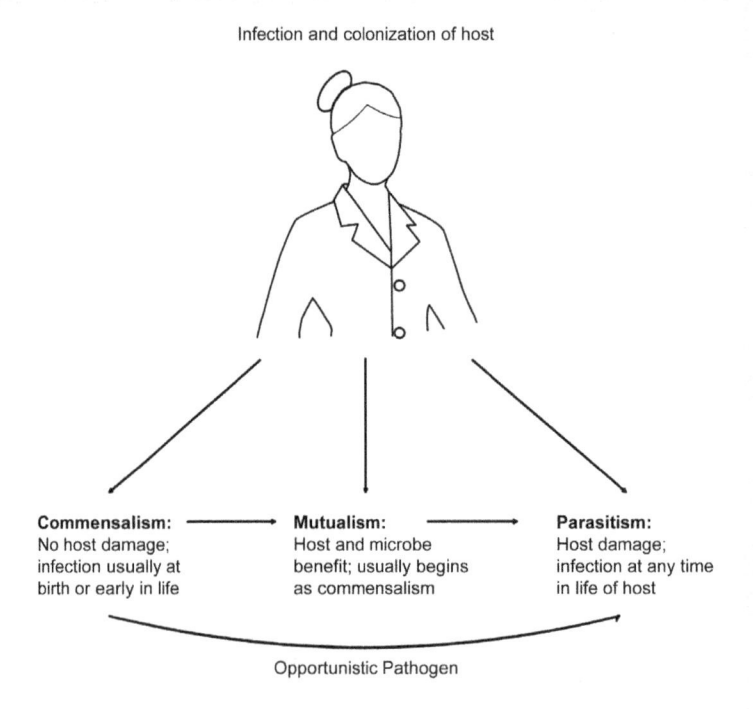

Infection and colonization of host

Commensalism: No host damage; infection usually at birth or early in life

Mutualism: Host and microbe benefit; usually begins as commensalism

Parasitism: Host damage; infection at any time in life of host

Opportunistic Pathogen

The symbiotic relationships of microbes and their human hosts can change over time if the immune system of the host becomes compromised or if the microbe is transferred to a different habitat in the host

FIGURE 7.1 Human symbiotic relationships

The benefits among the organisms living in commensalistic and mutualistic relationships are most often nutrient-based. Examples are stated in table "Symbiosis" in the *R & Q* section.

An oxygen-related example of a required commensalistic relationship is a strict anaerobe living in association with a facultative anaerobe. The strict anaerobe benefits from the fact that the facultative anaerobe is able to remove oxygen from the environment, thereby supporting survival and growth of the strict anaerobe.

Bacteria entering or living in a host are not always undesirable. We know this from the fact that microbes are already associated with human hosts at birth and within the first few years of life. The microbes that do not cause damage (or at least detectable damage) are living in a **commensalistic** relationship with the host. When such commensal microbes are settling in a particular part of the host, they are considered part of the normal microbiota. The natural microbiota benefit from their host by utilizing nutrients originating from the food eaten by the host, from dead cells, and from other waste products of the host.

When established as part of the normal microbiota, the relationship between the human host and the microbe can be described as **mutualistic**. Thus, both the host and microbe benefit. Often both organisms benefit nutritionally; however, the microbe also benefits from having a protected habitat in which to grow, and the host benefits from the ability of normal microbiota to inhibit colonization by pathogenic microbes. Many of the normal microbiota of the human gut assist with digestion of the food humans eat. This is also the case for strains *of E. coli*, which furthermore help the human body with the production and uptake of vitamin K.

However, if the balance of microbes in the host is changed for some reason (e.g., if the immune system of the host is compromised), the microbes may have opportunities to evade and settle in other parts of the host where they normally do not reside. Under such circumstances, both commensal and mutualistic microbes can cause host damage; this is often referred to as an **opportunistic infection**. An example of an opportunistic infection is if the bacterial organism *Escherichia coli*, which is part of the normal microbiota of the gastrointestinal tract (GI tract), become established in the urinary bladder. If this happens, the microbes most likely will cause a urinary tract infection. Thus, bacteria that become **opportunistic pathogens** now have a **parasitic relationship** with the host.

In symbiotic relationships described as **parasitism,** the parasite benefits and the host is harmed. Microbes that are parasites are also described as **pathogens**. The parasite benefits in two ways: it derives nutrition from the host, and it has a habitat in which it can grow. The host is typically much larger than the parasite, as in a bacterial parasite infecting a human host or bacterial viruses infecting a bacterial host.

In the exercises to follow, you will study examples of mutualism and parasitism.

Exercise 7-1

Mutualism

In this exercise, you will examine the highly specific mutualistic relationship that exists between leguminous plants (such as alfalfa, soybeans, and peas) and bacteria such as the species of *Rhizobium* or *Bradyrhizobium*. The bacteria reside within specialized plant structures called nodules. The nodules typically appear as bulbous swellings on the legume root surfaces.

The bacteria within the nodules are nitrogen-fixing bacteria, so the plant host benefits from the presence of the bacteria, since they fix free atmospheric nitrogen and thus provide nitrogen compounds that can be readily utilized by the plant. The bacteria benefit from the protection that the nodules provide, as well as carbohydrates produced as a result of the plant's photosynthetic process. Strictly dependent on the plant host for carbohydrates, the bacteria can utilize the energy generated from the carbohydrates for the nitrogen-fixation process.

This example of mutualism is an important step in the nitrogen cycle. It also improves soil fertility, which helps to reduce the use of industrial fertilizers, reduces water pollution, and keeps costs down for both producers and consumers.

Learning Objectives

To understand the concepts of symbiosis and microbial mutualism.

To gain knowledge about the symbiotic relationship between leguminous plants and their nitrogen-fixing bacterial symbionts.

Materials

- Photo of soybean roots with nodules
- Prepared slide of a root nodule

Work in pairs.

Procedure

1. Examine the external surface of the soybean roots on the photo Figure "Soybean Root." provided in the lab and in the lab manual. The nodules of this leguminous plant should appear as small bumps along the surface of the root.
2. Illustrate and describe your macroscopic observations of these structures in the R & Q section.
3. Examine the prepared slide of the cross section of a root nodule at 400X total magnification. Illustrate and record your microscopic observations of this cross section in the R & Q section.

Note: the close association with the vascular tissue of the plant, the xylem and phloem. This tissue resembles an "X" of large, reddish, thick-walled xylem cells, with small, green, tightly-packed phloem cells in all the angles. Food, water, and minerals are transported through this tissue of the plant.

4. Now observe the cross section of the root nodule at 1000X magnification. Illustrate and record your microscopic observations of this cross section in the *R & Q* section.

Note: the tiny, swollen, distorted, and often branched bacterial cells that are contained within the large, red-stained plant cells. Bacterial cells in this form are called **bacteroids,** which is the form that a bacterium takes inside a nodule. In the free-living forms, this organism will appear as bacilli. It is the bacteroids that are capable of nitrogen fixation.

R & Q

Macroscopic observation of soybean root with nodules
Illustration:

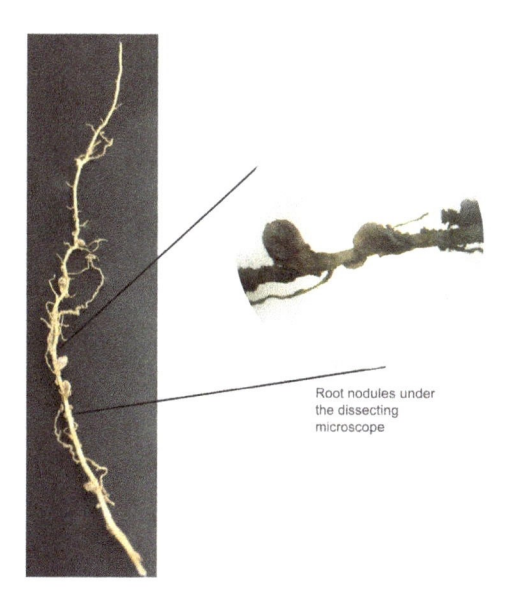

Root nodules under the dissecting microscope

Description:
_____
_____
_____

Exercise 7-1

Microscopic observations of a cross section of a root nodule, 400X

Illustration:

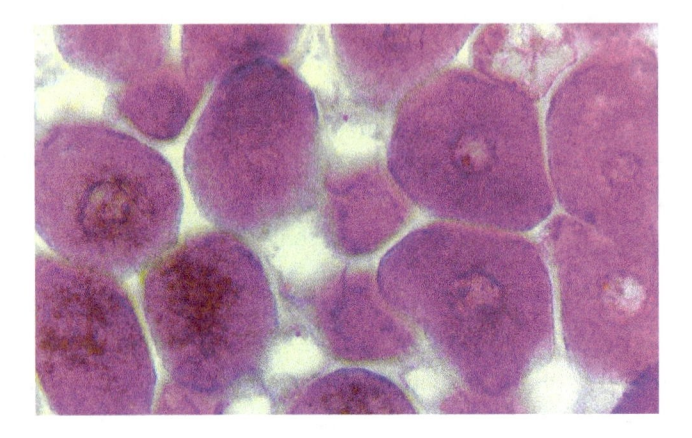

Description:
___
___
___

Microscopic observations of a cross section of a root nodule, 1000X

Illustration:

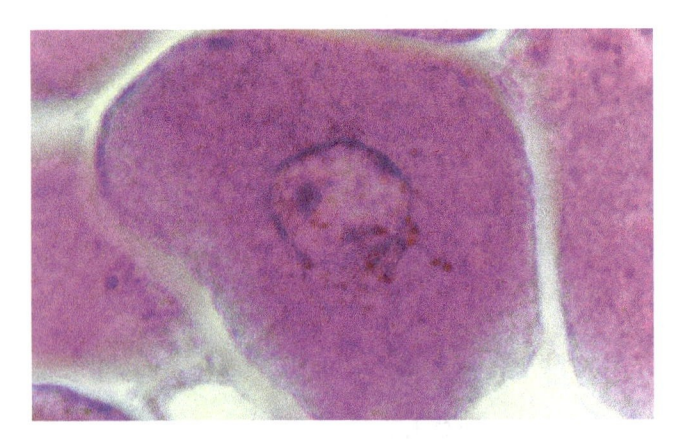

Description:
___
___
___

Exercise 7-1

Fill out the type of symbiosis in the table. Where appropriate, indicate "host" or "parasite" and any additional information in the boxes left empty.

Symbiotic bacteria	Type of symbiosis	Additional information
Bdellovibrio and various soil bacteria		*Bdellovibrio* attaches to host bacterium and penetrates the cell wall of the host cell; replicates in the space between cell wall and membrane; assimilates nutrients from host
Escherichia coli and T4 bacteriophage		
Cyanobacteria and fungi in lichen		The cyanobacteria benefits from fungal uptake of water, inorganic nutrients, as well as protection from drying. The fungi use photosynthetic products as carbon source
Bacteria of the genera *Rhizobium* or *Bradyrhizobium* and leguminous plants		
Chemoautotrophic bacteria and tube worm *Riftiapachyptila*		The bacteria benefit from worm's uptake of carbon and sulfite sources. The worms benefit from organic carbon and sulfite from bacteria
Endosymbiotic bacteria (ex. *Caedibacer, Hotospora*) and protist *Paramecium aurelia*		Bacteria benefit since they have gained a protective habitat. The benefit to *Paramecium* is either unknown or variable.

Which previous exercise described a symbiotic relationship between two organisms? Describe how the purpose of that relationship differs from those mentioned here.

_____
_____
_____

Parasitism

When considering parasitism between bacteria and a human host, the bacteria are the parasites. However, sometimes the bacteria are the hosts for example, when bacteria are infected by viruses. Such bacteria-related viruses are called **bacteriophages** or just **phages**.

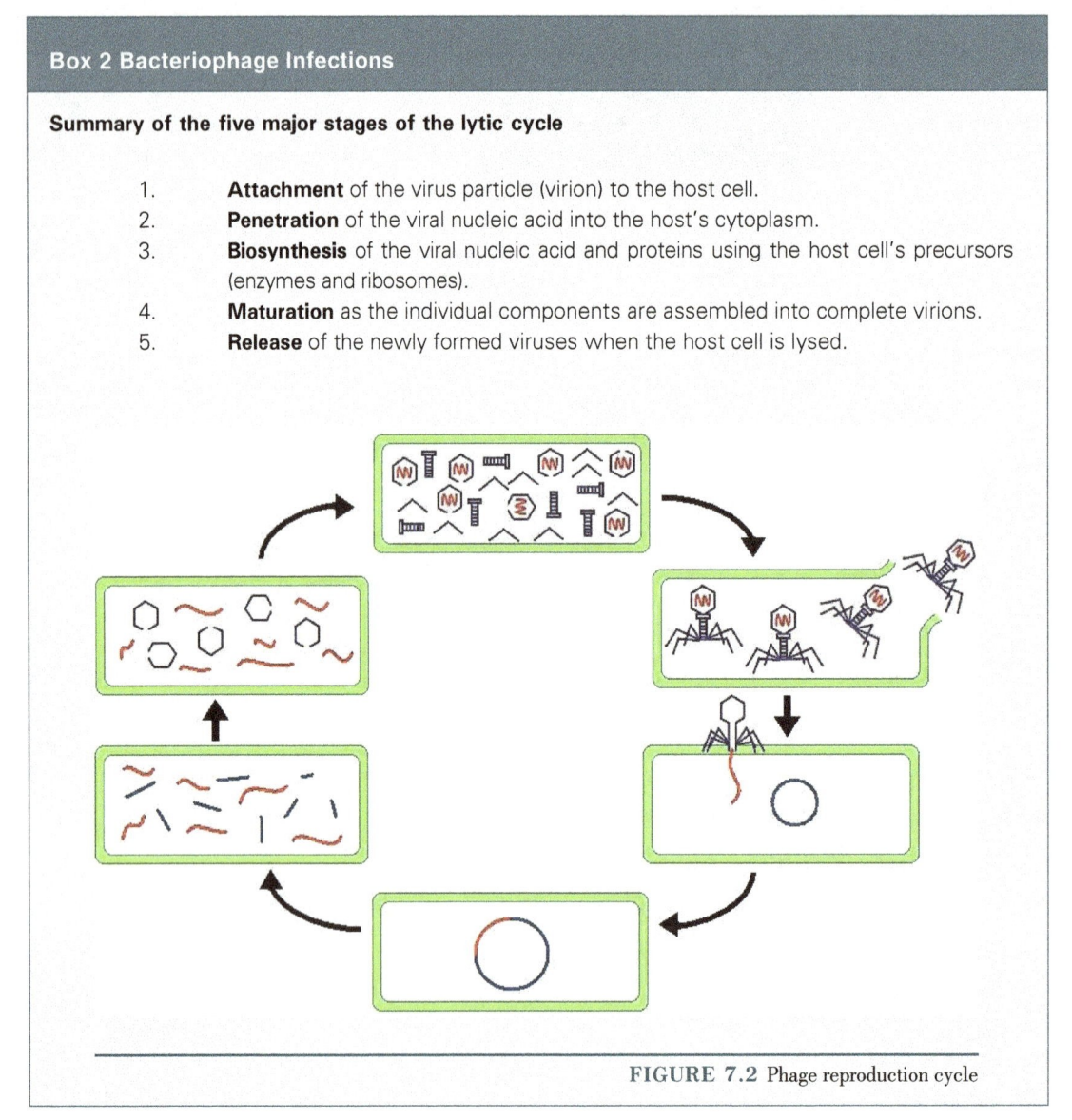

Box 2 Bacteriophage Infections

Summary of the five major stages of the lytic cycle

1. **Attachment** of the virus particle (virion) to the host cell.
2. **Penetration** of the viral nucleic acid into the host's cytoplasm.
3. **Biosynthesis** of the viral nucleic acid and proteins using the host cell's precursors (enzymes and ribosomes).
4. **Maturation** as the individual components are assembled into complete virions.
5. **Release** of the newly formed viruses when the host cell is lysed.

FIGURE 7.2 Phage reproduction cycle

Exercise 7-2

The attachment of a bacteriophage to a host cell is a highly specific process, with each type of virus attaching to only certain bacterial hosts. This specificity is determined primarily by the components on the outer surface of the virus, which interact with particular receptors present on the bacterial host's cell surface. The bacteriophage's ability to infect a host cell is so highly regulated that a bacteriophage that typically infects a *Staphylococcus aureus* cell will not have the ability to infect an *Escherichia coli* cell. There are also specific bacteriophages that only infect certain types of *S. aureus* or *E. coli* strains.. Such degree of specificity proves useful in the process of identifying certain types of bacteria.

In this exercise, you will test a bacteriophage's specificity for its host cell. You will also learn how to enumerate viruses (bacteriophages) by calculating plaque-forming units (PFU) that appear on an agar plate after bacteria have been infected with bacteriophages.

Learning Objectives

To understand the concept of parasitism.
To become familiar with the appearance of viral plaques and understand how they arise.
To be able to determine whether a certain bacterial species is susceptible or resistant to a given bacteriophage.
To learn how to enumerate viruses (bacteriophages).

Day 1

Materials

- TSB cultures of two different *E. coli* strains (2)
- T4 bacteriophage suspension
- TSA plates (6)
- 4.5 ml saline blanks (3)
- P200 and P1000 micropipttes
- Tips
- Alcohol jar
- Metal or glass spreader

Work in groups of four.

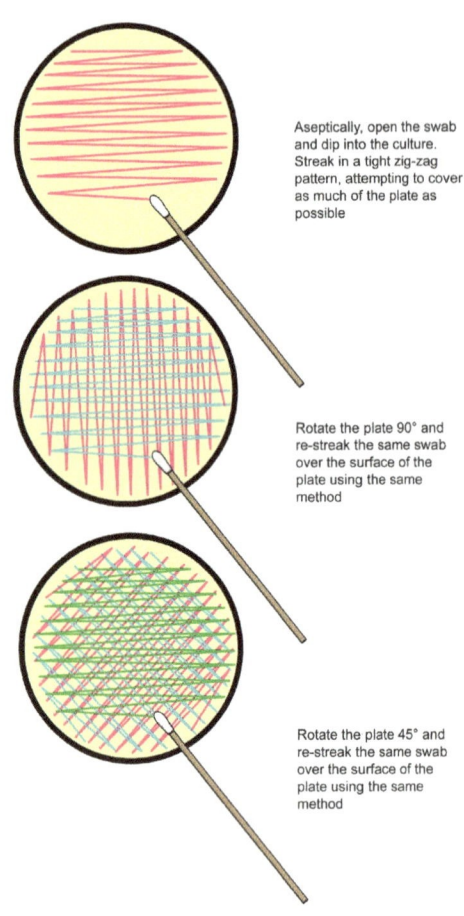

Exercise 7-2

Procedure

1. Label one set of three TSA plates for inoculation with *Escherichia coli* 455. Include all other information on the plate as previous. Using a sterile swab, make a spread plate of *E. coli* 455. It is important that the lawn of growth will cover the entire surface of the plate after incubation.

2. Label the remaining three TSA plates with *Escherichia coli* 363. Use a fresh sterile swab to prepare the second set of spread plates.

3. Prepare a serial dilution of the T_4 bacteriophage suspension. To obtain a 10x diluted bacteriophage suspension (10^{-1} dilution), transfer 0.5 ml of the bacteriophage suspension to a 4.5 ml sterile saline blank. Continue the dilution series as shown in Figure 7.3 "Serial Dilution of T_4 Bacteriophage."

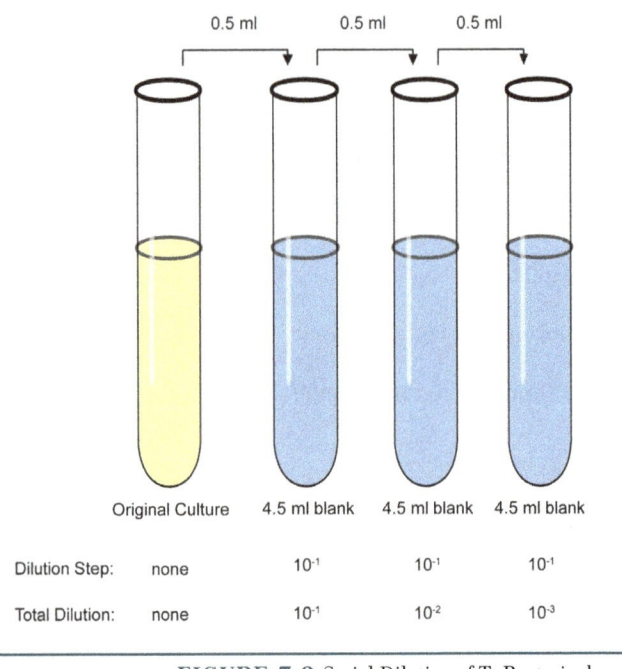

Aseptically, open the swab and dip into the culture. Streak in a tight zig-zag pattern, attempting to cover as much of the plate as possible

Rotate the plate 90° and re-streak the same swab over the surface of the plate using the same method

Rotate the plate 45° and re-streak the same swab over the surface of the plate using the same method

Finish inoculating the plate by running the swab around the edge of the plate

FIGURE 7.3 Serial Dilution of T_4 Bacteriophage

4. Ignite the Bunsen burner.
5. Label one plate for each dilution of the series. Include the volume of bacteriophage dilution to be plated.

    0.1 ml of 10^{-1} dilution
    0.1 ml 10^{-2}
    0.1 ml 10^{-3}

6. Plate 0.1 ml of each diluted bacteriophage suspension onto each of the respective plates inoculated with the *E. coli* 455. Use a sterilized bent glass or metal spreader to distribute the volume evenly over the surface of the TSA plate.
7. Reflame the glass or metal spreader, let it cool, and place it on the lab bench.
8. Repeat steps 5–7 in order to plate the diluted bacteriophage suspensions onto the respective plates inoculated with *E. coli* 363.
9. Incubate all the plates at 37°C for 24 hours.

    Note: In a real-life lab situation, you would use the average of multiple dilution series to achieve a more accurate count of the original concentration of phages (PFU/ml). You would most likely also use a different phage-plating technique that includes pouring a top agar containing the bacteriophage suspension onto the agar plates already inoculated with bacterial cells.

Day 2

1. Collect the plates from the previous lab period and examine them for the appearance of plaques.

    Note: plaques appear when infected bacterial cells are lysed to release mature viruses. The viruses that are released subsequently infect other bacterial cells in the immediate vicinity. As the number of lysed host cells increases, clear areas, or plaques, begin to appear. Thus, plaques will be present only if the bacteriophages are able to successfully infect the bacterial cells, replicate, and lyse the host cells.

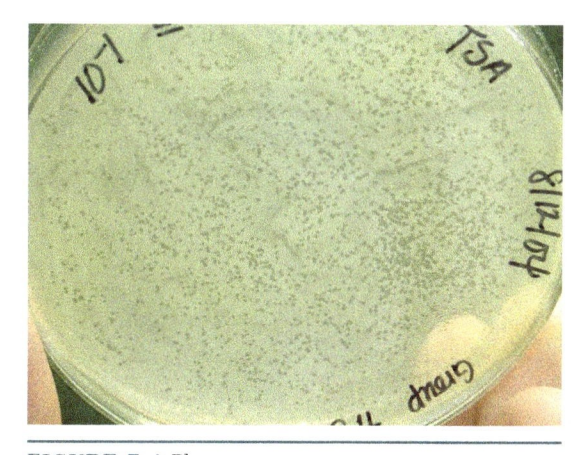

FIGURE 7.4 Plaques
Courtesy of The Ohio State University.

Exercise 7-2

2. Count the number of plaques present on each plate and record your result in the *R & Q* section.

Since it is assumed that each plaque initially arises from the infection of a single host cell by a single bacteriophage, the number of plaques present is directly related to the number of bacteriophages in suspension.

3. Select culture plates containing between thirty and three hundred plaques to determine the concentration of bacteriophages.

Similar to the bacterial colony counts, plaque counts in the thirty and three hundred range are sufficiently high to be statistically accurate and sufficiently low to prevent competition and overlap among the phages.

$$\frac{\text{Number of PFU}}{\text{Volume Plated} \times \text{Total Dilution}} = \text{Original Concentration of Phage (PFU / ml)}$$

4. To calculate PFU/ml, use the formula below:
5. Record your results in the *R & Q* section.

R & Q

Bacterial Strain	Viral Dilution Plated			Volume Plated
	10^{-1}	10^{-2}	10^{-3}	
Escherichia coli 455				0.1 ml
Escherichia coli 363				0.1 ml

Which bacteriophage dilution is most suitable for calculating the concentration of bacteriophages present in the original bacteriophage suspension?

___

Which *E. coli* strain is susceptible to the T_4 bacteriophage?

___

Give an explanation for the fact that only one of the two *E. coli* strains turned out to be susceptible to T_4 bacteriophages.

___

IMMUNOLOGY—NONSPECIFIC HOST DEFENSE

Pathogens penetrating the external defense systems of the human body trigger a series of **nonspecific host defense mechanisms**. Known as the **inflammatory response**, these mechanisms involve cellular and noncellular components of the blood and lymph systems that are relocated to the site of infection in an attempt to eliminate the evading pathogen. Among the cellular components of the inflammatory response are white blood cells, or **leukocytes**. **Neutrophils** and **macrophages** are the two major types of leukocytes that are recruited to the site of infection. Both neutrophils and macrophages are **phagocytes**, which means that they eliminate pathogens by carrying out phagocytosis (i.e., they surround and engulf invading cells).

The efficiency of phagocytosis depends upon a number of factors. Some components that are able to enhance phagocytosis are components of the immune system: **antibodies** and factors of the **complement system**. These components are able to bind to invading bacteria and attract phagocytes to the site of infection (a process called **opsonization**).

Phagocytic activity can also be negatively affected. This can occur when pathogens use their own defense mechanisms to affect phagocytosis in the attempt to escape elimination. Capsules are examples of bacterial **virulence factors** that help the bacterial invaders escape the phagocytic process.

The ability to evade host defenses often depends upon the virulence factors possessed by the pathogen. Thus, the virulence of an organism reflects the degree of **pathogenicity** (i.e., the ability with which the given organism can cause disease). **Pathogens** that are able to penetrate host defense systems with greater ease are said to be more **virulent**.

Other bacterial virulence factors include specific enzymes that affect the hosts in a number of different ways.

DNase, a virulence factor commonly associated with staphylococci and certain Gram-negative bacteria, is an extracellular enzyme (exoenzymes) that catalyzes the degradation of DNA. This process provides a nutrient source for the evading bacteria. The enzyme does not affect the DNA of living cells but hydrolyzes free DNA present in pus (fluid that accumulates at the site of infection and which typically contains dead cells and other cellular components). Because DNA is a very viscous macromolecule, a decrease in the amount of DNA molecules can ease the spread of invading microbes from the initial infection site. Thus, DNase increases the invasiveness of the microbes.

Fibrinogen is a soluble protein found in plasma. Fibrinogen, when converted to the insoluble form fibrin, is used in the process of producing blood clots, whose role is to prevent us from bleeding to death. Certain bacteria produce the enzyme **coagulase**, which catalyzes the conversion of fibrinogen to fibrin. In this scenario, fibrin forms a clot around the *bacteria*. Since the host's immune system does not recognize a clot as a foreign object, the bacteria, in this way, are "hiding" from the host's immune system. The inability of phagocytes to recognize fibrin-coated bacteria impedes the elimination process of the coagulase-producing bacteria and hence enhancing their virulence.

Bacterial **hemolysins** (toxins that affect red blood cells [erythrocytes]), are another type of enzymatic virulence factor.

In a host, the reduction of hemoglobin by **alpha-hemolysins** (α-hemolysins) will reduce the number of functional red blood cells in the body, resulting in a weakened response from the host to the invading microbes.

Besides eliminating red blood cells, **beta-hemolysins** (β-hemolysins) can also damage other cells and tissues in the immediate area, including phagocytes. Therefore, microbes that produce β-hemolysins can potentially affect phagocytosis, thereby facilitating further invasion of the pathogens into the body. Thus, besides weakening the overall ability of the host to respond to the presence of pathogens, phagocytosis may also be directly impeded.

Some bacterial species show a lack of hemolysin production that can break down red blood cells on the blood agar plate. Such bacteria produce **gamma-hemolysins** (γ-hemolysins).

The ability to cause hemolysis, as well as the level of hemolysis, can be used to identify and classify certain streptococci, including *Streptococcus pyogene*s, the causative agent of strep throat.

In the following two exercises, you will observe prepared slides of bacterial cells that have been phagocytized and examine selected bacteria for their virulence.

Exercise 7-3

Phagocytosis and Virulence Factors

Learning Objectives

To learn about phagocytosis and understand how virulence factors affect the phagocytic process. To interpret results that test bacteria for selected virulence factors.

Phagocytosis

Materials

- Prepared slide of phagocytes that have phagocytized *S. aureus* cells (Box 3)
- Compound brightfield microscope
- Demo plates of bacteria tested for DNase, coagulase, and hemolysins

Procedure

1. Observe the prepared slide using the compound brightfield microscope.

    Note: the macrophages will appear as relatively large, slightly pink macrophages with red nuclei. Inside the macrophages, you should see the dark purple, Gram-positive cocci cell (*S. aureus*).

2. Record your observations in the *R & Q* section.

Virulence factors

Procedure

DNase test

The following protocol was used to test bacterial cells for DNase activity:

1. Two organisms, *Serratia marcescens* and *Escherichia coli*, were streaked onto specific agar plates containing DNA.

Exercise 7-3

Box 3 Phagocytosis

Protocol used to prepare the slide of S. aureus cells phagocytized by macrophages

A mouse was injected in the abdominal cavity with 2 ml of thioglycollate broth to stimulate the movement of phagocytic cells into this region of the body.

Seventy-two hours later, the mouse was injected with 0.2 ml of an overnight culture of *Staphylococcus aureus* grown in TSB.

After 30 minutes, the mouse was euthanized, and cells were harvested from the abdominal cavity using a special procedure (called the lavage procedure, in which a mouse is injected with 3–5 ml of sterile saline and the abdomen is massaged to mix any cells present in the abdominal fluid with the saline). After removing the skin to expose the abdomen, a syringe is used to recover as much of the saline + peritoneal fluid cell suspension as possible.

Slides were prepared by spreading a single drop of the cell suspension over the surface of each slide, using the same technique that was used to prepare smears for capsule staining. However, unlike the capsule stain procedure, these suspensions were both air-dried and heat-fixed. The heat-fixed smears were then Gram stained.

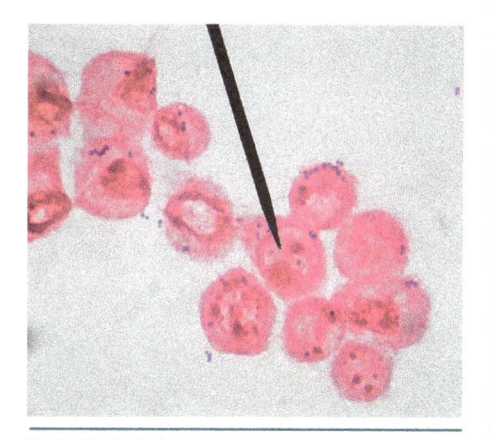

FIGURE 7.5 *S. aureus* phagocytized by macrophage 1000X total magnification

---

2. After incubation, 1M HCl was added to the plate.

   Note: Hydrochloric acid (HCl) causes intact (polymerized) DNA to precipitate, resulting in the medium becoming opaque. However, if the DNA has been hydrolyzed by DNase, the medium will remain clear upon the addition of HCl. Therefore, a clear area surrounding the bacterial growth on the plate indicates that the organism produces **DNase**. On the other hand, if the agar appears opaque after the addition of HCl, the result suggests that the bacteria do not produce DNase.

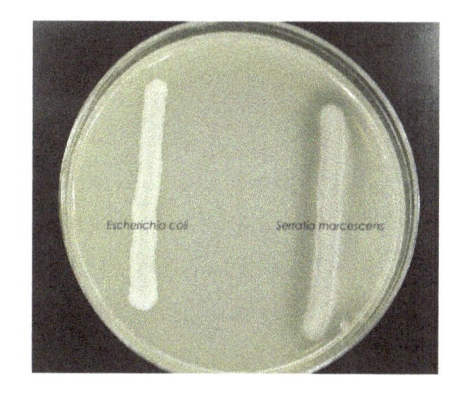

   FIGURE 7.6 DNase
   Courtesy of The Ohio State University.

3. Record your observations of Figure "DNase" in the *R & Q* section.

Exercise 7-3

Coagulase test

The following protocol was used to test bacterial strains for coagulase activity:

1. A sterile serological pipette was used to add 0.3 ml of a *Staphylococcus aureus* culture to one of two tubes containing blood plasma and sealed with parafilm. The blood plasma was mixed with the organism by carefully inverting the parafilm-sealed tube once.
2. Using a fresh sterile serological pipette, the second agglutination tube was inoculated with *Staphylococcus epidermidis*. This tube was also sealed with parafilm and carefully inverted once to mix the blood serum with the organism.
3. Both tubes were incubated at 37°C for 40 minutes.

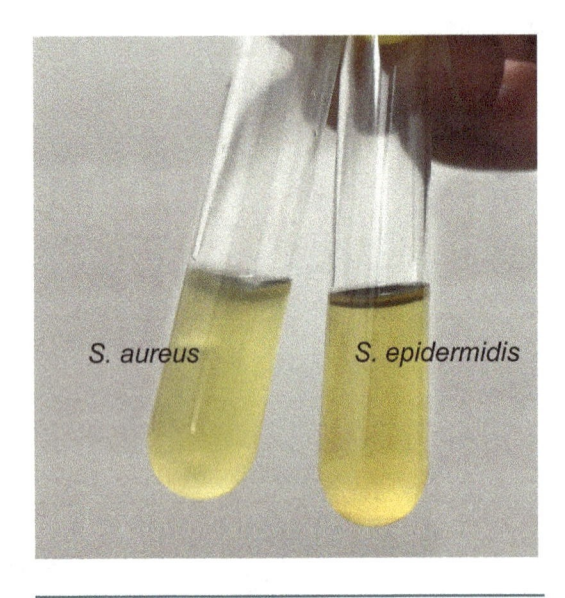

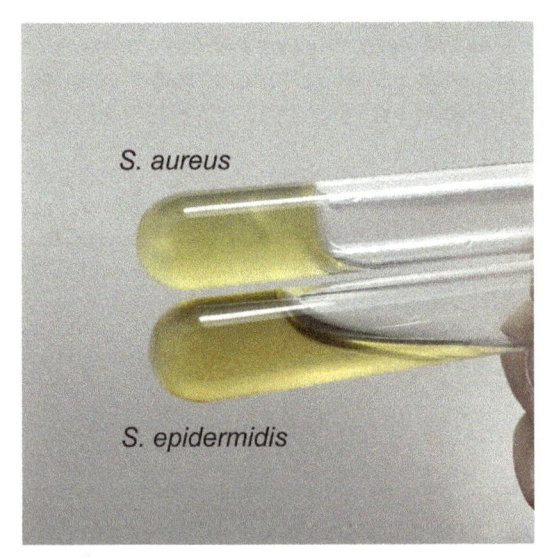

FIGURE 7.7 Test for coagulase activity

FIGURE 7.8 Test for coagulase activity severe tilt

4. Examine the results of the agglutination tubes in Fig 7.7 Test for coagulase activity. To evaluate if the formation of a plasma clot occurred in the tube, both tubes were tipped at a steep angle and compared. If the bacteria tested produce coagulase, the plasma clots or clumps. The absence of plasma clots leaves the plasma relatively fluid, and this indicates that the organism does not produce coagulase. See Figure 7.8 Test for coagulase activity severe tilt.
5. Record your observation of Figures 7.7 and 7.8 in the *R & Q* section.

Hemolysin test

The following protocol was used to test bacterial strains for α-, β-, or γ- hemolysin using blood agar plates:

1. Blood agar plates were streaked with each of the following organisms:

   Bacillus subtilis
   Streptococcus pneumonia
   Enterococcus faecalis

The blood agar plates were incubated at 37 °C for 24 hours.

Note: α- and β-hemolysins (or no hemolysin production [γ]) can be identified if the respective bacteria are grown on blood agar plates. If bacteria produce α-hemolysins, a greenish discoloration appears in the immediate vicinity of the colonies grown in this medium. β-hemolysis results in the complete lysis of erythrocytes contained in the agar. Therefore, if β-hemolysins are produced, colorless areas will appear in the blood agar surrounding the colonies in this medium. Lack of hemolysin production that can break down erythrocytes (γ-hemolysis) generates no change in blood agar within the specified incubation period.

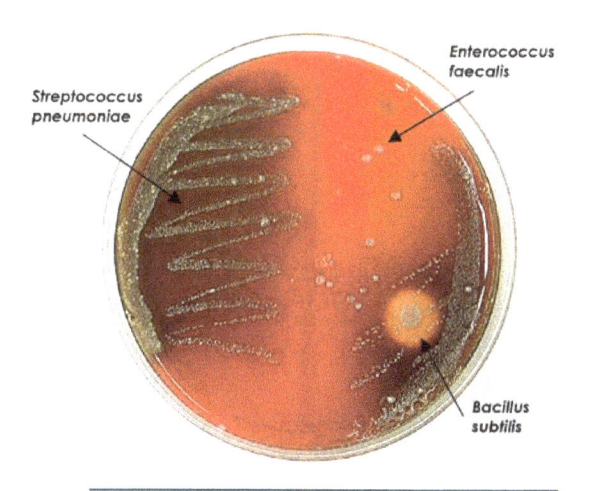

FIGURE 7.9 Blood agar plate with three different organisms showing alpha, beta and gamma hemolysis.
Courtesy of The Ohio State University.

In the R & Q section, record α (greenish), β (clear), or γ (no hemolysis) for each organism tested.

R & Q

Phagocytosis

Observation of Prepared Slide or Figure 7.5

       Specimen:

       Description:

Total magnification: _____ X

Exercise 7-3

DNase Activity

Organism	DNase Activity
Serratia marcescens	
Escherichia coli	

Coagulase Activity

Organism	Coagulase Activity
Staphylococcus aureus	
Staphylococcus epidermidis	

Hemolysin Activity

Organism	Hemolysin Activity
Bacillus subtilis	
Streptococcus pneumoniae	
Enterococcus faecalis	

IMMUNOLOGY—SPECIFIC HOST DEFENSE

The bodies of humans and other animals are protected from pathogens not only by the nonspecific host defense mechanisms but also by the **specific host defense mechanisms (i.e., the immune system)**. A major feature of this response is the production of antibodies (Ab), which are large, complex molecules, each made up of four polypeptide chains (Figure "Antibody"). Antibodies will react specifically with the substances (antigens [Ag]) that initially stimulated their production. Examples of antigens are non-host cell surface components or constituents exported from cells (e.g., toxins). Antigens are mostly proteins, but polysaccharides, glycoproteins, nucleoproteins, and glycolipids can also trigger antibody production. When antibodies react with their particular antigens, they form specific **antigen-antibody (Ag-Ab) complexes** that are vital components of the host-specific immune response. The complexes enable the body to eliminate unwanted invaders and their potential toxins. The various mechanisms responsible for eliminating the invaders include the following:

Precipitin Reaction: Ag-Ab complexes form when antibodies react with **soluble antigens**. The insoluble complexes precipitate from the solution and are removed from the body (e.g., by phagocytosis).

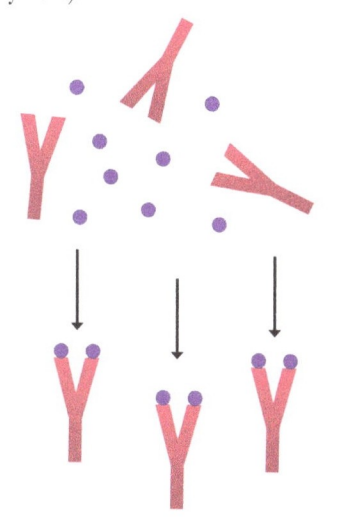

FIGURE 7.10 Precipitin reaction

FIGURE 7.11 Agglutination reaction

Agglutination Reaction: Ag-Ab complexes form when antibodies react with **insoluble antigens,** which are located on invading cells' surfaces. This reaction causes the cells to clump together (agglutinate), which makes it easier to remove the invaders sufficiently from the body by phagocytosis.

Opsonization: Ag-Ab complexes form and the antibodies, together with proteins of the **complement system,** build a "bridge" between antigens and phagocytic leucocytes of the body. This enhances phagocytosis of the antigens.

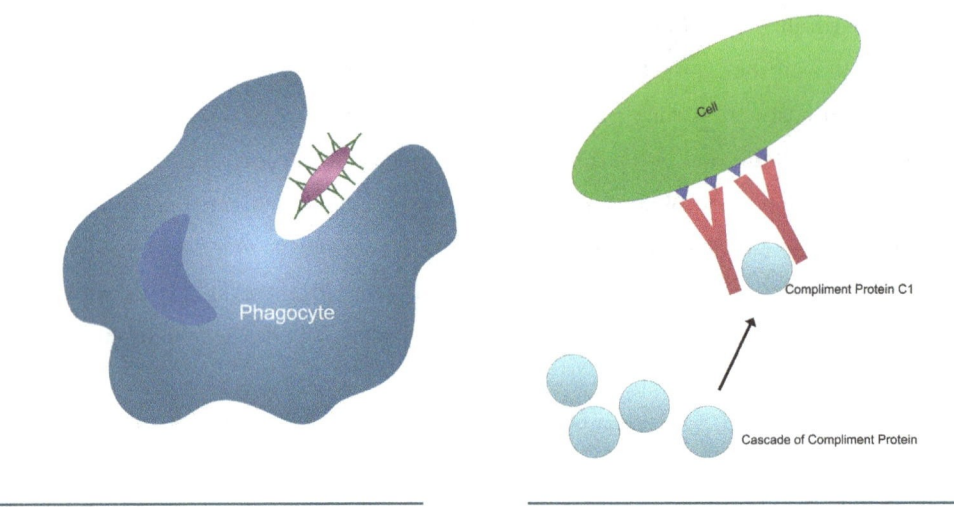

FIGURE 7.12 Opsonization

FIGURE 7.13 Compliment protein

Complement Fixation: Ag-Ab complexes trigger a series of reactions that take advantage of the entire complement system. The process causes the invading organisms to lyse.

The high specificity of the antibodies towards the antigen with which they interact is very valuable in clinical settings. It is essential for verifying exposure to infectious agents as well as identifying the specific disease-causing infectious agents.

To familiarize ourselves with antibody-antigen complex formation, we will perform precipitin and agglutination reactions in the following exercises.

Antigen-antibody Interactions

Precipitin test

For the precipitin reaction, you will employ a method involving a capillary tube. The method combines soluble antigen with serum (the liquid part of blood that does not contain blood cells or clotting factors) and allows you to determine if specific antibodies towards a certain antigen are present in the serum. This is done by examining if insoluble complexes precipitate from the solution. This procedure is somewhat similar to a test performed to determine if a patient has been exposed to the causative agent of Lyme disease, *Borellia burgdorferi*.

Agglutination test

For the agglutination test, you will perform a simulated blood-typing assay, comparable to testing for ABO and Rh factor antigens. These antigens, located on the surface of the blood cells, are important when determining blood types of individuals (e.g., when a blood transfusion has to be performed). A positive test for a hemagglutination assay appears as clumping (insoluble) red blood cells, easily visible to the naked eye.

Another example of an agglutination test is the detection of the animal pathogen *Brucella abortus* that causes spontaneous abortion in cattle. In order to examine if antibodies against *B. abortus* are present in a given cattle serum sample, an insoluble, nonvirulent antigen prep is combined with the serum. The presence of antibodies in the serum results in agglutination of the antigen. Thus, if the animal produced an immune response to the pathogen (*B. abortus*), it indicates that the tested animal is infected with *B. abortus*.

Learning Objectives

To gain knowledge about antigens and antibodies.
To understand the role of antibodies in the immune response.
To perform and observe precipitation and agglutination reactions.

Materials

- Capillary tube (1)
- BSA solution (1)

Exercise 7-4

- Rabbit anti-BSA serum
- Clay
- Simulated blood
- Antisera (3)
- Blood typing tray
- Toothpicks (3)

Work in groups of four.

Procedure

Precipitin test

Bovine serum albumin (BSA), a protein normally found in the serum of cattle, functions as the soluble antigen in this test. The source of antibodies that interact with the BSA protein originates from rabbit serum (antiserum). Before serum was obtained from the rabbits, they were injected with the (non-self) BSA protein from cattle, and anti-BSA antibodies were produced by the rabbit in response to the presence of the BSA protein.

1. Insert one end of a capillary tube into the tube of antiserum containing anti-BSA antibody. Allow the solution to be drawn into the capillary tube (see Figure "Precipitin Test").
2. Use a piece of gauze to gently wipe the excess antiserum from the outside of the capillary tube
3. Insert the same end of the capillary tube that you had inserted into the antibody solution in step 1 into the solution of BSA antigen.
4. Allow the antigen to be drawn into the capillary tube.

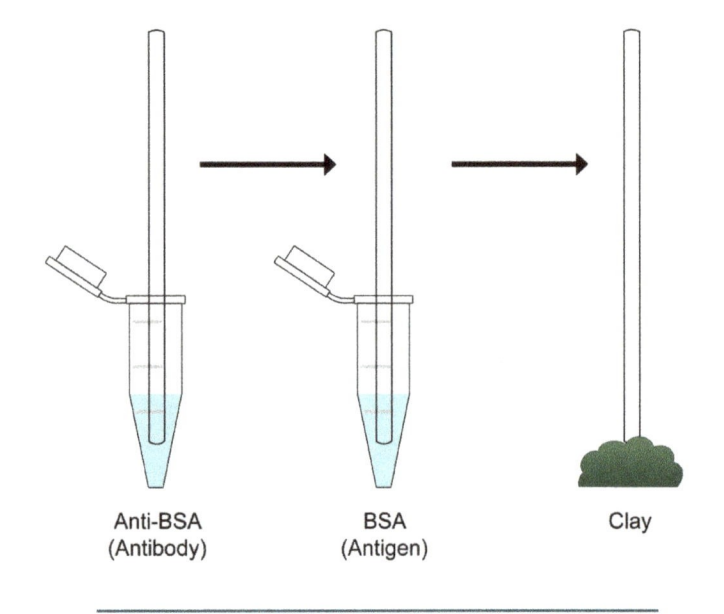

FIGURE 7.14 Precipitin test

Exercise 3-6

Although we will not taste the yogurt produced in this lab, we will perform tests that can inform us about the quality of our yogurt. The acidity (pH), diacetyl content, smell, and consistency of the yogurt product will be reported, and the results will be related to the success of the synergistic interplay between *S. thermophilus* and *L. bulgaricus*.

We will investigate the success of the symbiotic relationship between *S. thermophilus* and *L. bulgaricus* in the yogurt production by adding either one or both organisms to the milk samples prior to the fermentation process.

Day 1

Materials

- One tube of 2% milk (25 ml)
- Your assigned starter culture:
    - *S. thermophilus* or *L. bulgaricus*, or *S. thermophilus* and *L. bulgaricus*
- P1000 micropipette and tips or 1 ml serological pipettes

Work in groups of four.

Procedure

1. Add 0.5 ml of your assigned starter cultures to a tube containing 25 ml of 2% milk.
2. Mix bacteria with the milk by gently inverting the tube three times.
3. Incubate the tube at 40°C for 24 hours.

A "milk only" negative control will be incubated with the remaining inoculated milk samples.

Day 2

Materials

- Yogurt samples prepared in Day 1
- pH indicator strips (pH 2–9)
- Microfuge tube (2)
- 40% KOH

Work in groups of four

The Symbiotic Relationship of Bacteria in Yogurt Production

Learning Objective

To acknowledge the necessary symbiotic relationship between the two bacterial organisms involved in yogurt production.

Yogurt is a fermented milk product. The successful production of yogurt requires two bacteria, *Streptococcus thermophilus* and *Lactobacillus bulgaricus*, to coexist in a symbiotic relationship during the fermentation process. The sugar lactose, which is abundant in milk, is essential to the fermentation process. During yogurt production, lactose is catabolized to yield lactic acid, which is one of the components responsible for the characteristic sour taste of yogurt. Both *S. thermophilus* and *L. bulgaricus* are capable of fermenting lactose. The conversion of lactose to lactic acid occurs inside the bacterial cells after the lactose molecules have entered the cells. Once converted, lactic acid is then exported (secreted) from the bacterial cells into their environment, which results in an increase in acidity of the yogurt.

Streptococcus thermophilus: Enzymatic synthesis of formate (formic acid)

Lactobacillus bulgaricus: Enzymatic degredation of casein

Formic acid

Amino acids and peptides

The fermentation process takes place at 35–45°C and is divided into two distinct phases:

1. During the first phase, *L. bulgaricus* grows slowly, but as it grows, it produces peptides and amino acids. These peptides and amino acids stimulate the growth of *S. thermophilus*.

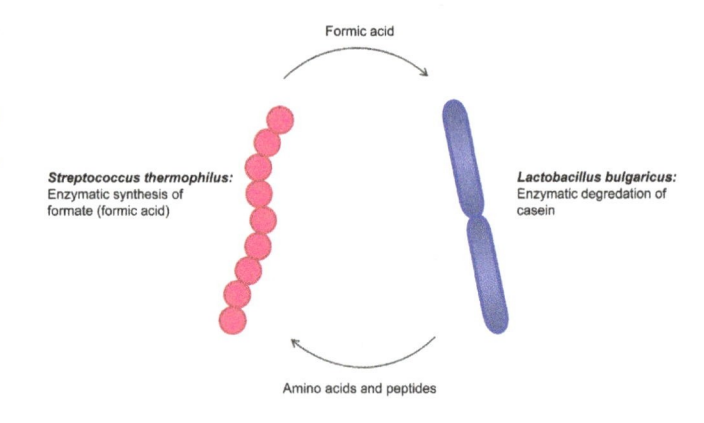

   Once *S. thermophilus* is stimulated and is growing efficiently, it quickly becomes the predominant organism, producing components such as lactic acid, acetaldehyde, diacetyl, and formate, which results in the pH change of the milk mixture from about 6.5 to 5.5.

2. The drop in pH and the presence of formate enhance the growth of *L. bulgaricus*, which now, in the second phase of the fermentation procedure, becomes the predominant organism.

   Due to lactic acid and acetaldehyde now efficiently being produced by *L. bulgaricus*, the pH drops further, and the optimal growth conditions for *L. bulgaricus* have been reached. This lower pH also affects the milk protein casein, causing structural changes that contribute to the formation of the solid curd of yogurt.

   When a pH of 4.2–4.3 has been reached, the fermentation process terminates and the resulting yogurt product has gained its characteristic consistency and sour, tart taste.

5. Plug the end of the capillary tube by placing it into a small amount of clay (see Figure 7.14 "Precipitin Test").

Examine the capillary tube. A whitish line of precipitate should become visible as the BSA antigen and anti-BSA antibodies from the antiserum interact.

> **Note:** View the capillary tube from several angles to better see the precipitate; holding the tube against a dark background can be helpful, too.

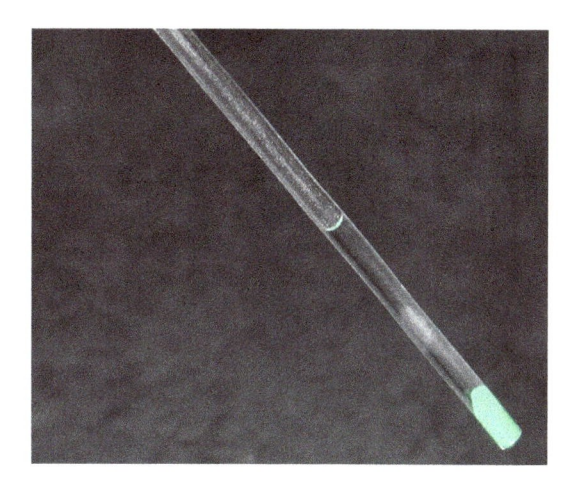

6. Draw and describe the area of the capillary tube in which precipitation occurred. Indicate where the serum containing the anti-BSA antibodies and the BSA antigen solution are positioned relative to one another.
7. Dispose of the used capillary tube in the red biohazard container.

Agglutination test

In this test, you combine an insoluble antigen with an antibody-containing serum. This sample contains the simulated blood cells (antigens) that will agglutinate if mixed with the correct antibody-containing serum.

Refer to the table below to obtain additional information about the simulated antisera used in this exercise.

Simulated Anti-serum	Contains components that mimic the action of...	Serum clumps, or agglutinates in samples that contain blood cells having...
A	Anti-A antibodies	"A antigens" on their surfaces
B	Anti-B antibodies	"B antigens" on their surfaces
Rh	Anti-Rh antibodies	"Rh antigens" on their surfaces

> **Note**: No biological components are used in this assay; therefore, it does not present any biological hazards.

Exercise 7-4

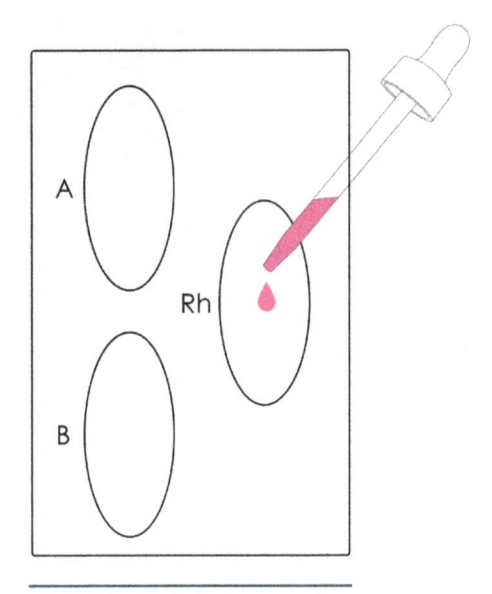

FIGURE 7.15 Agglutination Test

Place one drop of your assigned simulated blood sample into each well of the blood typing tray (see Figure 7.15 "Agglutination Test").

Place one drop of simulated Anti-A serum into Well A.

Place one drop of simulated Anti-B serum into Well B.

Place one drop of simulated Anti-Rh serum into Well Rh.

Use a separate, clean toothpick to mix the content of each well for 10 seconds.

Examine the wells for the appearance of clumping.

Record your observations in the *R & Q* section.

Exercise 7-4

R & Q

Pricipitin test
Draw your observations.

Agglutination Reaction

Sample Tested	simulated Anti-A serum	simulated Anti-B serum	simulated Anti-Rh serum

Individuals with Type A blood have A antigens on their blood cells' surfaces; those with Type B blood have B antigens on their surfaces; those with Type AB have both; and those with Type O have neither. What was the blood type in the sample that your group tested? Explain how you came to this conclusion.

_____
_____
_____

Exercise 7-4

Individuals with Type O blood are able to produce both Anti-A and Anti-B antibodies, while individuals with Type AB blood produce neither of these antibodies. Explain why you think this is the case. How does this relate to the idea that people with Type AB blood are often referred to as universal recipients for transfusions?

Individuals with Rh-positive blood possess Rh antigens on their surfaces. Did your sample test Rh positive? If an Rh-negative woman produces Anti-Rh antibodies, how might this affect her unborn child if it has Rh-positive blood?

How does the appearance of the agglutination test compare with that of the precipitin test?

EPIDEMIOLOGY

An **epidemic** is an outbreak of an infectious disease that rapidly spreads within a relatively short period of time and whose presence at an extraordinary high frequency within a given community is unusual.

Epidemiology is the study of epidemics, and **epidemiologists** are the professionals who watch and monitor populations for the occurrence of epidemics. They work on tracking down the causative agents when an epidemic occurs, determine the path of transmission of the infectious disease, and suggest ways to control the further spread of the disease. The work of an epidemiologist also includes identifying the index case: the very first reported incidence of the infectious disease within a given population.

In order to prevent further spread of an infectious disease throughout a population, it is important to isolate infected individuals. This entire process involves complex detective work that may include combined efforts of epidemiologists, pathologists, infectious disease specialists, and public health officers. The process is greatly facilitated by the assistance of the disease victims themselves, if this is a possibility.

Box 4 Lyme disease

One example of an epidemiological breakthrough is the identification of the spirochaete that causes **Lyme disease**. This took place in 1982 and included knowledge about the mode of transmission of the spirochaete (via the deer tick) and ways to prevent its transmission. This example is considered an epidemiological success because the epidemiologists involved not only came to recognize the definitive signs and symptoms of this infectious disease but were also able to identify the infectious agent that causes the disease. Another example of an epidemic disease is the plague in the mid-1300s caused by *Yersinia Pestis*. More recent examples are the Ebola virus, swine flu, and Zika virus epidemics.

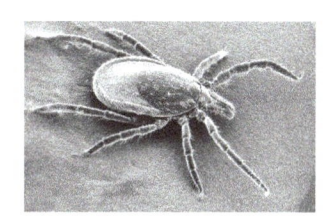

Copyright © Alan R Walker (CC BY-SA 3.0) at https://commons.wikimedia.org/wiki/File%3AIxodes-ricinus-female.jpg.

In this exercise, you will simulate the spread of an "infectious disease" within a "population," with the "population" being yourself and the students in your lab section.

The mode of transmission involves the exchange of fluids (solutions contained in test tubes). Instead of a disease organism, we will use an anti-BSA antibody solution. One person in the lab will be receiving the tube containing the anti-BSA antibody solution. This person is the index case.

The remaining students in the lab will receive a tube with a similar solution, but without anti-BSA antibody added. Everyone in the lab will thereafter start to exchange fluids by transferring 10 drops of his/her own solution to another person's tube, and vice versa. When a certain number of exchanges have been made, you will investigate which students have been infected and identify the index case—the person who initially received the tube with anti-BSA antibodies.

Although the transfer of antibodies does not cause disease, your immune system produces antibodies following exposure to a disease agent. As we previously saw in this module, if an individual has been exposed to a disease agent, the body will produce antibodies against the agent. Thus, in our exercise, the anti-BSA antibody solution mimics serum from an individual, and the BSA protein mimics the infectious agent.

After completion of the epidemiology simulation part of the exercise, you will examine if you and/or your lab partners have been infected by the disease agent BSA (or rather have received drops from a tube containing anti-BSA antibody). This examination will be achieved by performing a test called ELISA (enzyme-linked immunosorbent assay, see Box 6). You will finalize the exercise by analyzing the ELISA results collected from the entire class, and you will learn how to use this data to reveal who the index case is.

Box 5 Introduction to ELISA

As we saw earlier in this module, the precipitin and agglutination reactions are both useful for the rapid identification of invading organisms/pathogens through the detection of specific antibodies. However, their sensitivity is somewhat limited. ELISA is another test that takes advantage of the specificity of Ab-Ag interactions, but it comprises a much more sensitive detection system. So, whereas the precipitin and agglutination tests detect molecules in the 1–100 ng (10^{-9} g) range, ELISA detects molecules in the picogram (10^{-12} g) range. This major increase in sensitivity is accomplished by linking (conjugating) secondary antibodies to enzymes, fluorescent stains, or radioisotopes. The secondary antibodies are generated to react specifically with the antibodies in the initial Ab-Ag complexes.

ELISA may be used to assay for the presence of a variety of proteins, hormones, or drugs. ELISA can also be carried out to determine if an individual has been exposed to a particular pathogen since specific antibodies towards the pathogen have been formed. Therefore in this case, the assay depends on antibodies whose production was triggered by the disease agent (antigen). As an example, ELISA can be used to detect antibodies towards the Human Immunodeficiency Virus (HIV, the causative agent of AIDS), whose detection is an important first step in identifying HIV infections.

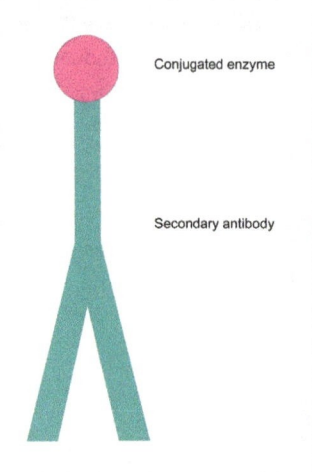

The ELISA procedure that you will perform in this exercise is similar, since you will attempt to detect the presence of anti-BSA antibody molecules.

Outline of ELISA

The following is a description of how ELISA is carried out when attempting to detect anti-BSA antibodies in solution:

1. The first step of the procedure is to coat the inner surfaces of small plastic wells with the BSA (the infectious agent or antigen). In this step, special techniques are available to enhance binding of the antigen to the wells.
2. The BSA-containing (antigen-containing) wells are then washed several times with a special wash buffer. These washing steps are important, since excess antigen that is unbound to the well surfaces will be removed.
3. Next, the solution (serum) to be analyzed for the presence of the anti-BSA antibody is diluted, and an aliquot is added to a BSA-coated well.

   Note: This step is equivalent to adding the primary antibody to the well. If anti-BSA antibodies are present in the solution, they will bind to BSA in the well during this step of the procedure.

4. A sample of solution without anti-BSA antibodies is added to a separate BSA-coated well as a negative control.
5. After an incubation step that allows the BSA and anti-BSA antibody complexes to form, the wells are washed several times with wash buffer. This removes any unbound anti-BSA antibody (primary antibody) from the well.

   Note: If antibodies in a given serum sample are not specific for (do not react with) the antigen that coats the wells, no Ab-Ag complexes will form in this step, and all antibodies will be removed during the washing steps of the wells.

6. In wells where the solution (serum) contains anti-BSA antibodies that specifically recognize (bind to) BSA (bound antigen), Ab-Ag complexes will form. These complexes will stay attached to the wells, and only excess, unbound antibodies will be removed from the wells during the washing step.
7. Following the addition of the conjugated secondary antibodies to each well, the mixtures are incubated to allow the secondary antibodies to react with the primary antibodies of any Ab-Ag complexes bound to the wells.

Note: Typically, more than one secondary antibody molecule will bind to each Ab-Ag complex. The binding of additional conjugated antibodies will produce a more intense (amplified) color, which makes it easier to detect the presence of the complexes.

8. The wells are washed once again to remove any excess, unbound, secondary antibodies.

   Note: This wash step is particularly important. The reason is that if the excess secondary antibodies are not removed, the enzyme still present in the well will react with the substrate added in the next step, and thus will interfere with the final result.

9. In this final step, a substrate of the enzyme conjugated to the secondary antibody is added to the wells. If present, the antibody-linked enzyme will catalyze a chemical reaction with the substrate, resulting in the formation of a color.

   Note: Since enzyme-linked antibodies would only be present after washing if they bound to Ab-Ag complexes, the detection of a color change of the solution in the well indicates that the target antibodies (anti-BSA antibodies) were present in the serum (solution) tested. If no color change occurs, it is assumed that Ab-Ag complexes were not formed and that the target antibodies were not present in the tested serum (solution).

10. The addition of a stopping solution reduces the probability of producing false-positive reactions.

    Note: Further testing using a procedure called a Western Blot can be done to confirm the ELISA results; this will also detect false-positive reactions.

FIGURE 7.16 ELISA procedure

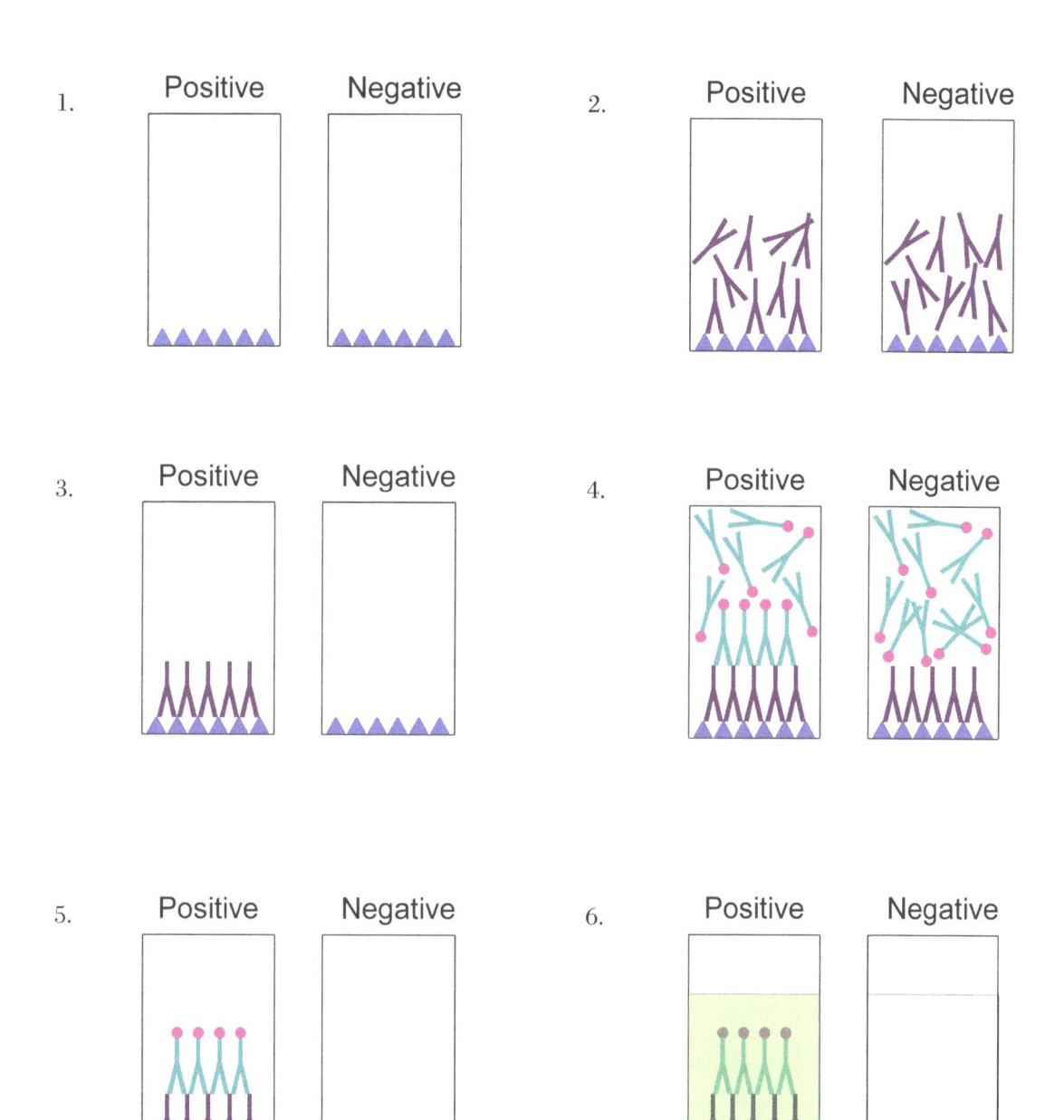

Exercise 7-5

Epidemiology and ELISA

Learning Objectives

To create an artificial epidemic.
To become aware of the rate at which infectious diseases can spread.
To become familiar with the basic principles behind ELISA.
To learn how to perform and interpret the results of ELISA.
To identify the index case.

Materials

Epidemiology:

- Dropper
- Numbered tube with solution tube

Work individually.

ELISA:

- Tube of control buffer
- Well strip precoated with BSA
- Microfuge tube containing secondary antibody
- Squirt bottle of wash buffer
- Microfuge tube containing substrate
- P200 micropipette
- Box of micropipette tips

Work in groups of four.

Procedure

EPIDEMIOLOGY

1. Collect one numbered tube and one dropper.
2. Record the number of your tube in the *R & Q* section.
3. Vortex the tube containing the fluid/solution.
4. Chose a student to exchange fluids with.
5. Simultaneously, place 10 drops of each of your fluids into the other student's tube (see Figure 7.17 "Exchange").

   Note: Place any fluid remaining in the dropper after the exchange in the test tube it originated from.

6. Record the number of the tube of the student with whom you exchanged fluids in the table "Exchange".
7. Cap the tube and vortex the solution.

   Note: In case you are infected, it is important mix the solution. Why?

8. Use the same dropper in all of the subsequent exchanges.

9. Repeat steps 4–7 for each exchange you make.

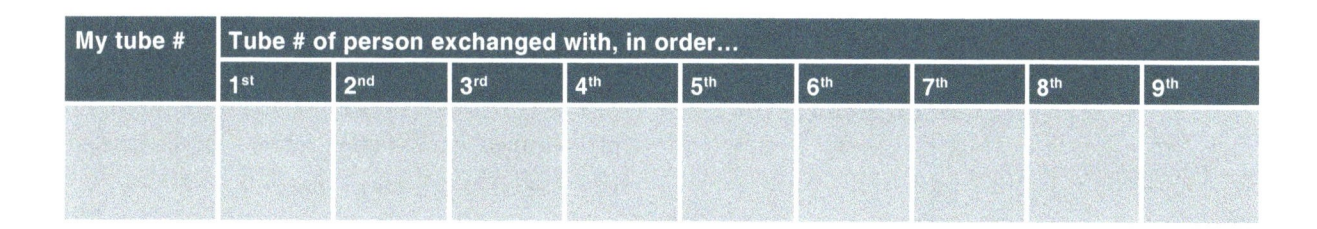

FIGURE 7.17 Exchange

My tube #	Tube # of person exchanged with, in order...								
	1st	2nd	3rd	4th	5th	6th	7th	8th	9th

10. When all exchanges are done, you are ready to perform ELISA to detect which students have been "infected" during the simulation.

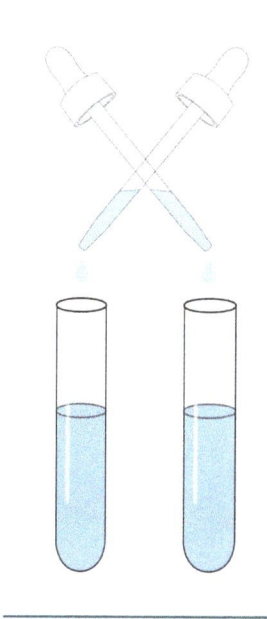

ELISA

11. Each student will perform ELISA on their own fluids/solutions.
12. You will share the strip of BSA-coated wells with your group of four. Refer to Figure for step-by-step instructions.

Note: These strips were prepared and incubated overnight at 4°C to ensure that the test antigen, BSA, adhered to the plastic surface of the wells.

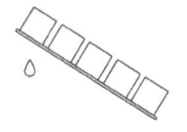

Invert the stip of wells over the sink and give it a single shake with a quick motion to remove excess unbound liquid BSA antigen remaining in the wells

Use a Sharpie marker to label one well for each student and one well for the negative control

Use the squirt bottle containing wash buffer to gently fill each well. Avoid overfilling the wells. Empty the wells by inverting the strip over the sink and giving it a single shake with a quick motion. Repeat a total of 3 times

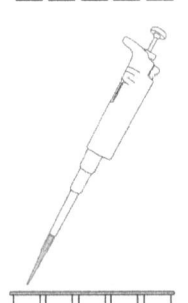

Use a p200 micropipette to add 100 μl of each student's sample to the designated wells as well as 100 μl of control buffer to the control well. Use a fresh tip for each sample. Incubate the strip of wells at 37 °C for 15 minutes

Wash the wells a total of 3 times by using the squirt bottle containing wash buffer to gently fill each well. Avoid overfilling the wells. Empty the wells by inverting the strip over the sink and giving it a single shake with a quick motion

13. Invert the strip over the sink and give it a single shake with a quick motion to remove excess unbound liquid BSA remaining in the wells.
14. Label wells, using a Sharpie to write on the plastic wells. Each student will use one well for each of the samples, and your entire group will share an additional well for the negative control.
15. Use the squirt bottle containing wash buffer to gently fill each well. Avoid overfilling the wells.
16. Empty the wells by inverting the strip over the sink and giving it a single shake with a quick motion.
17. Repeat the washing process twice, rinsing the wells a total of three times.
18. Remove the excess liquid remaining in the wells by firmly tapping the inverted strip several times onto a small stack of paper towels.
19. Using the P200 micropipette, each student adds 100 μl from their fluid/solution tube to the designated well. Use a fresh tip for each sample.
20. Use the P200 micropipette and a fresh tip to add 100 μl of control buffer to the control well.

Note: The control buffer is used to detect any potential color changes that can be appear as a result of the random binding of secondary conjugated antibody to the plastic.

21. Place the strip of wells into one of the white racks.
22. Incubate the strips at 37°C for 15 minutes to allow the primary antibody (anti-BSA antibody, if present) to bind to the antigen (BSA) adhering to the wells.
23. Wash the wells three times, as in steps 15–17. The wash steps will ensure the removal of unbound primary antibody from the wells.
24. Use the P200 micropipette with a fresh tip to add 100 µl of serum (containing the secondary antibody conjugated to the indicator enzyme) to each well.
25. Incubate the wells on your benchtop at room temperature for 15 minutes. During this incubation step, the secondary antibodies will bind to the primary antibodies, which, if present, are attached to the BSA antigen.
26. Empty the wells by inverting the strip over the sink, and wash the wells three times, as in steps 15–17.
27. Using the P200 micropipette and a **fresh tip**, add 100 µl of the **substrate** to each of the wells.
28. Incubate the well strip at room temperature for 5–10 minutes while watching for the development of green color in the wells.

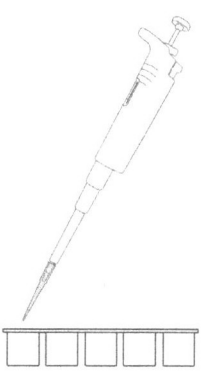

Use a p200 micropipette and a fresh tip to add 100 µl of conjugated enzyme to the designated wells. Incubate the strip of wells at room temperature for 15 minutes

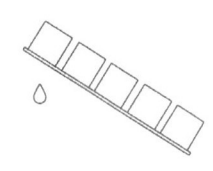

Invert the stip of wells over the sink and give it a single shake with a quick motion to remove excess unbound conjugated enzyme remaining in the wells

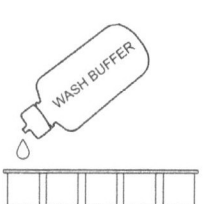

Wash the wells a total of 3 times by using the squirt bottle containing wash buffer to gently fill each well. Avoid overfilling the wells. Empty the wells by inverting the strip over the sink and giving it a single shake with a quick motion

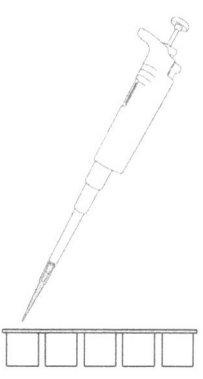

Use a p200 micropipette and a fresh tip to add 100 µl of substrate to the designated wells. Incubate the strip of wells at room temperature for 5-10 minutes while watching for development of green color in the wells

Note: The substrate will appear green in color when cleaved by the indicator enzyme that is conjugated to the secondary antibody. Thus, a green color in the wells indicates the presence of the conjugated secondary antibody. In our exercise, this indicates that formation of anti-BS antibodies and BSA complexes has occurred in the well. A positive ELISA result reveals that the given student is infected.

29. Record **positive** results in the provided Excel table.

    Note: if a student is infected, this could mean that:
    a. the student was the index case, or
    b. the student became "infected" during the simulation.

30. Add the class results to your table "ELISA Results" in the $R \& Q$ section. Record the order of exchanges in the second column.
31. Complete the epidemiology exercise by using the data to track the path of "infection" and determine the index case (original source of infection).

Exercise 7-5

327

R & Q

Number of tube with fluid_____

Tube # of "Infected" Individuals	Order of Exchanges

Exercise 7-5

Index case_____

Describe you view on how an infectious disease may spread quickly through a population.

_____
_____
_____

List several ways to control the spread of an infectious disease.

_____
_____
_____

Define the roles of the epidemiologist.

_____
_____
_____

Do some research and explain how an antibody can be produced that reacts with another antibody.

_____
_____
_____

Explain how a negative ELISA result of no color change is obtained when testing fluid (serum) from an uninfected individual in our lab.

_____
_____
_____

Exercise 7-5

EPIDEMIOLOGY PRACTICE PROBLEM #1

Difficulty Level – Easy: Use the following information to determine the path of infection and index case of a hypothetical epidemic. A group of people have broken out with a case of the YUKS. Use the table provided below and the diagram of the path of infection of this disease to determine the index case for this "epidemic".

Individual	Order of Contacts	Has the YUKS?
George	1st Gracie, then Bob	No
Gracie	1st Bing, then George, then Jack	No
Bob	1st George, then May, then Jack	Yes
Jack	1st Bing, then Gracie, then Bob	Yes
Bing	1st Gracie, then Jack, then Mae	Yes
Mae	1st Bing, then Bob	Yes

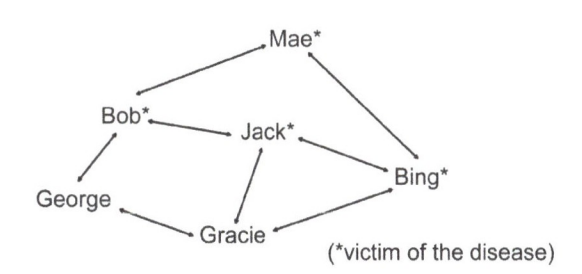

```
                    Mae*
       Bob*       /      \
          \  Jack*         \
           \  /  \          \
    George      \            Bing*
          \     Gracie
```
(*victim of the disease)

Index Case: _____

Answer: Mae

EPIDEMIOLOGY PRACTICE PROBLEM #2

Difficulty Level – Moderate: Use the following information to determine the path of infection and index case of a hypothetical epidemic. A group of people have contracted Luvtastudi Syndrom. Use the table provided below and the diagram of the path of infection of this disease to determine the index case for this "epidemic".

HINT: Determine if the infected individuals made contact with any uninfected individuals at any point in time. Then look at the sequence of contact among the infected individuals.

Individual	Order of Contacts	Victim of Luvtastudi Syndrom?
KA	JS, then LR, then JC, then BL	Yes
GS	JC, then CC	No
JC	GS, then CC, then KA	Yes
AD	BL, then LR	Yes
BL	AD, then RS, then KA	Yes
JS	KA, then TH	No
TH	JS, then RS	No
CC	GS, then JC	No
RS	BL, then TH	No
LR	KA, then AD	Yes

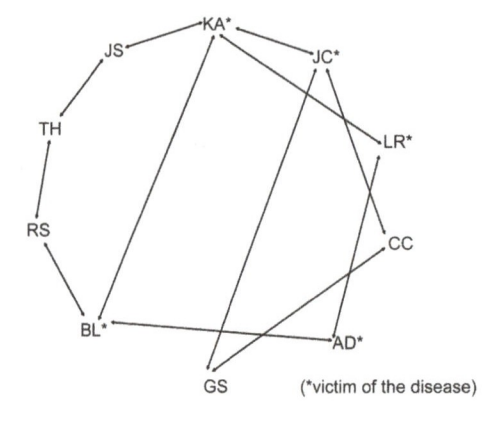

Index Case: _____

Answer: LR

Index

A

acidic dye, 77
A countable plate, 67
aerobic, 154
aerotolerant, 154
alpha-hemolysins, 303
anaerobe, 154
annular diaphragm, 14
antibodies, 302
antigen-antibody (Ag-Ab) complexes, 309
antigens, 309
antiseptics, 258
aseptically, 44
aseptic technique, 28

B

bacteriophages, 296
bacteroids, 293
Box 1, 155
Box 2, 155
Box 3, 156
Box 4, 156, 166
Box 5, 156
Box 7, 82, 88
Broad-spectrum antibiotics, 260
Brownian motion, 18

BSL1, 3
BSL2, 3

C

capsules, 76
cell concentration, 67
CFU/ml, 67
clean the oil objective last, 40
coagulase, 303
coliform, 142
commensalistic, 291
complement system, 302, 310
compound brightfield microscope, 12
contaminants, 41
current flow, 18

D

darkfield microscope, 12
differential, 155
differential stain, 77
disinfectants (Box 4), 258
DNase, 302, 305

E

Electron microscopes, 15
Emil Hansen (1842–1909), 42
endoenzymes, 170

endospores, 76
enumeration, 67
epidemic, 317
epidemiologists, 317
Epidemiology, 317
Equilibrium, 235
Etest strips, 280
eukaryote, 22
exoenzymes, 170
extracellular enzymes, 170

F

facultative anaerobes, 154
Figure legend, 171, 196
filter disk method, 267
fine-adjustment focus knob, 23
fine focus knob, 17
flagella, 17, 76
fluorescence microscope, 14
fresh tip, 325

G

gamma-hemolysins, 303
glycerol stocks, 43
Gram-positive cell wall, 79

H

Hans Christian Gram, 78
hay infusions, 17
hemolysins, 303
Hypertonic condition, 235
Hypotonic condition, 235

I

immersion oil, 17
inflammatory response, 302
insoluble antigens, 309

Intermediate (I), 281
intracellular enzymes, 170
inverted, 276
Isotonic condition, 235

J

Julius Richard Petri (1852–1921), 42

K

Kirby-Bauer method, 279

L

leukocytes, 302
Louis Pasteur (1822–1895), 42

M

MacConkey agar, 197
macrophages, 302
metabolism, 153
Microaerophilic, 154
morphology, 17
motility, 17
mutualistic, 291

N

narrow-spectrum antibiotics, 260
Neutrophils, 302
nonspecific host defense mechanisms, 302
normal microbiota, 257
numerical aperture, 16

O

objective lens, 16
obligate, 154
ocular lens, 16
OD, 238
opportunistic infection, 291
opportunistic pathogens, 91, 291

opsonization, 302
optical density, 238
Optical density OD, 68
Osmosis, 235
Osmotic pressure, 235

P

parasitic relationship, 291
parasitism, 291
parfocality, 17
pathogenicity, 302
pathogens, 291
Pathogens, 302
Paul Ehrlich (1854–1915), 76
peptone water, 140, 141
phages, 296
phagocytes, 302
phase contrast microscope, 12
phase-shifting element, 14
positive, 326
positive controls, 255
prokaryote, 22
protozoa, 22
Pseudomonas isolation agar, 196
pure cultures, 41

R

regular trash, 40
Resistant (R), 281
resolution, 16
resolving power, 16
Robert Koch (1843–1910), 42

S

selective, 155
selective-differential, 155
Selective-differential media, 196
Selective media, 195
serial dilution, 67
simple stain, 77
single isolated colonies, 44
soluble, 309
specific host defense mechanisms, 309
spectrophotometer, 238
spore, 102
spread plate, 69
Starch Agar, 196
sterile toothpick, 182
substrate, 325
Susceptible (S), 280
Symbiosis, 289

T

the immune system, 309
The Petroff-Hausser counting chamber, 68
The Total Viable Count, 67
three-phase streak, 41
total magnification, 16
transformation plates, 280
transient microbiota (Box 3), 257

V

virulence factors, 302
virulent, 302

W

Walter Hesse (1846–1911), 42

Z

zone of inhibition, 262, 267
zones of inhibition, 269, 272

CPSIA information can be obtained
at www.ICGtesting.com
Printed in the USA
LVHW010811170620
658069LV00001B/1

9 781516 544486